THE SOCIOLOGY OF HYPOCRISY

For Margaret, Helene, and Karen

The Sociology of Hypocrisy
An Analysis of Sport and Religion

STEPHEN G. WIETING
University of Iowa, USA

Routledge
Taylor & Francis Group

LONDON AND NEW YORK

First published 2015 by Ashgate Publishing

2 Park Square, Milton Park, Abingdon, Oxfordshire OX14 4RN
52 Vanderbilt Avenue, New York, NY 10017

Routledge is an imprint of the Taylor & Francis Group, an informa business

First issued in paperback 2019

British Library Cataloguing in Publication Data
A catalogue record for this book is available from the British Library

The Library of Congress has cataloged the printed edition as follows:
Wieting, Stephen G.
  The sociology of hypocrisy : an analysis of sport and religion / by Stephen G. Wieting.
    pages cm
  Includes bibliographical references and index.
  ISBN 978-1-4724-1922-4 (hardback)—ISBN 978-1-4724-1923-1 (ebook)—ISBN
978-1-4724-1924-8 (epub) 1. Hypocrisy—Case studies. 2. Sports—Moral and ethical
aspects. 3. Hypocrisy—Religious aspects. I. Title.
  BJ1535.H8W54 2015
  306.4'83—dc23

                                                                          2015011905

ISBN 13: 978-1-4724-1922-4 (hbk)
ISBN 13: 978-0-367-27172-5 (pbk)

Contents

List of Figures and Tables

Figures

Tables

Acknowledgments

Old Icelandic proverbs can usefully constrain and prod our actions. They also can add texture to attempted expressions of deep feeling, in this case appreciation. Three are helpful here: "Many a person seizes the lock for the door" (*Grettir Saga*); "No tree falls at the first stroke" (*Njal's Saga*); and "Old friends are the last to break away" (*Grettir Saga*). With these aids, I want sincerely to thank: Ben Earnhart, Makur Jain, Robert Baller, Christoph Weismayer, Paul Sturgis. Simona Ionescu, Thor Aspelund, Helene Wieting, Evans Ochola, Parang Kim, J. Tyler Leverty, Mary Noonan, Fred Mims, Monica Mims, Bogdan Vasi, Thórólfur Thórlindsson, Viðar Halldórsson, Steven Hitlin, Jeff Lucas, Jennifer Glanville, Michael Sauder, Arron Wings, Erlendur Már Antonsson, and Neil Jordan.

Chapter 1

Introduction: Is Hypocrisy So Ordinary as to Ignore or the Second Worst Vice?

Hypocrisy: The Question[1]

On November 16, 1940, Cornell University received a Fifth Down (due to a referee error) in a collegiate football contest in the United States with Dartmouth College in Hanover, New Hampshire and scored a touchdown with the extra chance. The immediate result was that the favored Cornell team defeated Dartmouth 7–3. The next day, officials noticed the error. With the knowledge, the Cornell players, their coach, their athletic director, and the president of Cornell sent a telegram to Dartmouth offering to forfeit the game in Dartmouth's favor, allowing them to win 3–0. Dartmouth accepted.

On October 9, 1990, the favored University of Colorado football team received an extra (Fifth) down due to a referee's error. They scored on the play in the waning minutes of the contest and were declared the winner, 33–31, against the University of Missouri in Columbia. The head of the University of Missouri, Chancellor Haskell Monroe, Jr., appealed to the Big-Eight football conference ("Eight" referring to the number of institutions within this conference at the time) about the fairness of the result. The conference upheld the conclusion of the game. "Colorado football coach Bill McCartney … did little to sooth the controversy. When, asked whether he would consider forfeiting the game, McCartney declared that he had considered it but decided against it because 'the field was lousy.'"[2]

Few fans, journalists, or researchers would deny there are differences here. (The attendance in Missouri was 46,956; the capacity today at Dartmouth Memorial Field is 13,000.) Considerably fewer researchers would consider these differences "make a difference." The judgment in this project is that the differences do "make a difference."

Hypocrisy occurs when a person or institution who has moral currency acts in such a way that contradicts the basis of the currency. In the course of one's life,

---

1 Portions of this chapter were presented during the Nordic Sociological Association meetings, Reykjavík, Iceland, August 2012 (with the original title of "Hypocrisy in Religion and in Sport: Individual and Institutional Implications").

2 "Fifth Down Game" (1990). "Closure came in the summer of 1998—four years after [Bill] McCartney retired as the [Colorado] Buffs' head coach—when he admitted to making mistakes and being saddened by the Fifth Down fiasco. McCartney made the remarks at a Promise Keepers gathering at the site of the controversy in Columbia, Missouri."

everybody displays in some way such contradictions. We cannot do otherwise if we aspire to moral elevations on one hand, and realities assure that human frailties (or uncontrollable circumstances) may compromise the heights we have reached or aspired to, on the other hand. Further to demonstrate the generality of the phenomenon, like the occurrence of lying, which is often used effectively to efface another (Bok, 1999), frequently the assignation of "hypocrite" is used as a favored rhetorical ploy to best an enemy or competitor.

Despite the real prospects of common individual occurrences of hypocrisy and the popularity of the designation in rhetorical contests, there is a lack of systematic attention to the origins, patterns, and implications of hypocrisy within sociology. Literatures from many fields are used here; this book carries the explicit burden—from the title—of honoring existing materials from sociology but also noting lacunae in this field.

The project is programmatic. As programs portend, there is a motivation for the effort: sociology *should* do this. There is also in programs warrant for the claim of responsibility: sociology *can* do this. Some of the reasons as will become apparent come from the inclusion of the work on hypocrisy within politics and political science, literary criticism, and philosophy. By default, the intimation is that those traditions have supplanted or pre-empted what sociology might do.

The title of the book is literal, and the motivation for the coverage and organization come from the sense of responsibility and competence. Programs have minimal elements; but programs are always essential to complete or proceed toward a valued objective. Programs, big and small, must contain the *should* and *can* elements. Opening the first entry in Jess Walter's short-story collection, *We Live in Water* (Walter, 2013: 1), the elements of programs for survival whether at the lowest or highest levels appear:

> BIT [short, and reductive of Wayne Bittenger, a central spokesperson] HATES going to cardboard. But he got tossed from the Jesus beds for drunk and sacrilege, and he's got no other way to get money. So he's up behind Frankie Doodle's, flipping through broken-down produce boxes like an art buyer over a rack of paintings, and when he finds a piece without stains or writing he rips it down until it's square. Then he walks to the Quik Stop, where the fat checker likes him. He flirts her out of a Magic Marker and a beefstick (Walter, 2013:1).

Jess Walter, like effective writers of fiction, can encapsulate practical human problems and doable solutions in an economical manner. Mr. Bittenger is out of money, and he needs to advertise for contributions. By experience and creativity he knows how to do this. He has a program.[3]

---

3   Jess Walter is an American writer whose most recent novel, *Beautiful Ruins*, 2012, was a number one *New York Times* best seller. It received acclaim as *Esquire*'s Book of the Year and National Public Radio Fresh Air's Best Novel of 2012.

Hypocrisy and One Instance of the Sociological Program

So, here is what the program of the sociology (of hypocrisy) should do and can do. This is the coverage and sequence of the material on the sociology of hypocrisy.

1. Sociology looks at the context of actions as one productive means for interpretation.
2. Sociology, with the notions of ideal types and strategic cases, defers from talking about everything, and alternatively looks methodologically to cases with reduced variance, representative of the salient theoretical questions in view, and which are strategically placed in social systems.
3. Sociology by definition acknowledges the role of social organizational factors in the determination of interactional patterns of social actors.
4. Sociology does not always do this, but I am going to attend to the sometimes mentioned mandate, to look for the implications and consequences of patterns of hypocrisy within society.
5. Sociology in principle intends theoretical yield from guided and systematic research.

Contexts and Writing about Hypocrisy

First, I note some productive intellectual traditions for the study of hypocrisy. Sociology has given irregular attention to hypocrisy. There is variable attention and disparate definitions of the term. Fields such as politics, political science, the history of manners, literary criticism, and ethical studies within philosophy have given more attention to the topic of hypocrisy than has sociology. One consistent yield of these traditions (illustrative work exists in Runciman [2006, 2008], Shklar [1984], and Davidson [2004]) is the importance of cultural contexts in adding variation to the meanings of hypocrisy. While sociology generally has circuited attention to hypocrisy, the field offers as a strength an awareness of cultural contexts. Hence, sociology provides resources for showing recognition of such contextual influences. Chapters 2 and 3 attend to variations of context in the meaning, attention, and anticipated consequences of hypocrisy. The salience of hypocrisy or, as Judith N. Shklar (1984) describes the condition of *exigency* surrounding the deceits, adds variation to the influence of culture on hypocrisy and is a central theme of this first portion of the program of coverage.

1. Contexts that have high valuation for performance, particularly evaluated in relative terms, create exigencies for hypocrisy in institutions, such as in sport and religion.
2. Some individuals have a distinct willingness to assure accomplishment, and proceed to seek it without reservation of effort or expense.

3. The individuals on the path to accomplishment have the cognitive capability and are structurally situated in institutions where they can compartmentalize promised or claimed achievement and documented, objective achievement.
4. Individuals and the surrounding institutions have the resources to control how publically available information is framed and accessed by publics.
5. Individuals and the surrounding institutions have the resources to persist in the maintenance of the putative valorized performance even as evidence and outside knowledge about its falsity grows.

Strategic Cases in the Study of Hypocrisy: Sport and Religion

Secondly, I examine some cases where hypocrisy is evident at the public level. Sports and religion are two institutions given primary attention here. While hypocrisy may occur in many institutions, these two appear to be productive research sites that illuminate the contradictions that hypocrisy embodies. In each, leaders are institutionally charged with displaying and maintaining high moral conduct. So, when compromises occur in individual acts or institutional manifestations, the contradiction between promised high morality and acts that are at variance with the standards stands in clear relief.

I have excluded hypocrisy in politics from the book. The large volume of material could be a reason for doing so. But there is a qualitative issue that provides a stronger warrant for the exclusion. It is true as David Runciman has nicely documented (2006, 2008) that hypocrisy as a topic for intellectual discourse was closely associated from the seventeenth century on with politics. This was the period of developing ideas about republics. Leaders should be valued by the worth of their credentials. And these credentials should be transparent to what was viewed as the emerging popular electorate. In *The New York Times*, from which a systematic set of cases has been drawn, there are at least as many instances of hypocrisy mentioned within political stories as with religion and sport. In Runciman and related analyses the seriousness of hypocrisy by politicians and in institutions continues. But at the same time, the spread and indeed the ubiquity of hypocrisy in politics suggests its commonality is now becoming coincidental with modern politics (at least in the United States). As such the value of looking at hypocrisy in politics is commensurately reduced as an important desideratum of social order.

For slightly different reasons, hypocrisy in business should be omitted as well. When we consider the legal conception of the corporation, the idea that deceptive practices by business corporations would be an unusual occurrence is a *non-sequitur.* Corporations exist to make money for their shareholders; they do not exist to represent the moral standards of a culture. Perhaps the tobacco industry would be the clearest example of formally hypocritical acts as to be so numerous and expected that to focus on identifying them, let alone correcting them, is folly. Robert N. Proctor's book, *Golden Holocaust: Origins of the Cigarette Catastrophe and the Case for Abolition* (2011) persistently documents the deceits of the industry through the nineteenth, twentieth, and current centuries. The Legacy Tobacco Documents Library (http://legacy.library.ncsf.edu), which has developed an archive of documents mandated by successive court cases against tobacco manufacturers, lists 6,784 documents with the invocation of "hypocrisy" in a key word search.[4]

The reason I have elected to focus on hypocrisy in religion and sport is that these two institutions represent in their proclaimed purposes and generally attributed social obligations levels of honesty and opposition to deceit that make them unique. If hypocrisy has consequences in institutions—as will be described in the project—then a defensible first step is to consider these institutions as "limiting cases." If hypocrisy exists in these two institutions where such hiding of information and manufacture of information is essentially considered anathema, then this gives us a starting point to assessing degrees of hypocrisy and consequences of hypocrisy where such formal denunciation of hypocrisy does not exist.

The general principles of case selection in play here lie within sociology. Source material must be available. The cases should represent relatively unmitigated forms of the institutional characteristics in view. Max Weber's ideal type is instructive. Sources of meaning infusing human conduct play into his analyses and interpretations of society, giving his distinctive term of "social action." One prototypical example—his ideal type—of such a source of meaning of human conduct came from Reformed Protestantism. As defined here, sport and religion in their ideal typical composition represent institutional instances that should eschew hypocrisy.

Particular attention focuses on religion and sport cases that are visible. The choice of these cases of pedophilia, Penn State, the Tour de France, and Hillsborough meet the necessary requirements of case selection. Records exist both for the individual actors and for the surrounding organizations. Each accommodates to the requirements of the ideal type, in that the public remonstrances of members and the official postures of the organizations claim honesty. The idea of the book being programmatic—providing an outline of work—obviously includes an invitation for continued collaborative efforts within sociology. Therefore the existence of cases that not only are prototypical and have a history of available records but are also ongoing contributes to this invitation for continued collaborative work within the discipline.

---

4   Note: A recent publication of documents from Boy Scout organizations in Oregon (USA) suggests one more ostensive service agency to be doubly fallible in its hypocrisies. Fifteen thousand pages of documents kept by the Oregon chapter of the Scouts describes abuses by 1,247 leaders of member scouts over a period of 1959–85. News agencies sought the release of documents. Not only did the abuses by leaders occur (as described in the documents), but the scouting organization resisted for decades the obligation to publicize the misdeeds. Now called "The Perversion Documents," essentials of the documents began appearing in the United States in October 2012.

The Importance of Organizational Settings

The social context of hypocrisy includes, as well as culture, the institutional setting of acts of deceit. Institutions may be faulted for lies; common use of the term "hypocrite" much more frequently attempts to make an individual culpable. But when an individual is labeled with the term, it is of great importance to be sensitive to the institutional arrangements within which such lies occur. The surrounding institution may, alternatively, hide, nurture, constrain, or punish the individual lies. Considering the attention to the contexts of hypocrisy and looking at the strategic cases of sport and religion as the initial foci of the project, the third facet of the book program will be to consider the role of organizations in the patterns of appearance of hypocrisy and the contribution to the persistence of hypocrisy. This material appears principally in Chapter 4 but also in Chapter 5.

Some Consequences of Hypocrisy

Fourthly, hypocrisy like lying (or fraud or theft) is consequential. It is consequential for the individual who must either find ways to rationalize or cover up his or her contradictions or face them and experience the harsh blow of a diminished self. It is consequential for the institution because its effectiveness as a moral guardian becomes liable to loss of public trust, or, as with individuals, the institution must scurry to establish further mechanisms to neutralize its contradictions. Chapters 4, 5, and 6 address types of implications and consequences. For one example, societal reaction in the form of increased security occurs in Chapter 4. Hypocrisy and other kinds of dishonesty may appear as recognition of cheating occurs in a sport, and representative cases appear in Chapter 5. Hypocrisy (and related violations of truth) which provide insight into general discussions of trust and documented reductions in public trust is the focus of Chapter 6.

Hypocrisy and Sociological Theory

The fifth obligation (and prospect) for this program on hypocrisy is to draw out consequences for how theories of human action and institutions within sociology proceed. The interactionist tradition, particularly associated with the work of Erving Goffman, is one alternative discussed. There are also alternatives associated with the conflict tradition within sociology and from what are termed contract theories of social order. These are elaborated further at the end of this chapter and make up the core of Chapter 7.

Opening Examples of the Sociological Program

Hypocrisy within the Sociological Tradition: Some Attention—with Notable Omissions

As represented by writing such as that of David Runciman (2006, 2008), hypocrisy has been a durable theme of political philosophy. With the rise of thinking about republics, ideas for optimal societies entail a market where success of the ideas required fidelity to preferred individual and institutional standards of morality. There is not a literature within sociology on hypocrisy.[5] The absence is cause for some reflection. Sociology focuses on matters of social order, changes of these orders, and threats to the order. Stability, ordered change, and breaches hinge on some condition of trust: agreed upon norms, new ones duly negotiated, or norms compromised. Hypocrisy assumes trust to begin with and then disappoints trust, hence the apparent relevance to traditional sociological concerns.

The work of Erving Goffman would seem to be full of allusions to hypocrisy. However, treatments such as *The Presentation of Self in Everyday Life* (Goffman, 1959) and *Stigma* (Goffman, 1986) make no use of the term. These two books suggest two standpoints toward the manipulations of information that in substance are involved in what other writers call "hypocrisy." The juxtaposition of the two, preoccupation with hypocrisy versus considering hypocrisy as part of general social artifice opens up ideas relevant to general theories about organization, trust, and deceit which will be treated at the end of the book in Chapter 7.

If Goffman's posture toward lying has informed or reflects the traditions of sociology, then the absence of sociological treatment is not an anomaly at all. Goffman's approach from the beginning of his rich production of insights and terminology considers all social life as artifice. In his whole scheme, the meanings of hypocrisy as probed here are ordinary and predictable. When we find in *The Presentation of Self* the terms for disruption (inconsistencies or contradictions) in "face," for example, these are not problematic for society in terms of lost trust and cynicism. Rather the valence of treatment is that these are flaws in the maintenance of a social conspiracy erecting a social order.

Goffman assumes the performance of all actors is not problematical with deceitful acts. By contrast, critics of hypocrisy see these as the fissures that can doom society. What is problematical for Goffman in the deceits is the discovery. This can only be resolved or repaired by a recovery individually created or aided by allies. The valuation of this deception is somewhat altered in *Stigma*. Here one's identity personally and socially can potentially become at risk. So one must work to "fit" into society. One learns to "pass" or to "cover" questionable acts and appearances.

In short, then, the threats to public order that hypocrisy formally poses, on one hand, but the spreading occurrences on the other hand (perhaps diluting its

---

5 An accounting of this lacuna within sociological writing occurs within Chapter 5.

importance for some) create some context for understanding the mixed character of sources on the topic. As Runciman and others demonstrate, the importance of hypocrisy within political theory assumes salience in the seventeenth century and continues, at least in his analysis, into the twenty-first century. Moral philosophers such as Bok treat hypocrisy as an important component of lying and concealment. It would seem that sociology would foreground the topic. However, it may be that there is a sufficient heritage of cynicism about artifice in institutions and in human conduct that sociology avers to the "generality, therefore irrelevant" standpoint. Erving Goffman's work from *The Presentation of Self* and *Stigma* through *Frame Analysis* (1986) would be one major example of this stance.

There are some concepts that are attended to within sociology generally that may carry some insights on hypocrisy such as "demand characteristics," "side bets," "commitment," "ambivalence," and "hypocrisy as a context for evil." There are a few isolated experimental studies such as those of Lammers et al. (2010). The relevance of power placement of an individual for anticipating greater predisposition toward hypocrisy exists in this instance. But there is no intellectual stream of work. Inventories of survey studies such as those of ICPSR (Inter-university Consortium for Political and Social Research) in the United States give no listing of the concept. The consequences for institutions discussed in this chapter and throughout the book do receive some attention in survey studies of loss of public confidence (of government, banks, journalists, jurists). Chapters 6 and 7 explore implications for social science research that the deficit of attention to hypocrisy holds.

Religion, Sport, and Organizational Imperatives

Religion
This famous definition by Clifford Geertz shows the central role of religion in culture: "Religion is (1) a system of symbols which acts to (2) establish powerful, pervasive, and long-lasting moods and motivations in men [and women and children] by (3) formulating conceptions of a general order of existence and (4) clothing these conceptions of such an aura of factuality that (5) the moods and motivations seem uniquely realistic" (Geertz, 1973: 90). One might construe "religion" as used here as "that which concerns us ultimately," to invoke Paul Tillich. I use Clifford Geertz's definition of religion because I believe this has broad use by researchers who want to identify common components of religion in doing comparative research. While cryptic, Tillich's conception certainly is discriminating in identifying beliefs, rituals, and teachings which official religions maintain and which cannot be casually applied to the institutional purposes of other institutions.

Denying one's self or an act (dissimulation) or adopting a self-characteristic or act that is not so (simulation) are lies. As such, religions condemn these conditions as they condemn all artifice. The Bible, in several versions, cites instances that are deemed wrong. As Runciman makes evident, political discourse of the seventeenth and eighteenth centuries made hypocrisy in politics highly salient. The relative occurrence of "hypocrisy" in the King James Version of the Bible compared to its appearance in later versions shows the salience Runciman describes. The concordance for the King James Version lists 42 entries; the Revised Standard Version lists 21. Consistent with Christianity's negativity toward hypocrisy, the Koran lists 37 instances with associated indictments.

The strong condemnation of hypocrisy by religions illuminates a dynamic that the extent of censure may insure preoccupation with it; and in ideological conflicts may lead to preoccupation with hypocrisy. Judith Shklar notes this dynamic within politics: "Our levels of moral exigency clearly determine what we do or do not regard as hypocritical. Ideological conflict, however contributes as much as moral rigor to making it the chief of the vices. When political actors disagree about right and wrong, and everything else, they can only undermine each other with the revelation that their opponent is not living up to his own professional ideal" (1984: 47, 48).

Religions whose essence stresses moral purity are a more extreme example of an institution where fear of hypocrisy is escalated and charges used as a tool against opponents. Shklar continues: "The striving for religious perfection is interminable, and the demand for fidelity is ever more exigent. The stricter these requirements of faith are, however, the more likely real or imputable pretense becomes. But the only weapon against it is to insist on even greater efforts, which in turn encourages the very vice that is to be extirpated. Exigency creates hypocrisy as one of its inevitable by-products and Puritanism is invariably accompanied by hypocrisy and duly ridiculed for it" (1984: 49).

The words "hypocrite" and "hypocrisy" have roots in fourth-century BC Greek use within the theater, where an actor is providing a fiction of an ostensive reality in the drama, and an actor's interpretation, one of alternative meanings; and also within the combination of the words "hypo," signifying under and "krinein" meaning to decide: hence a deficiency in judgment. The meanings from scholarship on the seventeenth- and eighteenth-century use and public preoccupation done by Runciman (2006; 2008), Shklar (1984), and Davidson (2004) combine the practice of dissimulation, where an unfavorable characteristic is hidden, or simulation where a favorable characteristic is claimed falsely.

The term always has some negative component. However, as commentary on contexts of use shows the meanings can be mixed. Runciman, Shklar, and Davidson note contending positions about the meaning of hypocrisy. While hypocrisy challenges fidelity, some forms of hypocrisy may be evaluated as a matter of results of democratic choices and necessary for the continuities of some interactions. Some key relationships appear in an analysis of the eighteenth and nineteenth centuries. Sincerity versus politeness captures on one side the emphasis on unadulterated honesty versus withholding a criticism of another's appearance which would disrupt an interaction. Runciman describes the existence of two orders of hypocrisy, which contrast in seriousness. "First-order hypocrisy is the ubiquitous practice of concealing vice as virtue, which makes up the parade of our social existence. Second-order hypocrisy is concealing the truth about this practice, and pretending that the parade itself is a form of genuinely virtuous, and therefore self-denying behavior" (Runciman, 2008: 53, 54). The difference between dissimulation and simulation occupies Francis Bacon (Bacon, 2008). Those who acquiesce in the necessity of first-order hypocrisy, further emphasize that behaviors and claims which may be technically dishonest eventually may become habits and hence in a regularized form show verifiably honorable conduct.

In a body of broad journalistic representation in North America, *The New York Times* offered 121 separate statements on religion and hypocrisy from 2002 through 2011. This preoccupation appears continuously for 50 years, with decade by decade figures from 1962 being 122, 116, 101, and 135 preceding the last decade figure. These consistently portrayed hypocrisy as negative in its occurrences.

The continuing scandal of priests abusing parishioners in the Roman Catholic Church, and the persistent pattern of superiors masking egregiously bad acts by priests was one of the most glaring examples of deceits within the protection of power. Priests hold authority on the basis of power and reputation. Recognition of abuses occurred by 1950. "By 2011, allegations had been made against nearly 5000 priests, and over 15,000 individuals had testified to being victimized. (Estimates of the actual number of victims range as high as 280,000)" (Schneier, 2012: 163).

Figure 1.1   Timeline of Catholic priest pedophilia[6]

Date	Event
5/25/48	Priest letter intimating pedophilia from 1948; released on 9/21/05.
1993	Bishop Mahoney writes to Vatican about pedophile priest.
2000s	Recognition of Vatican and Episcopal protections of priests. Secret archives opened; settlements with victims begin.
2003	BishopsAccountability.org: http://www:bishop-accountability. org/AtAGlance/timeline.htm (note the organizational response in other cases later, for example, Boy Scouts, USA Swimming).

------

6   The provision of timelines to complement the narrative within each of the major cases covered serve at least three of the five program goals: illustrating the role of context on the appearance and meaning of the hypocrisy; showing how the surrounding organizations both protect and then violently oppose the hypocrisies; and suggesting possible consequences of the initial act and the organizational involvement. There are three isolable source streams for the items in this figure and the text material. One is the trail of instances that come from a combination of both church admission/acquiesce and acts of the legal system which initially appear in news accounts. The now frequent coverage of these cases by news outlets is a start-point with the coverage of claimed abuses among Boston clergy by the *Boston Globe* (the first in January 6, 2001). A second comes from developing research literature: for example, Jason Berry and Gerald Renner, *Vows of Silence: The Abuse of Power in the Papacy of John Paul II* (New York: Free Press, 2004) and Philip Jenkins, *Pedophiles and Priests: Anatomy of a Contemporary Crisis* (Oxford: Oxford University Press, 2001).

3/2010	Report that Lawrence C. Murphy, a priest at a school for the deaf in Wisconsin assaulted boys, 1950–74. Case was forwarded to Congregation for the Doctrine of the Faith, headed by Cardinal Ratzinger (future pope Benedict XVI), but office did not act.
9/2012	Bishop Robert W. Finn, bishop of Kansas City-St. Joseph, convicted for failure to report child abuse (first act toward Bishop in US).
1/2013	A report about a telephone "hotline" in Germany, which received 8,500 calls about abuse. The report itself contained information from 1,824 callers, 1,165 with claims of being victims of abuse.
2/2013	Cardinal Keith O'Brien resigns over charges he protected pedophiles while a bishop in Scotland.
2/2013	Roger M. Mahoney, bishop of Los Angeles, relieved of duties for protecting pedophile priests.
2013	Range of costs totaled. Includes settlements to victims; priest destructiveness; suicides of victims (chronicled in Victoria, Australia); loss of revenues and defections from Catholic Churches); after Milwaukee Diocese goes bankrupt, one estimate for Roman Catholic Church is $3 billion in settlements.
2/2013	Pope Benedict XVI resigns.
3/2013	Jorge Mario Borgoglio elected Pope, as Francis.
7/2013	Pope Francis of gay priests, "Who am I to judge?"
7/14/2014	Affidavit filed in Ramsey County, Minnesota by Jennifer Haselberger.

A third can be described as an advocacy literature coming from self-defined caretakers of Church members, and sometimes the very name of the Roman Catholic Church. BishopAccountability.org, begun in 2003 and located in Massachusetts, is one visible example. This organization, incorporated and claiming to be non-profit, describes itself as an educational institution. The sources for these items on the timeline come mainly from published accounts that are journalistic reports, but include on-the-record acts of the Church and civil or criminal legal actions. The beginning event reported in "A Documentary History of the Crisis" from BishopAccountability.org is from an archive entry provided in a letter by Rev. Joseph P. Gausch of Philadelphia written to a fellow priest. A useful illustration of the many parties to the discovery, concealment, and then excusing and/or apologizing for priest and administrative activities in abuse cases exists in the recent court statement by Jennifer M. Haselberger who was a Canon Lawyer working in the Archdiocese of Saint Paul and Minneapolis, Minnesota ("Affidavit of Jennifer M. Haselberger Filed in Second Judicial District Court, 7/14/14 in Ramsey County Civil Court, Minnesota).

Sport

Sport essentially is physical, intrinsic, rule governed, and consummative. It is a moral preserve because it requires to maintain its venerated status as a means of cultural memory (along with appealing to all the senses and being a source of common conversation topics), preserving intact rules that define practices and outcomes. The purity of the activity serves as a kind of moral preserve making sporting acts the medium of metaphor and accounts serviceable as cultural memory.

For a definition to be useful it must refer to something and exclude something else. I believe my definition of sport as: physical, intrinsic, rule governed, and consummative does capture how sport was known from early records of the Olympics in the eighth century BC, and how it usefully can be used at present with the "boundaries in use" criterion along the lines of Durkheim's definition of moral systems. The boundaries of elite athletics (Olympic Games or Tour de France) are illuminated when violations are cited. These same essential components of sport appear in gymnasia all over the world on Saturday mornings where "pick-up" games of hand-ball, soccer, or basketball occur without formal referees. If rules regarding local court access, team selection, appropriate accommodation to common rules, or lack of adequate physical effort (which can mitigate a team's chance of winning) are compromised, penalties are stiff, immediate, and consequential. Losing a pick-up basketball game does not rest on extrinsic rewards of money; but losing may end access to a court, yield loss of reputation defined by sex, class, race, age, department affiliation, or disallow bragging rights for a day, a weekend, or a lifetime. Anybody who has participated in such weekend sport activity knows these realities clearly.[7]

When coaches, players, or officials compromise these elements, it often is a moral stretch that may exceed criminal or civil penalties. Perhaps the biggest event in North America in the last year is the prospect of Jerry Sandusky's acts toward children under his care and the implications for Penn State University and the Penn State Football Program.

The Pennsylvania State University case which emerged in late 2011 continues to provide a template for charting the expanding institutional implications of a personal act of hypocrisy. Jerry Sandusky, a former assistant football coach at Pennsylvania State University was indicted on several criminal charges for coercing and having sex with minor males. The hypocritical elements of his acts exist in the fact that he was able to gain access and trust from the boys because of his reputation and status as a coach and later through his work in an ostensive philanthropic organization which helped boys with problems. The organization, "The Second Mile," was founded by Sandusky in 1977; it ceased to operate after November 2011. An assistant coach was asked to resign following the

---

7 Note: for printed illustrations of the formidable constraints of rules in informal sport, one can look at David Halberstam, *The Amateur* (1996) or Pete Axthelm, *The City Game: Basketball from the Garden to the Playground* (1970).

arrest and indicting of Sandusky because some years earlier he (the younger assistant) saw one of the acts and did not intervene appropriately; nor was he considered to have adequately reported the act. Following this, the university also fired the head coach, Joe Paterno, who had coached at the institution for 60 years, 45 of which he acted as head coach. Not judged criminally culpable, Paterno was considered not to have acted directly enough to constrain Sandusky and had compromised the university. In turn, the institution fired Graham Spanier, president of the university. Again, his inaction in the scenario and even indications of his predisposition to hide the incidents were among the faults eventually attributed to him.

Initial consequences of the abuse cases and the improper handling of knowledge in 1998, 2000, and 2001 by administrators at Penn State have been widely reported. Joe Paterno (coach), Graham B. Spanier (president), Tim Curley (athletic director), Gary Schultz (vice president), and Thomas Harmon (university police chief) all were forced out of the university. Coach Paterno has died, and Curley and Schultz have been indicted for criminal culpability in the history of the administrative handling of the abuse and for perjury. (Footnote 6 contains additional details, and specific sources.)

Within two weeks of the report of the Freeh investigation (July 12, 2012), an independent inquiry,[8] the NCAA penalties were exacted.[9] These included: a $60 million fine; disqualification from post-season games for four years; a fine of $13 million for four years from the Big Ten Conference (of which Penn State is a part); a loss of 10 scholarships for football for four years; and the requirement that victories of Coach Paterno be vacated during the period of 1998–2011. The university expunged a major part of Paterno's visibility on the campus by taking down a statue honoring the coach. Institutions, one being the University of Wisconsin, began revising their reporting and controlling procedures of acts of sexual harassment.

---

8 The "Freeh Report," as it is referenced colloquially, carries the formal title, *Report of the Special Investigative Counsel Regarding the Actions of the Pennsylvania State University Related to the Child Sexual Abuse Committed by Gerald A. Sandusky.* The report covers allegations about Sandusky, the early investigation by Penn State of Sandusky in the 1990s, Sandusky's retirement from that university, and the series of actions over the past three years by Penn State toward Sandusky's record, actions which have been criticized and which have brought criminal litigation against Penn State officials.

9 I.e. the National Collegiate Athletic Association, the principal governing body of university athletics in the United States. It is mentioned further in footnote 10 below and in Chapter 2.

Figure 1.2   Chronology of Penn State situation[10]

Date	Event
1994	Sandusky inappropriately has contact with a boy (he has befriended) in a shower.
1998	Sandusky showers with an 11-year-old boy. Mother is told, and she reports incident to Penn State.
5/98	Detectives listen to phone conversation with mother; Sandusky admits contact and admits it was wrong.
6/1/98	Sandusky is interviewed by State Department of Public Welfare and a Penn State University police detective. Says he will not shower with children any more.
1999	Sandusky assaults a boy multiple times in a Pennsylvania State University facility.
1999	Paterno tells Sandusky he will not be next head coach; Sandusky retires.
Fall 2000	James Calhoun, a janitor, sees Mr Sandusky in the football locker room's shower, performing oral sex on a boy. Mr Calhoun tells his supervisor and other janitorial staff, but a formal report is never made.
3/1/02	McQueary, a graduate assistant, sees separate shower incident with Sandusky and boy (dispute remains about different reports he made of the incident).

---

10   The timeline of the Penn State Scandal runs from 1994 to the present. Principals in the narrative and in the summary items in this figure include Jerry Sandusky, Joe Paterno, Graham Spanier, Cynthia Baldwin, Tim Curley, Gary Schultz, Mike McQueary, the Paterno family estate, Louis Freeh, and approximately 26 unnamed victims of Sandusky's assaults. Jerry Sandusky started as a coach at Penn State in 1969. He started the Second Mile program as a charity for underprivileged youth. The program ended in 2012. Joe Paterno was the head football coach at Penn State University from 1966 until November 8, 2011 when the Penn State Board of Trustees fired him. He died in January 2012. Graham Spanier was president of Penn State University from September 1995 until November 9, 2011, when he resigned. Cynthia Baldwin, an attorney, has entered the sequence because of a disagreement over her representation in the 2011 Grand Jury process. Part of Spanier's, Schultz's, and Curley's defense in August 2013, uses their claim that Baldwin's testimony against them in the Grand Jury proceedings was a conflict of interest, because they understood that she, as a Penn State attorney, was defending them during the 2011 Grand Jury processes. Timothy Curley became athletic director at Penn State in 1993. His testimony about knowledge and acts associated with Sandusky in the Grand Jury trial was impugned and he was indicted for perjury. He was placed on administrative leave, and Penn State did not renew his contract when it expired in June 2013. Mike McQueary was a student assistant in 2002; in March 2002, he observed Sandusky in a compromising position. He has testified to this effect in 2010. The Paterno family has taken steps to challenge the Penn State firing of

3/2/02	McQueary (who became wide-receivers coach and recruiting coordinator in 2004) reports incident to Mr Paterno at his house.
3/3/02	Paterno reports incident to Timothy M. Curley, athletic director.
Mid-3/2002	McQueary meets with Curley and Gary C. Schultz to discuss incident.
Late 3/2002	McQueary informed Sandusky's keys taken, and incident reported to Second Mile.
2002	Spanier is notified of the incident and approves of how it was handled.
2008	Mother of high school freshman reports inappropriate acts of Sandusky to high school. They contact police.
2009	Pennsylvania District Attorney begins an investigation.
12/10	McQueary testifies at grand jury.
1/12/11	Schultz and Curley testify they were not told by McQueary about any sexual conduct.
2011	Spanier testified he was never informed the incident was sexual. Says he was not aware of police investigation in 1998.

Coach Paterno, and they commissioned a report challenging the Freeh report, their report headed by Dick Thornburgh (November 2013). Louis Freeh was director of the United States Federal Bureau of Investigation from 1993–2001. He was commissioned by Penn State University to investigate the Sandusky scandal, and he issued his report in July 2012. The dates reported in this timeline through the Sandusky sentencing and the immediate aftermath come from a consensual record in *Report of the Special Investigative Counsel Regarding the Actions of The Pennsylvania State University Related to the Child Abuse Committed by Gerald A. Sandusky* (Freeh Sporkin & Sullivan, July 12, 2012); *Paterno* (Posnanski, 2012); and relevant portions of "Penn State Child Abuse Scandal" (Wikipedia, last modified on July 21, 2014). Gary Schultz had been a Vice President at Penn State during the events scrutinized by the Grand Jury. He was indicted along with Curley, and following the Grand Jury statement he resigned. The series of responses and individual legal actions by these principals receive coverage in general media such as *The New York Times*, and in sport media such as publications by ESPN. Access for the key moments in the timeline since the Sandusky sentencing come from "Penn State Child Abuse Scandal" (Wikipedia) and "Graham Spanier" (Wikipedia, last modified on August 11, 2014). Four specific sources show how the principals' efforts to extricate themselves from the charges of lying or inappropriate behavior continue: for the 7/14/14 entry regarding Paterno's efforts at a settlement ("Paterno Won Sweeter Deal Even as Scandal Played Out," *The New York Times*, July 14, 2012, http://www.nytimes.com/2012/07/14); regarding the McQueary case (Don Van Natta Jr., ESPN The Magazine, 3/4/14, http://espn.go.com/espn/featurestory); President's Spanier's life ("The Trials of Graham Spanier, Penn State's Ousted President," Michael Sololove, *The New York Times*, July 16, 2014, http://www.nytimes.com/2014/07/20/magazine); and reaction and some political efforts regarding Spanier's fate (Jack Stripling, "Behind an Ex-President, a Band of Loyalists," *The Chronicle of Higher Education*, August 11, 2014, http://chronicle.com/article).

11/4/11	Prosecutors file 40 charges against Sandusky for conduct toward eight boys; file charges against Curley and Schultz, saying they lied and failed to report incidents to law enforcement agencies.
11/5/11	Sandusky arrested, released on $100,000 bail.
11/6/11	Spanier supports Curley and Schultz, who step down.
11/7/11	Curley and Schultz surrender to police.
11/9/11	Penn State Board fires Spanier and Paterno.
11/11	President and CEO of Second Mile, Jack Raykovitz, steps down.
1/2/12	Tom Corbett, Pennsylvania Governor, sues NCAA over penalties levied against Penn State.
1/14/12	Sally Jenkins interview with Joe Paterno.
1/22/12	Paterno dies.
2/17/12	Penn State countersues Pennsylvania Manufacturers' Association Insurance Co., because PMA has declined to pay for defense costs associated with misconduct of Sandusky. "PMA argues that it is not obligated to pay out on policies written after 1991 because of exclusions for 'abuse or molestation,' 'intentional acts,' 'known loss.'"
7/12/12	Louis Freeh report delivered.
7/14/12	"Mr Paterno was said to be paid $3 million at the end of the 2011 season if he agreed it would be his last. Interest-free loans totaling $350,000 that the university had made to Paterno over the years would be forgiven as part of the retirement package. He would also have the use of the university's private plane and a luxury box at Beaver Stadium for him and his family to use over the next 25 years."
10/2/12	McQueary sues Penn State for defamation and misinformation (seeks $4 million).
10/9/12	Sandusky sentenced to 30–60 years by Judge John M. Cleland for 45 counts of abuse.
11/1/12	Spanier charged.
11/9/12	Spanier "... was arraigned and released on bail at a brief court appearance Wednesday on charges he lied about and concealed child sex abuse allegations involving former assistant football coach Jerry Sandusky."
2/2013	*Critique of the Freeh Report: the Rush to Injustice Regarding Joe Paterno* appears.
3/12/2013	Sandusky scandal has cost Penn State $41 million.
4/2013	Penn State fights McQueary lawsuit
5/2013	Paterno's family sues Penn State.
7/15/13	Spanier sues Louis Freeh for slander/libel/defamation from Freeh Report.
7/30/13	Spanier, Gary Schultz, and Tim Curley ordered to stand trial by Judge William Wenner.

7/30/13	Perjury charge entered in court for Graham Spanier (contesting his April 2011 testimony).
8/5/13	Lawyers for Spanier, Schultz, and Curley are asking that testimony of Cynthia Baldwin (in 2001 the Penn State General Counsel) be ruled inadmissible, since she could have been representing the three when she heard them discussing Sandusky in 2001.
8/7/13	Spanier, Curley, and Schultz enter pleas of "Not Guilty."
8/18/13	First of 26 claims settled. Multi-million settlement for 26-year-old man, who was attacked in August 2001. Penn State has allotted $60 million total for the settlements.
8/24/13	Seven victims settle. These include Sandusky's son, Matt; and includes Victim 2, who as a child Mike McQueary said he saw being attacked in 2001. (McQueary at the time was a student assistant, and later testified about what he saw.)
8/2013	Sandusky criticizes first Penn State settlements.
9/2013	NCAA criticizes Paterno family lawsuit.
3/4/2014	Update of McQueary firing and lawsuits.
8/11/2014	News account of loyal supporters of Spanier.
8/16/2014	News account of Spanier post-career experiences.

Consequences and Implications of Hypocrisy: Delaying and Concealing Revelations

Hypocrisy is lying. Information denied or finessed about a negative characteristic is dissimulation. (This may appear when another is condemned by somebody who displays the same basis for condemnation, but denies it in himself or herself.) In simulation, as contrasted with dissimulation, where somebody tries to hide an unfavorable act or condition, an actor or an institution make claims about themselves that are not true. An effort is made, that is, to fabricate a credential. Hypocrisy has the special ingredient from general forms of deceit in that the actor or institution profits directly from the hypocrisy. Denying or concealing something negative in the past assures benefit through the denial in the hypocrisy: the negative element cannot be a liability. Claiming a characteristic yields a good to the hypocrite in the form of moral, judgmental, or material coin, even though the gain is unwarranted. In a social arrangement where cynics argue the generality of deceit, hypocrisy carries an especially strong breach of trust (still occurring, as argued, in religion and sports, if not politics). This is because the claim, either of purity from a wrongful past or possession of a valued characteristic, implicitly or explicitly, may elicit honor, loyalty, and trust by consumers, clients, or publics.

In social and cultural terms, the implications of hypocrisy connect crucially to a sequence of commission, initial response to the ostensive hypocrisy, the discovery, and the reception by various audiences and constituencies. The following figure arrays some of the factors in the sequence.

Figure 1.3   The acts, discovery, and dissemination

<table>
<tr><td>

The Act
↓
The Cover-up Power of institution (or person)
  • Control of information by institution (or person)
↓
The Discovery
  • Early institutional whistle-blower (note Penn State)
  • Enforcement officer
  • Victim
  • Media representative (find out status, type of organization)
↓
The reception
  • Must include audience receptivity (to gossip, rumor, failures of others, themselves being hypocritical)
  • Audience must have literacy and access to technical discovery resources

</td></tr>
<tr><td>

Note that the chance for cover-up may be contingent on an actor's sense of guilt or obligation to confess. (John Profumo [d. 2006], Secretary of State for War, was caught in a sex scandal in 1963, and acknowledged his culpability as a matter of honor; Armstrong, Landis, Suzy Favor, and Tyler Hamilton, and other cyclists [discussed later] have tried to lie their way out of their predicaments until they were formally caught or charged.)

</td></tr>
</table>

The timing of the process denoted in Figure 1.3 bears on the magnitude and breadth of the implication, as is evident in these prototypical cases and will also be evident in the cases discussed in Chapter 5. Organizational literature that deals with anticipating factors and consequences of scandals that occur in institutional settings shows consistently that the longer the act or acts persist, including organizational efforts to conceal or re-frame the events as at least neutral, the negative consequences are greater.

In the central cases in this introduction, the length of time that elapsed before discovery and dissemination of the news is substantial. Looking back, the initial event that defines the eventual arrest of Sandusky in 2011, and the events that continued, originally occurred in 1998. A police investigation occurred, but no action within the athletic department at Penn State appears to have followed. The incident that, again retrospectively, is focused on as determining dangers from Sandusky is dated February 2001. In the progression to the crises erupting in 2011, looking back, again, a Vice President for Student Affairs hired in 2003, claims she alerted her superiors about favoritism within the football program during her tenure, but was opposed by Coach Paterno. She resigned in 2007, but became a central figure in 2011 when she distributed information that she had opposed Paterno, and accused Paterno of "favoritism and meddling" (Posnanski 315).

The religious cases introduced as prototypical, again, show long periods of concealment and efforts of the surrounding institutions to downplay the seriousness of the charges of misconduct. In the sizable delays, not only do the original perpetrators of deceit become subject to public censure, but the institutional guardians also have become targets of criminal prosecution.

Revelations of claims of assault and pedophilia toward Church members by priests in the last three years illustrate essential aspects of the sequence of the impropriety, followed by detection and attempts to stop the person, hesitancy or outright gate-keeping of Church authorities, and eventually broad dissemination of events in a report and sanctions against individuals responsible for the original acts and those considered to have covered these up. Notable Dioceses include Kansas City-St. Joseph, Minneapolis-St. Paul, and Los Angeles in the United States, and Berlin in Germany.

Implications for the individual

Self-deception   Self-deception occurs among hypocrites who recognize their deceits or are discovered in their deceits. Sandusky claimed innocence at his sentencing, angering both the presiding judge and the victims. Coach Paterno acknowledged that he should have done more to constrain Sandusky's activities, but showed no recognition of the severity of the Sandusky case.

Guilt and remorse   Fear of a hypocritical act or recognizing oneself as displaying such a deceit can have varying consequences depending on the personal saliency and cultural meaning of a particular kind of integrity. For the Puritan, while the exigencies of the culture may drive one to zealousness and then only pretended zealousness (and success), hypocrisy when recognized may be catastrophic. Calvinistic theology rigorously condemns suicide. But the recognition of the excessively self-conscious person that he or she has deceitfully hidden a vice or dishonestly claimed a virtue has to have consequences.

A Catholic priest may be driven by analogous impulses toward purity and constancy in maintaining his vows. Again, when confronted with evidence of failure or violation of vows, the person may turn public censure into personal censure in the form of attempted suicide. Marion Jones confessed guilt for drug usage; Vince Foster committed suicide (potentially faulted in a scandal during Bill Clinton's Presidential administration); J. Clifford Baxter (Enron executive) was a possible suicide; Kenneth Lay died months after confession of Enron guilt; Father Shawn Ratigan (Kansas City), upon being suspected of creating and storing child pornography, attempts suicide.

If the cultural expectations are strong and personal conformity to them highly salient, one may also tend toward self-destructiveness within sport. During the Cultural Revolution in China which began in 1966, Mao Zedong included table tennis as a banned activity for its possible association with bourgeois values.

Major table tennis players were condemned. Three evidently took to heart the regime condemnation and committed suicide: Yung Kuo Tuan, Fu Qifang, and Jian Yongning. They, alternatively, could have exacted the ultimate self-destruction rather than be forced (as some colleagues did) to honor the definitions and restrictions of the Cultural Revolution. Either way, the exigency of the cultural expectations defined a radical act of self-destruction, one possible consequence of hypocrisy.

Relatives and friends of the hypocrite may experience some guilt, but more often feel remorse at the hypocrite's acts. The father-in-law of Floyd Landis (disqualified winner of the 2006 Tour de France) committed suicide. The son of Bernard Madoff, the imprisoned financier, committed suicide. The son of Jeffrey Skilling (head of Enron) committed suicide.

The dynamic of: culturally-defined high standards, internalization of them by members, a necessary shortage of success on some accepted measure, and, with the shortage, a person being excluded from some form of compensation yields other outcomes than lying and literal suicide. The dynamic may lead to costly forms of escape in the form of some self-injury or renunciation. Judith Shklar speaks of this mixture as a basis of a moral exigency or intense sense of obligation not to fail. The very idea of participation in an activity, such as sports, can carry with some paradox this kind of exigency. Yes, sporting activities are, in principle, intrinsic: "it is just a game." But the rule governed character, another defining dimension, can impose a special sense of accountability for success that is more intense than within an activity that may be evaluated as conditioned by chance. Further drawing on the component of sport as consummative, for those that participate success really does matter and the higher the level of competition the higher are the valuations given to success.

Three examples from within university competitive settings in the United States prove useful. "Sharon [Jarrell] took first [in the cross-country race]. But for years, the scene I would remember most vividly would be the sight of the second-place runner who finished just a few yards ahead of me. The girl, a senior from another school, had run so hard she passed out and crumpled to the ground just after crossing the finish line ... Her example was enough to convince me that cross-country competition needed to be an all-or-nothing proposition. And I determined to do whatever it took to succeed" (Wazeter, 1989: 18). On February 4, 1982, Mary Wazeter, during a walk with her dog in Wilkes-Barre, Pennsylvania, jumped from a bridge into the Susquehanna River. "That night she leaped from the railroad bridge, suffering six broken ribs, collapsed lungs, a broken arm and a shattered vertebra when she hit the ice 35 feet below, ironically lying in the hospital and fighting for her life did more for Mary's mental health attitude than all the preceding therapy" ("A Lethal Quest for the Winning Edge," 1983: 3). Ms Wazeter had been a star high school runner in high school and cross-country races, and in large summer road-races such as the L'eggs Mini Marathon in New York before earning an athletic grant-in-aide to Georgetown University in Washington, DC. Her promise as a runner was cut short by self-doubts in her ability at the school, and compromising habits such as anorexia nervosa during her first prospective cross-country season. She left school and was receiving treatment for her eating disorder: factors immediately preceding her jump from the bridge.

Kathy Ormsby from North Carolina State ran among the leaders in the 10k NCAA championship race underway the evening of June 4, 1986 at Indiana University in Bloomington. Two thirds of the way through the race, Ms Ormsby left the track, traversed a seven-foot fence, ran for several minutes, found a bridge 35 feet above the White River and jumped. Having been located by a concerned coach and taken to a hospital, assessments included a fractured spine and a punctured rib. She was paralyzed from the waist down. As a high-school runner and as a collegiate Ms Ormsby was superb. She was the NCAA, Division I record holder in the 10k, an accomplishment from a meet five weeks before the Indiana University meet.

Suzy Favor competing for the University of Wisconsin won nine NCAA championships. She competed in the Summer Olympic Games in 1992, 1996, and 2000 either in the 800m or 1,500m events. She did not win a medal and she has admitted deliberately falling during the 1500m final in 2000.

A popular culture website, "The Smoking Gun," reported on December 20, 2012 that Ms Suzy Favor Hamilton, under the occupational alias of Kelly Lundy, had been working as a $600 escort with a major service located in Las Vegas ("The Smoking Gun," 2012: 1 ff.). In the aftermath of the news, her accounts included information about depression after her child's birth, sadness over her own brother's suicide in 1999, and tension between her and her husband, Mark, about her double life. Following the news, the Big Ten Athletic Conference in the United States removed her name from the award, which she had won three times, honoring the female athlete of the year.[11]

---

11 Athletic competition within colleges and universities in the United States is regulated by the National Collegiate Athletic Association. Within this general organization, schools participate in one of three divisions (I, II, and III) basically determined by the size of the school and the amount of revenue expended and generated by athletic participation of the respective school. Within these three divisions, groups of schools are further organized around conferences. The criteria for a particular grouping would include the choice of division and historically included geographic proximity, hence the idea of an organization of schools known as the Pac-ten referring to schools near the Pacific Ocean. Now conferences configure themselves additionally with attention to how pairings of schools contribute to market advantages from media coverage. Originally geographic proximity was a strong factor in the constitution of the Big Ten, a grouping of universities primarily in the middle states in the United States. Penn State University was added in 1990, the University of Nebraska was added in 2011, and the University of Maryland and Rutgers University were added in 2014, the latter two particularly affording expansion of media opportunities from East Coast audiences. Johns Hopkins University was added in 2014 with men's lacrosse; this addition served both market interests and competitive advantages for the conference because only a few of the original group of schools sustained men's lacrosse teams. "Big Ten" is still used as an identifier despite the fact that there are now 15 schools in the association. A useful overview of history and present organization of the conference exists in "Big Ten Conference," http://en.wikipedia.org/Big_Ten_Conference, last modified on 8/20/14.

Integration of keen obligations toward perfection exist in all three biographies. Mary Wazeter's home background contained strong influences of the Roman Catholicism of her father and the Welsh-Presbyterianism of her mother. "Running had provided my identity. And I thanked God for the special ability he's given me. I was Mary Wazeter, promising young runner. Now I had only to fulfill the promise" (Wazeter, 1989: 27). "As a high school senior, [Kathy] Ormsby was youth co-pastor and a choir member at a Baptist church. She set three North Carolina high school track records and graduated first in a class of 600. At North Carolina State, when she found a rare break in her schedule, she felt guilty. 'I never felt I was good at anything,' she said, 'I always felt I had to work hard to do well'" ("Runner Recounts Leaving Race and Leaping Off Bridge," 1986: 2).[12]

Implications for institutions

Hypocrisy—the act and the discovery—yields several negative consequences for institutions. First, diminution of trust between institutions can occur as was the case when major umbrella institutions governing collegiate sport in the United

---

12   The three examples occurring with university athletes can be judged to carry an added pressure of a sense of obligation to succeed for the benefit of the school being represented. The dynamic of a compulsion that may include notable violations of the norms that give purpose to the very activity being engaged in exist in the following additional running instances. Thirty-six thousand runners were scheduled to compete in the 118th running of the Boston Marathon on April 21, 2014. Training for this event is physically demanding, the event can be enormously discomforting, especially as glycogen levels drop dangerously low in the last four of the 26.2 miles. Recovery from the experience may last two weeks. There is no external reward for the vast majority of these people; their investment in the preparation, pain, and even danger comes from the consummative character of sport. The consummative sport and the complex of a personally propelling need to be seen as completing the event have in a few instances led some individuals to claim to have finished when they have not. On casual acquaintance with such instance, one might say "Why in the world bother with such a feigned accomplishment?" The fact that it has happened, even with great rarity, provides one more clue to the potency of sport to evoke extreme steps in the process of competing: lying, yes, as in the instances of hypocrisy discussed throughout the book, self-destructiveness as in the instances of Ormsby, Wazeter, and Favor, and even lying about even competing and finishing such arduous events as the marathon.

Thirty-four years ago prior to the day of the 2014 marathon (April 21, 1980) Rosie Ruiz Vivas (born 1953 in Havana, Cuba) crossed the finish line of the Boston Marathon as the ostensive winner, with the fastest Boston on record. Suspicions followed: she was not sweating and had a resting heart rate of 76 (high compared with customary female standards of a rate in the 50s). She had not been seen by legitimate leaders of the female section of the race, Jacqueline Gareau and Patti Lyons. Two Harvard students had seen her run out of a crowd of spectators on Commonwealth Avenue (a half-mile from the finish). Ms Ruiz was justly disqualified from the race.

Mark Singer writes in *The New Yorker* (Singer, 2012) of a Michigan dentist who appears to have fabricated finishes and competitive times for himself in several moderately sized marathons, and larger ones including the Boston Marathon.

States delivered large sanctions on Penn State University. Both the National Collegiate Athletic Association (NCAA) and the Big Ten Conference levied large penalties and fines against Penn State. Secondly, there can be loss of valued members of the institution as with players leaving Penn State during and after the Sandusky affair. Church members left the Lutheran Church in Iceland over the Bishop scandal (discussed in later chapters). Commentators report losses among Roman Catholic Church members where scandals occurred. Thirdly, there is a reduction of resources as efforts may be increasingly invested in damage control. In some cases, involving the Roman Catholic Church, finances dwindled and some churches were closed. Fourthly, there can be financial losses to an institution. There has been an immediate, substantial cost to Penn State; but long-term costs of loss of game revenue, civil suits, and alumni support could last for ten years. Fifth, there can be a cost for like-institutions from a "warning effect." As mentioned, Wisconsin and other institutions began their own revision of structures to prevent such costly circumstances as occurred at Penn State.

All of the institutional implications noted here are in process and may continue indefinitely, with reduction of donations, loss of student applicants, loss of players, and civil suits from victims claiming abuse. (The sequence is schematized with additional notes in Figure 1.3 above.) Sandusky has been convicted on 45 of 49 criminal charges and in October 2012 was sentenced to at least 30 years in jail. Following the Freeh report, Tom Kline, a lawyer for one of the victims said: "I believe the report is a road map, a resource manual and a guidebook to the civil litigation."

One of the characteristic patterns of the cases described here is an exponential growth of reaction and new action by parties in the hypocrisy context. Even if the events were long-standing and concealed, once the revelation (often provoked by a journalist) occurs parties work to redirect attention and re-frame the discovery to neutralize culpability.

With respect to the Penn State case in particular, the expansion includes the following sequence, in summary. Graham Spanier, the sitting Pennsylvania University President, was indicted (November 1, 2011) on charges of grand jury perjury, obstruction of justice, child endangerment, failure to report child abuse, and conspiracy in connection with the scandal. Curley and Schultz were also indicted for these charges. President Spanier was then forced to resign as president of the university on November 11, 2011.

In 2012, Joe Posnanski published a long-developing biography of Joe Paterno (Posnanski, 2012). Along with a developmental trajectory in the material, in which Coach Paterno was collaborating, there is a turn at the end for inclusion of material on the Penn State crisis which was prompted by the unexpected disclosures about, and the arrest and sentencing of, Sandusky. Looking back to front, from Paterno's death (January 12, 2012), the events in 2011 and 2012 defined the last quarter of the book and surely prompted an earlier publication and different conclusion than Mr Posnanski had originally envisioned.

On October 2, 2012, Mike McQueary, the assistant coach who had been pivotal in initiating original events in the sequence by reporting a sighting of Sandusky's fraternization with a child in the football locker room, filed a defamation law suit against Penn State.

By February 2013, news sources have reported that as many as 28 alleged victims of the scandal have sued either Sandusky, Penn State University, "The Second Mile" (the philanthropic association associated with Sandusky), or a combination of these targets. Eighteen persons have been added to the 10 originally mentioned in the trial of Sandusky. Reports in July 2013 authorized by the Penn State Board of Trustees estimate settlements of about $60 million for about 24 claimants.

The governor of Pennsylvania, Tom Corbett, on January 1, 2013 sued the NCAA "... on behalf of the people of Pennsylvania, alleging that it was 'overreaching and unlawful' in how it punished the university, and that it broke antitrust laws and harmed residents in the process)" (Steve Eder, *NYT*, 1/2/2013).[13]

The length of time the factors of the Penn State situation took, and the duration of the reported claims about priest abuse, prompt the question for institutional care-takers and a variety of inquiries from outside about long-term liability to these and other institutions. In general, there is no insurance for these types of issues. The reason for this is that they are not accidental and as a result are not insurable. Thus, insurers exclude intentional acts. Insurance policies also exclude criminal acts, abuse and molestations. (Leverty, personal communication, 2013). In recent negotiations over coverage of damages by State Farm of Sandusky's acts, the insurance carrier filed a motion in Pennsylvania to receive that as a company they are not liable. Following this suit, the Sandusky estate and State Farm Fire and Casualty Company resolved their dispute. Relatedly, Pennsylvania Manufacturers' Association (PMA) Insurance Company has sued to be divested of claims on its coverage or any liabilities. Penn State has countersued to maintain the coverage.

The Roman Catholic Church insures itself. So though technically they are "covered" for these eventualities, the pool of resources to deal with these risks comes from the Church itself.

Hypocrisy and the Problem of Trust in Societies

Despite hypocrisy being common across many societies, it is generally condemned. Philosophical ethics has considered it among the worst human vices.

---

13   In February 2013, a report from a committee sustained by the Paterno family appeared: "Critique of the Freeh Report: the Rush to Injustice" (totaling some 240 pages of text and documents authenticating the credentials of the committee members). Louis J. Freeh, the lead author of the group generating the original report, in turn distributed to the press a defense of the "Freeh Report."

Complementing the seven deadly sins of Christianity, Judith N. Shklar (1984) lists, in order of seriousness, the "ordinary vices" of cruelty, hypocrisy, snobbery, treachery, and misanthropy. The texts of world religions condemn hypocrisy. In the overview of major news sources' allusions to "hypocrisy" in its connection to either religion or sport, the consistent negative valence of hypocritical acts is unavoidable.[14] Considering implications for both persons and institutions at the hypothetical level and with empirical examples shows psychological costs and often huge institutional costs. Despite this weight of opprobrium, though, hypocrisy persists. Why? And what is to be done with an eye to improving and maintaining trust levels?

The *Why?* question receives some illumination from the very generality of hypocrisy and the inherent contradictions described above. Hence, resolution in the interest of heightening trust offers at first two discouraging possibilities.

From Machiavelli until the current day, commentators on politics would seem to suggest that in that institution, hypocrisy is so common that it is generally assumed. While political spokespersons may both dissimulate and simulate, the generality may mean that nobody expects better and so when it occurs offenders may claim harm is mitigated. The same diminution of negative consequences may be argued within both sport and religion as well.

More complexly, prospects for hypocrisy may be tied to customary and sometimes honorable practices such as aspirations and self-promotion. Such was the case with the Puritans in England and the new North America. Puritans sought purity and distinctness, and many analyses cite the associated expectations and discipline as reasons for Puritan successes. But failure and compromise can occur, so the vulnerability to personal and public claims of "hypocrisy" for Puritans emerges.

Trust depends on knowledge about others and extrapolations leading to assumptions about others that allow assessments of costs and rewards in cooperation. Hypocrisy perverts the mechanism: denying or hiding negative attributes (dissimulation) or inflating positive attributes (simulation) makes safe calculation of cost/reward in cooperation impossible. In Bruce Schneier's (2012: 139, 140) comments on trust maintenance, a person may defect (by lying hypocritically) for selfish needs or because they think somebody else is effecting deceit and may in the process best them. Hypocrisy may be a means for an individual, group, or organization for self-preservation. One can, thereby, be caught between two competing moral demands: the demand for moral purity and the demands for success.

Along with these two discouraging prospects, one can identify a few practical alternatives that may reduce hypocrisy in the interest of trust. Short of a cultural change, some institutional protections could on empirical and theoretical grounds

14   These news sources, representing the United States, France, and Iceland in the comparisons of sport and religion in the countries in Chapters 2 and 3 are: *The New York Times*, *Le Monde*, and *Morganblaðið*.

suggest that centralization of power increases the chance of hypocrisy. In the Penn State University case, the NCAA, the regents of that university, and the conclusions of the independent group investigating the scandal (Report of the Special Investigating Counsel, 2012) all pointed to the seriousness of the destructive acts being centrally tied to the arrogance of power at the university (and by intimation the power allocated to football programs at other universities). The president of the NCAA's comment was mirrored by other college presidents: "Football will never again be put ahead of educating, nurturing and protecting young people," Mark Emmert [the NCAA president] said (Emmert, 2012). Similarly, "We've had enough," Edward Ray, the president of Oregon State and the NCAA executive committee chairman, said of the ethical lapses that have disfigured big-time college sports in recent years. "This has to stop" (Ray, 2012).[15]

Use of technology to guard against deceits can occur. Technology can, of course, be exploited by and save those who want to conceal unwanted information or who intend to burnish modest credentials in the public domain. But technology can also make known hypocritical acts of simulation and dissimulation. The tool "Politifact" is one such resource: http://www.politifact. com/, especially see the Truth-o-meter, http://www.politifact.com/truth-o-meter/ statements/. A similar resource is Factcheck.org, but their measurements aren't as easily quantified: http://factcheck.org/. Chapter 4 will examine the balance of aid that elaborate technologies provide to those who want to conceal facts about themselves in juxtaposition with those who have the facility to use technologically-aided searches to uncover acts of deceit of individuals and institutions.

Finally, with an eye to combining both variations in centralized power (a source of potential deceits) and access to factual information one can combine knowledge of centrality using the GINI Index with a measure of corruption. One useful representation of corruption is available in: http://www.transparency.org/ research/cpi/overview/. Chapter 6 will examine literature on trust within societies, and discuss implications that hypocrisy holds for confidence that publics have in institutions and leaders.

---

15 The statement is representative. President Ray occupies a highly distinguished position in America's system of higher education. The position requires the support of collegiate athletics at his institution. He complements his acknowledgement of the importance of sports at Oregon State University with a further commitment in his oversight work within the NCAA. But even as he speaks, the NCAA itself is being sued, and successfully, as will be discussed in Chapter 2, for violation of the US Sherman Anti-trust Act. Further, by the fall of 2014, the NCAA has violated its own claims for oversight of athletic scholarships and mechanisms of "competitive balance" by ceding discretion over the amount of money given students to five special conferences and the schools which are members of those conferences.

Theoretical Stakes in the Investigation of Hypocrisy across Cultures: a Return to the Work of Sociology

Runciman, Davidson, and Shklar explain, from their research on politics in the seventeenth and eighteenth centuries, that hypocrisy can have different meanings, even some with opposed values. "O.K.," one might say, "then why bother with or worry about the negative valence?" This predisposition exists in material such as an essay in *The New York Times*, entitled "Hypocrisy Has Its Virtues" (Alan Ahrenhall, February 6, 2001). "Hypocrisy" as an appellation to criticize another person is used relatively frequently in US commentary compared to other cultural settings (Tables 2.1 and 2.2 in the book). "So," one can say, "the ubiquity should prompt reduction in preoccupation with the possible negative consequences of hypocrisy. Indeed, it appears to be all around us and so we should not bother with it." "Hypocrisy," the lexical item, is treated quite differently by lines of literature discussed in this book. *Words that Work: It's Not What You Say, It's What People Hear* (2007), the work of Frank Luntz, the publicist for many Republicans in the US; George Lakoff, identified as a cognitive scientist (*Moral Politics, How Liberals and Conservatives Think*, 2002; *The Political Mind*, 2009); or Sissela Bok (1999) display these differences. The approach to the use of language of Luntz, for example, lies within the Goffman tradition: language is artifice. The consequence of import is if one's client inadvertently becomes labeled as a hypocrite, and then the label elicits negative evaluations from constituencies. Pre-emption, here, is essential so within the pragmatics of language word preference prompts the attempt to label one's political opponent as a hypocrite. From a conflict standpoint, the assumption of social action always open to artifice is replaced with the assumption that words as a form of capital should be used honestly to ensure fairness in the exchange of this capital. But conflict theory sees that conditions of inequality of access, designations of meanings, and capabilities of distortions of truth exist in the exchange of information.

The main literature on hypocrisy that I have reviewed in politics, political science, the history of manners, and literary criticism makes the point that Person X can say one thing and then Person Y can say another about hypocrisy, contrasting or with a variation in meaning in their respective usages. "Isn't this interesting; how ironical?" Yet none of this literature tries to detail consequences from the negative side, the lying for instance. I am reading this to be a characteristic of the approach taken in the literature. That is to say, it observes the "interesting variations, but does not consider negative consequences. Sociology has omitted attention to this altogether. I write, as I should, trying to be faithful and dispassionate in representing other authors' work and in describing the various cases within the book. But I resist the idea that "mixed meanings," ubiquity, inattention, or cynicism obviates consequences of this kind of lying. People kill themselves, people violate the trust of intimates, institutions are compromised and sustain huge losses or cease to exist. Alternative, general approaches lie in these first four facets of the sociological program on hypocrisy which have been sketched (contexts, ideal-typical cases, organizational influences, consequences such as threats to trust).

The fifth component of the program of sociology being outlined is to draw out some stakes within general theoretical alternatives alive in sociological work. Here are three alternatives which will be developed more fully in Chapter 7. Importantly, each gives different interpretations of hypocrisy; each makes different assumptions about the range of social responses available to societies; and each holds different expectations about the potential social efforts have for reducing the negative consequences of hypocrisy that are discussed in Chapters 5 and 6.

Option No. 1: Erving Goffman and the Sociological Premise that Artifice is Normative

The work of Erving Goffman would seem to be full of allusions to hypocrisy. However, treatments such as *The Presentation of Self in Everyday Life* and *Stigma* make no use of the term. These two books display two standpoints toward the manipulations of information that in substance are involved in what other writers call "hypocrisy." The juxtaposition of the two—a preoccupation with hypocrisy versus considering hypocrisy as part of general social artifice—opens up ideas relevant to general theories about organization, trust, and deceit which will be treated in the final chapter.

It is worth noting in advance an item of terminology, useful for distinguishing Goffman from an alternative view of hypocrisy and its consequences, has emerged recently within the large number of articles in US news sources recounting the "fall" of Lance Armstrong from the circles of professional bicycle racing. Lance Armstrong's case as discussed in Chapter 5 is introduced to aid the identification of hypocrisy and its implications. This terminology ("fall") moves Armstrong and the other principals in the Tour de France towards the already-considered instances of hypocrisy in the Roman Catholic Church and at Penn State University, and additionally it serves to distinguish between Goffman's position and an alternative, as depicted in the final chapter. Such articles have noted that if Armstrong had had access to a "damage control expert" working on his behalf, then he could have avoided some of the extremely costly penalties exacted on him. Specifically, this commentary construes Armstrong's predicament as a matter of public relations (as Goffman would). The problem is not Armstrong's deceits; the problem—now correctable by a skilled "damage control expert"—is that he must repair his "face" and "cover" his deceptions more effectively.

Option No. 2: Schneier: Bounded Rationality

Theoretical ideas that essentially align with conflict theory represent a second alternative. This material comes from sources that include variables of differences in relative access to technologies that allow hiding information. But the technologies can also allow detection and publication of hidden information, and subsequently allow consumption of the information. A representative statement used in Chapter 7 is that of Bruce Schneier (2012): *Liars & Outliers: Enabling the Trust that Society Needs to Survive.*

Option No. 3: A Social Contract where Pretense is Modulated and Evaluation of Shortcomings Attends to Context

Based on the research from three countries and across two institutions, the latter portions of the book will suggest entertaining a different approach to the study of social order than that of Goffman and from that of many conflict theories. If Puritanism (and similar contexts that induce exaggeration and unrealistic claims) is supplanted by a moral context that emphasizes candor and realistic claims) then the prospects for hypocrisy when unrealistic claims are not realized are reduced. In turn, if social audiences approach plans and claims of individual and institutional actors with a realistic eye born of attention to complex contexts, then the external demand for actors to over-promise could be reduced.

There is a political philosophical tradition providing a basis for what will be the argument for this alternative to Goffman's approach. The foundation here will draw from John Rawls' *A Theory of Justice* (1999). Also, an integration of Rawls' work with some sociological theories, which will be used here, exists in "Morality, Justice, and Social Choice: Foundations for the Construction of Social Order" (Condon and Wieting, 1982).

For purposes of the program of the project, a crucial matter once we acknowledge the import of context is to work to identify instances where some variations exist over conditions that heighten the dishonest elements of hypocrisy and exacerbate the consequences. Here is where Shklar's point about conditions of contexts enters. Her term of "exigency," which is a variable, stands out as crucial. To consider contexts as Chapters 2 and 3 do, some variation of this element of exigency is important. Additionally, there needs to be some availability of records and records that can be compared. This undergirds the choice of the US, Iceland, and France in the process of illustrating cultural influences on the salience and preoccupation for actors and publics with hypocrisy.

With respect to implications from the theories elected, first, even though Goffman's work is historically tied to the social behaviorist tradition of the United States, in form it is a functional theory. There is no way cleanly to test it, because the outcomes are always foretold by the assumptions. But the design of this project at least allows us to describe some cultural influences (from three national sites, deployed for some comparison) on the strategies that are used to maintain social order when truth claims are questionable. Disruptions of the social fabric are repaired by actions by self and other; but the quality of these and the pace of success can vary by culture. Anticipating material in the chapters to follow, here are outlines of examples developed more fully later. These examples suggest that in spite of cultural variation, social contracts and agreements can exist and be maintained to ensure relative honesty and transparency in exchanges. Several of the Tour de France riders within Lance Armstrong's team wrote, with co-authors, biographies after the drug use sanctions occurred. Armstrong himself, in one of the latest book-length statements about him, *Wheelmen: Lance Armstrong, The Tour de France, and the Greatest Sports Conspiracy Ever* (Albergotti and O'Connell, 2013), and in almost all of his public statements up to the moment, attempts to give a particular kind of account to explain away his culpability. He says repeatedly, in his defense, that all the other riders were using drugs; and he effectively offers the rhetorical proposition to readers, "If you were in my place, you would have used drugs also." Tyler Hamilton, in his tell-all book (*The Secret Race*, 2012), also makes the same claim that he should not be held culpable for cheating and lying about it because others were doing the same thing and, tells the reader, again in substance, "Don't judge me negatively, until you have been in my shoes" (e.g., Hamilton and Coyle, 2012: 246, 253). To expect assent of these kinds of accounts assumes from the reading culture that, under certain circumstances, cheating and lying should be expected. In David Millar's (a former Scottish rider) biography (Millar, 2011) and in George Hincapie's biography (Hincapie and Hummer, 2014) this form of account does not occur. Within the whole moral tenor of each book, such a defense of cheating and then lying about it would appear incongruous. Hincapie is originally from Columbia, thus, like Millar, representing cultures outside the United States.

Complementing these contrasts in types of accounts within a single sport, descriptions of curling later, a decidedly Canadian sport in its development, show that the very prospect of violating a rule, let alone not calling the penalty on oneself, is unthinkable to curling participants and those who consume the sport as spectators. There is a detailed history of athletic events within Icelandic culture in later chapters. Rather than the assumption of infidelity (again, "Everybody is doing it!") within the sports, and the efforts at defending cheating and lying, a rule violation between competitors is fundamentally wrong because it violates the cultural norm of trust between two or more actors within the sport.

Secondly, conflict theories are less determinative. The idea that conflict over control of information as capital will continue (as progenitors of fictions are discovered and constrained by security), the pace, complexity, and relative success both of infractions (liars and outliers) and those responsible for security can be assessed both across time and culture.[16]

Thirdly, research on the contract view of negotiated decisions to be honest and integral has identified variables that account for more and less cooperation. These variables include complexity, scale, and history and length of interaction; all of which can be seen to vary for test across time and space in the design of the project.

---

16 Note: For hypocrisy to have social consequences, relevant consumers must have access to the description of hypocrisy. The sequence includes variable access of hypocrites to mechanisms of concealment, and then variable access of publicists such as journalists to the information, and then variable access of consumers through levels of literacy and physical access to media carrying the information. This is so since Shakespeare and Molière's *Tartuffe*.

Continuation of the Program: Context (A) and Cases (B)

Five sociological topics in view in the book connect within societies and appear with connections throughout the following chapters. But the structure of the treatment gives specific attention to each within select chapters.

First, "hypocrisy" is a symbol in use in societies with variable references, and, within the tradition of pragmatism and social behaviorism in sociology, "hypocrisy" carries different meanings and serves different purposes. This social process is a fundamental ingredient of the creation of society and is the first sociological question addressed. Illustratively, social conditions of reference and pragmatic use occur differently through time and across cultures, so matters of exigency within these settings from ranges of time and space appear in Chapters 2 and 3.

Secondly, while the weight of valuation of hypocrisy consistently carries some or entirely a negative component, broad research and public sentiment acknowledge the wide distribution across societies and institutions of hypocritical acts, which may allow conclusions of decreasing saliency and worry about control within societies. To consider the differentiating potential of hypocrisy, if there is one given this generality, religion and sport are examined as ideal cases where hypocrisy in principle should be avoided. Thirdly, individual persons and groups who betray the deceits labeled "hypocritical" find that surrounding institutions act toward the hypocrisy in the forms of detection and penalization, but also protection and enhancement. This organizational imperative occupies Chapters 4 and 5. Fourthly, sociology, while reflecting societies' repugnance toward hypocrisy, has not sorted out the consequences of lying. Some consequences and implications appear in each chapter, the fourth substantive focus. One significant consequence is the loss of trust, and this topic appears as Chapter 6. The oddity of sociology recognizing the commonness of hypocrisy while delaying careful analysis leads to the topics of Chapter 7. There I consider prospects of available theories for illuminating the components of hypocrisy.

The contexts, the two institutions of sport and religion, and the illustrative cases come from decisions based on practicality, theoretical requirements, and programmatic goals of the project. To display variation of social demands for perfection and rigid sanctions for failure, exigency as Shklar terms it, allows the selection of the US, Iceland, and France. Practically, these provide comparable running records that serve as bases of comparison. Their respective cultural histories surrounding sport and religion allow comparison of what exigency refers to. The choices of sport and religion, as anticipated earlier in the chapter, provide examples of institutions where integrity is valued in a society. Such integrity is essential to the meaning of the institutions by definition. These are ideal types in terms Max Weber intended (e.g., essays in Weber, 2011). If the variable hypocrisy (integrity vs. lying) matters in theoretical terms then hypocrisy should in principle be excluded in sport and religion.

The ways hypocrisy appears, is sustained, and eventually is responded to within sport and religious institutions holds requirements for illustrative cases, here principally Penn State University, the Tour de France, the Roman Catholic Church, and the Hillsborough deaths. These cases afford the expanse of time needed to see the processes of institutional response to acts of hypocrisy. They allow exposure to a fair volume of source records and not just journalistic reports (original sources denoted in the bibliography). The cases allow access to different viewpoints of actors within different levels of the organization. They allow exploration by readers because the cases continue to unfold. This possibility of shared sociological investigation coincides with the programmatic goals of the project. Sociology should address the occurrences of hypocrisy and has tools to do so as a discipline; so the cases provide an invitation for continued sociological effort in the study of hypocrisy.

The selectivity of cases, hence, allows illustrations of the organizational influences operating in the origin and maintenance of hypocrisy. The source material from these cases (e.g., secondary literature, biographies, historical records, journalistic accounts, institutional records, legal holdings, sport-juridical judgments, expert correspondence, and video materials) allows future researchers to continue along the research lines begun here. These organizational factors add to the prospect of general consequences of hypocrisy, such as impingement on levels of trust in society.

Contexts, strategic cases, organization imperatives, and threats to trust lie within the purview of sociology, both in disciplinary obligations and disciplinary capabilities. Attention to these four topics press sociological work to examine, in turn, theoretical options for understanding and explaining the illustrations here and complementary cases.

Chapter 2
Sport and Religion in the United States

Introduction: the Dark Side of Perfection

Hester Prynne (a central figure in Nathaniel Hawthorne's novel written in 1850) lived out her life in seventeenth-century New England with the weighty sense of the shame of her adultery, a sentiment that was reinforced continually by a social environment that reminded her of her error. Her partner in her deviancy, the young pastor of the local church, Arthur Dimmsdale, for a period resisted acknowledging his culpability even while appreciatively (and respectfully) experiencing Hester's bravery in not naming him as the father of Pearl, the child born of their adultery. The Reverend Dimmsdale eventually deteriorated in health and came to the decision to confess his partnership with Hester in illicit sex. The sin, the deviancy, was first born by Hester and the consequences for her reinforced by the judging community. But the denial by Dimmsdale—the hypocrisy—carried an even more potent consequence. In a community that honored purity and personal fidelity, his gradual recognition of his status as a hypocrite brought emotional and physical costs on him in excess of those brought on Hester by her bad behavior.

The awareness of wrong warped Hester's entire life, recognition of hypocrisy by Dimmsdale brought about his downfall. Beyond both, though, was the most potent fear of all in Hester Prynne: "She was terror-stricken by the revelations that were thus made. What were they? Could they be other than the insidious whispers of the bad angel, who would fain have persuaded the struggling woman, as yet only half his victim, that the outward guise of purity was but a lie, and that, if truth were everywhere to be shown, a scarlet letter would blaze forth on many a bosom besides Hester Prynne's?" (Hawthorne, 2013: 39).

Hester had a double apprehension with her insights. On one hand, she was aware of hypocrisy all around her, thus contextualizing her own error. However, she was partly recuperating from the belief that others' penalizations of her represented some overall social standard—to be believed in. But if this standard was false, then the foundation of her faith was gone. "Her imagination was somewhat affected, and, had she been of a softer moral and intellectual fibre, would have been still more so, by the strange and solitary anguish of her life. Walking to and fro, with those lonely footsteps, in the little world with which she was outwardly connected, it now and then appeared to Hester—if altogether fancy, it was nevertheless too potent to be resisted—she felt or fancied, then, that the scarlet letter had endowed her with a new sense. She shuddered to believe, yet could not help believing, that it gave her a sympathetic knowledge of the hidden sin in other hearts" (Hawthorne, 2013: 39).

Sport is physical, rule-governed, intrinsic, and consummative. Of the 10,998,815 students in United States four-year colleges and universities, approximately 4 percent participate in intercollegiate sport in 23 different sports. 28.8 percent of this 4 percent receive an athletic scholarship, 55.07 percent of whom are male and 44.93 percent of whom are female (considering recipients of sex-divided sports and excluding the 620 scholarships for non-sex-based events, bowling and equestrian). The majority of the news about college athletics focuses on a little over 1 percent of college and university students, therefore (that is, the ones receiving scholarships). 32,089 men in football and basketball, on scholarship in the elite level, Division I schools, occupy the most attention, or 0.29 percent of the college and university students.

This group (the 0.29 percent) wants more money and material return for their participation in sport as organized in the United States. The National Collegiate Athletic Association[1] and some university athletic departments are the targets of the plaintiff athletes. The exchange of claims and counter-claims illustrates key dynamics of exigencies that affect hypocrisy within the NCAA oversight of sport beginning early in the twentieth century. This chapter looks at hypocrisy in both sport and religion in the United States, as a step in the comparison of three contexts where cultural and organizational factors can bear on the meaning, appearance, and consequences of hypocrisy. Considering sport to begin with, emphasizing three aspects of sport in the US allows a basis of comparison between the US and then Iceland and France. These three features include: the tension between sport and academics within colleges and universities; the resistance and slow accommodation to gender equality; and the connection of college sport and professional sport in the US. The first part of the chapter introduces the background of the three. The history and current issues surrounding these three features give definition to the stakes and bases of argument now occurring between student athletes and the NCAA (particularly visible during 2014) and form a second segment of the treatment of sport in the chapter. The cultural exigencies Shklar describes, that create predispositions to hypocrisy, are durable and consequential. The exigencies and the associated patterns of hypocrisy—both being durable and consequential—are stressed throughout the book. The historical treatment gives a view of the cultural and organizational components of US sport; the strength, durability and consequences from the setting appear currently in high-stakes contests over sport activities and benefits from sport. From Hawthorne (1850) to

---

1   The National Collegiate Athletic Association, NCAA, to recount from Chapter 1, oversees collegiate sport in the United Sates. In originating under a different name in 1906, the NCAA title continues since 1910. The discussion of the activities of this organization occurs below within the treatment of the distinguishing features of United States sport. Figures for scholarship recipients show consistency from three sources consulted: http://scholarshipforathletes.com; a personal communication from the NCAA records department; and *Student-Athlete Participation 1981–1982, 2013–2014: NCAA Sports Sponsorship and Participation Rates Report*, 2014).

athletic lawsuits in 2014 is an expanse of time, but a short distance in substance connection. This particular line from the past to the present is one among others which show how the exigencies noted by Shklar from US history continue to define current contests over both moral and financial capital within US sport. The consideration of religion later in the chapter requires, too, a combination of attention to the religious context in the US, and also ways in which the traditions affect patterns of hypocrisy in the present.

Anthropologists make the priority of unraveling the complexities of cultures distinct from their own; an admonition of this book is that sociologists should, and can, do some of this as well. A colleague outside of the US looking at this set of circumstances (where beneficiaries challenge the beneficent institutions) would be tested. From one reasonable vantage point, the colleague would see a tiny fraction of men, who have had their college education totally paid for, who have been selectively attended to, favored, and envied by millions of students and athletic consumers, all made possible by the organization they now are suing or demanding more money from. Fairness cannot deny that some of this minority of men (0.29 percent of the college and university population) might have been given more for their time playing college sports. The realities of the legal world into which they have entered to sue the NCAA or to gain the status as a union, giving them a favorable hearing, come largely through the principles of a particularly American legal structure—the Sherman Anti-trust Act.

This said, in deference to their cases, their posture, from the outside, from the vantage point of our guest analyst requires some culturally-specific information to illuminate these lawsuits. The dimensions of American society Hawthorne focuses on through Hester's anguished thinking helps this outside investigator. Dimmsdale eventually acknowledges his culpability in the sin, and he pays from both the sin and the hypocrisy in denial. Hester knows she has violated prevailing norms and she has paid with community censure. She suffers alone, knowing full well that despite others' disdain toward her, they, too, are worthy of the epithet, "hypocrite." While cynicism might allow some respite for her, she will not indulge in it because she continues to believe in the harsh standards of her community and a difficult, but deserved, penalty the standards have imposed on her.

The analogies, with the use of Hawthorne, exist in the lawsuits and claims against the NCAA. The charges of the plaintiffs against the NCAA, which are described fully below, claim long-standing contradictions within NCAA policy—dissimulation and simulation, yes, the components of hypocrisy. In the O'Bannon case, one of the three described below, the Federal judge concurs with the attributions. The lawsuits within the perspective of Hawthorne become more intelligible because the plaintiffs know that the NCAA has been good to them during their athletic and academic histories (if they are honest). They also know that the wealth of the NCAA, which they seek to tap, comes from an organization that has been hugely successful within American higher education and from which they personally have profited a great deal. Hester is profoundly conflicted by her knowledge of hypocrites among her persecutors, and her desire yet to believe in the system around her. The plaintiffs seeking to tap into the wealth of the NCAA now, show less acuity in the understanding of the contradictions of their own actions.

Religion as a system of beliefs and practices that gives great support to individuals to contend with tragedy and the uncertainties of life presents itself through institutions that are honest and safe. Both sport and religion, as selected out in Chapter 1 as ideal-typical cases where hypocrisy should not occur, manifest different patterns of appearance of hypocrisy in different contexts. This chapter describes cultural conditions of sport and religion that associate with high levels of the kind of exigencies Judith N. Shklar stresses as fostering hypocrisy, described in this chapter here in the US. Chapter 3 uses information from France and Iceland as a reference point for assessing possible contextual differences in appearance, forms, and consequences of hypocrisy.

Some prospects for what the comparison of the three contexts, the three countries, might help illuminate are foregrounded in the following tables. The tables document incidents and preoccupations with hypocrisy within three comparable news organs in the three countries: *The New York Times*, *Le Monde*, and *Morgunblaðið*.

Hypocrisy, to emphasize, is consistently condemned in religious texts. Thirty-seven citations and condemnations of hypocrisy occur in the Koran. Twenty-one occur in the Revised Standard Version of the Bible. In the early seventeenth-century version, The King James Version, terminology is selected for 42 hypocritical acts—all condemned. Hypocrisy is bad, in the evaluations of major religious cultures. In the Christian culture of seventeenth-century England, and in the settlements of Puritans in Massachusetts it is not only bad, but a preoccupation. Sermons of the period brand hypocrisy as the most damnable of human vices. Hypocrisy, either as denial of a wrong, or as a claim of an ability not actually possessed, has consequences at every level of social organization. Material in the sequence of chapters describes some of these. The additional question, so interesting, yet so difficult to resolve is how different cultural settings, defined either by time or location, give greater or lesser intensity to hypocrisy. Hypocrisy from its appearance in seventeenth-century Puritan North America, was a repugnant and oft-condemned failing. Did this early cultural valence continue through US society in the institutions where intrinsically it could, with expectation, continue: sport and religion? Or did its salience and meaning change, adding illustration to the factor of exigency, or relative salience, that Shklar and others have intriguingly noted.

Over the last 50 years, hypocrisy has remained in the public domain of discourse as morally reprehensible acts. In *The New York Times*—as one visible, continuous, and representative medium—the term persists within materials on sport and religion.[2]

---

2   In the interest of due consideration of goal two of the set of five in the book program listed in Chapter 1, news sources that are as comparable as possible and allow access over at least a half century are required, hence the selection of these three. *The New York Times*, now with a general circulation within the United States, was founded in New York City and

Table 2.1 *The New York Times, Le Monde, Morgunblaðið* **sport and hypocrisy allusions 1962–2011**

	United States Sport	France Sport	Iceland Sport
1962–1971	114	33	5
1972–1981	155	59	2
1982–1991	143	45	3
1992–2001	165	48	6
2002–2011	189	64	6

Table 2.2 *The New York Times, Le Monde, Morgunblaðið* **religion and hypocrisy allusions 1962–2011**

	United States Religion	France Religion	Iceland Religion
1962–1971	122	58	1
1972–1981	116	68	7
1982–1991	101	65	9
1992–2001	135	74	7
2002–2011	121	92	8

Numerical comparisons between institutions and across time for sport and religion may carry some substantive meaning. Additional analytical potential lies with comparison among the three countries. While Chapter 1 introduces the importance of hypocrisy for examining trust in institutions, Chapter 2 provides a presentation of how hypocrisy insinuates itself into the institutions of religion and sport in the United States. Prior discussions of hypocrisy, such as those of Judith Shklar, have noted how certain types of moral contexts may induce hypocritical acts. Implied in her discussion is the prospect that changes in moral contexts may affect the incidence and character of hypocrisy.

has been continuously published since September 18, 1851 (http://en.wikipedia.org/wiki/The_New_York_Times). *Le Monde*, a widely circulated French newspaper, was founded in 1944, first published that year on December 14, and has been published daily since. One report estimates circulation of 323,039 per issue in 2009, with 40,000 sold outside France (http://en.wikipedia.org/wiki/Le_Monde). *Morgunblaðið* was first published in Iceland in November 2013. The paper has been published continuously since, with qualification that publication did not occur on Mondays, until full-week publication started in 2003. Circulation is approximately 50,000, a substantial proportion within a population of 350,000 (http://en.wikipedia.org/wiki/Morgunbla%C3%B0i%C3%B0).

Hypocrisy, again, is condemned by major world religions. As introduced in Chapter 1, hypocrisy can have several social consequences, and personal ones as well. Open for exploration are the correlates of hypocrisy, and, as they gradually can be ferreted out, some conditions. What is emerging thus far, from both Chapter 1 and the beginning of this chapter, are these associated factors. Hypocrites tend to lie while in positions of power. They have high expectations for what they are doing. They have the capacity to compartmentalize the standards identified with errors and inadequacies and when unsuccessful in achieving these standards themselves, might then betray them. The contexts of hypocrites and hypocritical acts contain cultural elements (cultural values within Puritanism, for example) and social organizational elements. Cultural mandates of religion with a Puritanical core present the expectations to superior performance to adherents, and may in turn carry the opprobrium and censure when adherents under-perform. The higher the hypocrite is in an organizational structure and the more vested the organization is in the performance of the actor, the more likely the organization can be tempted or predisposed to conceal the deceitful acts of the hypocrite.

Appearance, frequency, persistence, and seriousness of consequences of hypocrisy are not automatic as the cases in Chapter 1 show. They are variables, and the weight of the variables come from social context factors. So to pursue the correlates of hypocrisy and to move gradually toward understanding conditions of appearance, the project includes the design that builds in variation by time and a modest amount of variation by national context. These tasks occupy the project in Chapters 2 and 3. The selection of the two countries of France and Iceland is purposive in foregrounding their salience for a comparison with the United States. The point here should further be stressed that the choice of sport and religion as sites for examining hypocrisy does not deny the appearance and even commonness of hypocrisy in other institutions. Religion and sport by their very character assume participants are truthful and are the earliest to condemn and admonish liars within the two institutions. So, sport and religion are limiting cases of hypocrisy: if there is anywhere where deceit should not occur within human activity it should be in the church, mosque, or synagogue; and on the athletic playing field.

Sport in the United States: "Winning is not everything, it is the only thing" (American proverb)

In this and the following chapters, information on sport and religion in the United States, France, and Iceland will be presented. As the discussion starts, the final demurral is that obviously the scope of treatment of the institutions in the three countries is modest. That said, the choices of substance for sport and religion in the United States, France, and Iceland are analytically strategic for the consideration of how contextual exigencies can nurture and exacerbate hypocritical behavior, and alternatively may be able to contain and correct these kinds of deceit within sport and religion in the countries. Material on the two institutions in the three countries stresses differences among the three countries being compared. The different aspects of sport and religion in the three are salient as potential correlates and conditions of the appearance, frequency, persistence, and consequences of hypocrisy just noted. The conditions of sport and religion foregrounded deal with power, moral focus (exigency), temptations and opportunities of actors to compartmentalize aspects of their lives, and conditions where institutional surroundings of persons culpable of hypocritical deceits may themselves create an "organizational imperative," where the deceits are accommodated to with concealment, deflection, and hyperbolic dismissal. The components or specific *moments* of sport and religion within the United States, France, and Iceland appear in Table 2.3. As stated, three unique sport patterns in the United States will be given special attention: sport within American colleges and universities; the special social and legal effort to equalize sport for women in the United States; and the structure of business organization within professional franchises of sport.

Table 2.3   Some notable features and events in sport and religion in the United States, France, and Iceland

	US	France	Iceland
Sport	Sport within the college system	The Modern Olympics	Sport in early history and Glíma
	Title IX and women in sport	The Tour de France	Strongman and Strongwoman
	Franchises of professional sport	Les Bleus, 1998	Team Handball
Religion	Puritan heritage	Catholic church/ state	Religion in country identity
	Persistence of religious commitment	Church and secularism	Moderate religious interest

Organized Sport within American Colleges[3]

An important intention of this project is to describe the social implications of hypocrisy. Sociologically, since ostensibly good and well-intentioned actions have

---

3   The sequence of work on college sport which figures prominently here as background includes the studies of Murray Sperber (Sperber, 1990, 1998, 2000). Complementing Sperber, a professor and cultural historian, the view-points of administrators used come from Shulman and Bowen, 2001 and Bowen and Levin, 2003. An early, and critical, overview of the volatile tension between sports and academic priorities is Howard J. Savage, *American College Athletics* (1929). A responsible and thorough treatment of the anticipation for, enactment of, and aftermath of Title IX is Welch Suggs, *A Place on the*

led to very bad outcomes, this is an example of a domain of responsibility for the discipline. Despite the demonstrated social implications (see Chapter 1 for some examples), the prospect of sociology's systematic study of the factors associated with these bad, but non-obvious, outcomes has not been realized. Attached to the focus on describing these moderately recognized outcomes, curiosity and theoretical requirements demand that an effort be made at least to clarify some steps that lead to these bad (but, again, non-obvious and unintended) outcomes. From Shklar, and now from the description of religion in America that shows the paradoxical pattern of hypocrisy (two forms of lying) related to culturally valued characteristics of individuals and institutions, attention can turn to one other general condition that bears on the occurrences of hypocrisy and the seriousness of consequences.

Hypocrisy depends on the ability to compartmentalize bodies of information, the capacity to control the distribution of contradictory information, and the potential to alter public evaluations when discrepancies in information exist. The one small study mentioned in Chapter 1 notes power differentials allowing these privileges. In the examination of the structure of sport in the United States, some elaboration of what this kind of power can mean, especially in so far as power includes considerable control of valued resources, appears first in the special characteristics of US sport, which in turn give definition to very recent legal contests over college sport resources. The first special feature of sport in the United States (sport in higher education) includes debates over the independence of athletic departments, payments to student athletes, and degree of academic success of athletes.

The Status and Isolation of Athletic Departments in Major US Universities

Athletic contests between universities started in 1852 with the sport of rowing. As other sports were incorporated into higher education, discussions grew about monitoring the balance of academic priorities and athletic priorities of these institutions. The first intercollegiate football game was played on November 6, 1869 with a score of Rutgers 6 to Princeton's 4. The first intercollegiate basketball game was played at The University of Iowa on January 18, 1896, with the University of Chicago defeating The University of Iowa 15–12. In 1906, the Intercollegiate Athletic Association of the United States was formed as an administrative context for such oversight; in 1910, the name was changed to the National Collegiate Athletic Association (NCAA). This organization acts as the official organizational oversight of collegiate sport in the US governing 23 sports at three levels, Division I, II, and III. Member schools in the successive divisions are 340, Division I, 312, Division II, and 442, Division III. The differentiation of the three divisions

Team: the Triumph and Tragedy of Title IX, 2005. For a recent and nicely focused recent source on football specifically, Dave Revsine, *The Opening Kickoff: the Tumultuous Birth of a Football Nation*, 2014, is serviceable.

primarily includes the availability of maximum scholarships and participation in a total slate of conference sports for Division I, lesser number of scholarships, and a small range of sponsored sports for Division II, and generally no scholarships for specific athletic acumen for athletes at Division III schools.

The range of organizational activities which must conform to this institution illustrates the amount of control of sports afforded the NCAA. The salary patterns of coaches of these teams compared to salaries of leaders at these universities primarily concerned with education in its entirety, the college presidents, shows the centrality of influence of some sports, particularly American style football at Division I universities. The following summary table shows the salary differentials of the two roles of several major universities.

Table 2.4   Top 10 football coach salaries and associated university presidents' salaries[4]

School	Football Coach (2013)*	President of Institution**(2013)
Alabama	$5,545,852	$550,000
Texas	5,453,750	628,190
Arkansas	5,158,863	320,000
Tennessee	4,860,000	394,956
Oklahoma	4,773,167	434,905
Ohio State	4,608,000	851,303
Louisiana State	4,459,363	600,000
Michigan	4,154,000	603,357
Iowa	3,985,000	493,272
Louisville	3,738,500	500,000

Payments to Students for Athletic Participation

One major reason for the special feature of US higher education incorporating sports into student life and organizational features of colleges is student interest, both as participants and as spectators. But schools have found increasingly that the economic yield from putting on major sport events justifies the expense for development, programming, and maintenance of revenue-production from sports. The central role sports plays in these instances links with subsidies given to athletes, including general gratuities which may be large or small, and have

4   * USA Today Sports college football coaches salaries database. Note: Can be arranged by school, conference, coach, and varieties of revenue stream. ** *Chronicle of Higher Education* survey; figures are base pay (recent source is *Chronicle of Higher Education*, May 16, 2014).

been sources of disagreement within society and among donors, governments, and school officials. Now the NCAA attempts to define the limits of these subsidies. Some schools by election do not give subsidies purely on the basis of athletic ability. A few other countries, including Canada, Britain, and New Zealand give such sport subsidies, but on a considerably reduced scale compared to institutions in the United States. This system of reward, and, of course, criteria for recruitment in sport in the US is quite unique.

Successes and Failures of Chances for "Student Athletes"

One can view the subsidization of college athletes in various ways. Some may see the subsidies—purely for physical accomplishment—inimical to the historical purposes of the university. Scholarships, that is, in this view could be given for academic records, for artistic prowess, or even demonstrated need; but physicality alone the argument persists should not be a criterion. A common basis for the reticence to subsidize college athletes has been the perceived or real academic performances of these students. Through the period of review of news items attributing hypocrisy to educational coaches and administrators, the contradictions and indeed deceit of the term "student athlete" has been frequent. There are many visible stories of contradictions built into the ineligibility of athletes or the false assignment of passing grades to athletes. The NCAA has a record of modifying policies and increasing surveillance in the interest of purifying the concept of being both an athlete and a legitimate student.

Charges of deceit, either when bad acts are hidden or good acts falsely claimed should be viewed within the factual realities in the context as well as what is being here defined as overblown expectations—exigency. Colleges are implicated of course in the creation and maintenance of sports programs, if only because of the potential revenue produced and as a basis for reputation. The NCAA itself is an organization governing activities but it is an organization made up of colleges as institutional members as well. So the NCAA has a strong interest in reducing the gap between claims about the "student athlete" and outcomes. In a word, the NCAA keeps records to justify the continuity of support of sports. From the early 1970s, considerable attention has been given to rules governing payment, eligibility, monitoring, sanctioning, and also recording. The mechanisms of detection as a central ingredient of control of deceits as described in Chapter 4 occur with refinement in the NCAA's work.

The criterion of academic performance for athletes is graduation. The Graduation Success Rate (GSR), and the Academic Progress Rate (APR) which refers to academic progression of teams, apply to all participating athletes. Two standards have been used: one is the Federal graduation rate, which is the percentage of persons (athletes and non-athletes) who graduate in six years. Another more recent rate-figure which attempts to take into account athletes who transfer to another school before graduating became more commonly used starting in 2005 for Division I schools. The index further attempts to credit athletes in good standing by not placing in the denominator of the index any students who leave, so long as their academic records are sound. As a representation of trends—generally improving—of graduation rates for student-athletes figures using both the Federal rate and the GSR appear in Table 2.5 for the schools noted above, with high coach salaries. The table records rates for all athletes at the schools and for football.

Table 2.5   Athlete graduation rates at select Division I schools*

Schools	2006		1998	
	All	**Football**	**All**	**Football**
Alabama	86/68	73/57	69/55	39/39
Oklahoma	76/56	51/42	62/56	51/38
Ohio State	89/75	75/58	78/62	54/49
Louisiana State	81/57	74/44	66/54	51/54
Iowa	88/71	81/66	74/68	58/53
South Carolina	82/65	65/51	75/58	62/55
Auburn	75/59	70/61	72/55	59/46
Oregon	81/63	72/57	75/64	63/66
Texas Christian	88/70	85/80	86/67	86/70

* Note: Paired figures are for the GSR/Federal figures; for all athletes and then for football athletes; using dates when athletes entered schools, 1998 or 2006 (most recent figures). From Trends in Graduation Success Rates and Federal Graduation Rates at NCAA Division 1 Institutions. October 2013. Regular publication From NCAA Research, prepared by NCAA Research Staff.

Title IX and Gender Equality

The legal designation of "Title IX" figures prominently in discussions of the history of sports in the United States. The designation refers formally to Title IX of the United States Amendments of 1972, Public Law No. 92–318, 86 Stat. 235 (June 23, 1972). The central proposition of the law says: "No person in the United States shall, on the basis of sex, be excluded from participation in, be denied the benefits of, or be subjected to discrimination under any education program or activity receiving Federal financial assistance."

Title IX follows a trajectory of civil rights legislation in the United States, both drawing on this legislation as precedent but also drawing energy from perceived inadequacies in these precedents. The Fourteenth Amendment was added to the US Constitution in 1868 following the US Civil War with an express focus on redressing conditions and legal status of slaves. The amendment has served as precedent in some civil rights cases addressing women's rights, as in Roe v. Wade 1973 (asserting women's right to have an abortion, under specified conditions). The lack of specificity about equalizing the status of women with men has also been seen as an inadequacy (bearing on efforts to pass an Equal Rights Amendment for women, which was never passed in the US, albeit first introduced into Congress in 1923 and following years of subsequent legislative efforts toward passage, until passage by Congress in 1972, and then failing ratification from the required number of states).The Civil Rights Act of 1964 passed by Congress as Public Law 88–352 (78 Stat. 241) included a provision prohibiting discrimination on the basis of sex (as well as race). But the condition was added late, and some scholarship on American law claims the condition was added in an effort to reduce support for the law by conservative members of Congress.

The wording of Title IX addresses equality goals in all aspects of university life. The most controversial component has turned out to be the matter of equality in intercollegiate sports for men and women. The controversy prompted a relatively long period of time before the specific aspects of the provision about sex could be spelled out, remains frequently contested by layers of sport participation and administration of college sport, and may be relatively less successful than other endeavors within college life that were the target of Title IX. For example, the resulting increase of proportion of women generally in college has led to more women now in college in the US than men. Too, high salaried professions like law and medicine which long have favored men in their respective graduate programs for advanced degrees now show nearly equal proportions in law schools and medical schools of men and women.

Lingering cultural resistance to institutional changes within the sport administrations such as the NCAA, amongst political spokespersons, and the schools themselves appears in the long period of time that took place first to articulate the conditions to demonstrate equality for sport (not until 1975) and then the continuing legal battles initiated by interest groups to assure compliance to Title IX.[5] For example, even today, 42 years after initial passage, discussion and debate continue among interested parties. This includes legal challenges by women, arguments from men from less-visible sports such as wrestling who feel sex-balancing efforts have affected their participation chances, and college administrations defending their records on how the three fundamental criteria of compliance are being met at the institutional levels.

A major criticism of sport within the United States over the past half-century addresses the history of and continuation of mixed opportunities available for females in schools and society as a whole. The Olympic Games, discussed in Chapter 3 as a particular contribution of French society, has grown as an international event, which began with a clear bias against female participation; and its popularity and geographic spread provide a common reference point for progress or lack of progress for women within organized sport. Table 2.6 summarizes female to male participation over the history of the summer Olympic Games for Iceland, France, and the United States. Women's participation relative to that of men since WWII has grown regularly with figures across countries now

---

5   Suggs, 2006; Cohen v. Brown, 1996.

Table 2.6   Men/women participation and success at Summer Olympic Games[6]

	1896		1900			1920	
	M	**W**	**M**	**W**		**M**	**W**
Total French	64	0	491 (Total)	?		296	8
Total US	14	0	65	10		274	14
Total Iceland	0	0	0	0	(Iceland first enters in 1908.)	0	0

	1932		1948		1956		1968	
	M	**W**	**M**	**W**	**M**	**W**	**M**	**W**
Total French	97	6	279	37	119	18	169	31
Total US	400	74	262	38	251	46	274	83
Total Iceland	0	0	17	3	*		5	2

	1980		1992		2004		2012	
	M	**W**	**M**	**W**	**M**	**W**	**M**	**F**
Total French	98	23	241	98	195	113	183	147 (W=44%)
Total US	–	–	355	190	613 total	?	261	269 (W=47%)
Total Iceland	9 Total		4	1	21	5	22	6 (W=21%)
US Medals							45	58

* Participation figures not available for Iceland in 1956; however, first of four medals for an Icelandic athlete, Vilhjálmur Einarsson. Iceland has competed continuously since the 1932 Olympics.

showing females comprising 44.2 percent of the participants—compared to none in 1896, and 2.2 percent in 1900. Participation in sport has grown strongly for women in child venues, secondary education, and in colleges over the past 50 years. One of the central reasons has been a concerted effort within universities—both to increase participation and through provision of advocates of equality. A major vehicle has been a federal Law, Title IX, which has been pushed by advocates, enacted by colleges, and affected female participation in sport.

6   For comparisons between the United States and France and for comparisons between males and females (participation and medals), Wikipedia organized sites for the Summer Games from 1896 through 2012 are largely complete. Lacunae exist, though. France as the host of the 1900 Games, where women first participated, brought a large majority of participants. But the exact number of French women participants is not certain. The Wikipedia site for the US team in 2004 gives a total participation figure of 613, but it does not denote an exact division of male and female participants. Information for Iceland is the

Careful assessment of development of female participation in elite sport for women shows stagnation and pockets of inequality (Hogshead-Makar and Zimbalist, 2007; Suggs, 2005). But the aggregate is notable; and relative to the overall data for the Olympics, and for the countries to be compared in Chapter 3, France and Iceland. Title IX as instigator plays a part in the relatively strong record of the United States. Female to male participation trends in the three countries give this evidence in Table 2.6.

The Unique Status of Major League Baseball, the National Football League, and the National Basketball Association[7]

Professional sports in the United States fall within the corporate category. As noted in Chapter 1, profit, by law, gives priorities that circuit the public interest and candor. The leagues, National Basketball Association, the National Football League, Major League Baseball, and the National Hockey League, assume a monopoly form with their franchise rights (and restrictions on growth from the collective organizations). They further can receive tax and subsidy benefits for the purchase, building, and maintenance of stadia.

Despite the earlier stated reasons for excluding business from the limiting cases of religion and sport, these businesses depend on the organization and services of colleges for labor production. Hence, the character of American sport shows, again, a unique fixture of sport business that is connected to and dependent on the features of athletic recruitment and scholarships in colleges. Because of the franchise protections (essentially creating monopolies for the finite number of teams and within geographical markets, and assuring large fan interest), salaries for labor are high. Labor opportunities, though, are extremely modest, which is a feature often overlooked by young males within the United States who envision such labor opportunities. Specifically, there are 3400 player jobs in this labor market.

Efforts from the colleges have shown some tendency toward protecting the chances of student athletes, against the unqualified labor preferences of the professional leagues. Within the NBA, players who are drafted by teams must be at least 19 years old in the year of the draft. Additionally, excluding international players, a player must be at least one year past his high school graduation class. Within the National Football league, individuals who have been out of high school

---

most accessible from: *Hagskinna*: Icelandic Historical Statistics. 1997; and the *Statistical Yearbook of Iceland*. Continuous from Hagstofa Ísland.

7   The Sherman Antitrust Act passed the United States Congress in 1990. In one summary, http://en.wikepedia.org/wiki/Sherman_Antitrust Act: "It prohibits certain business activities that federal government regulators deem to be anti-competitive, and requires the federal government to investigate and pursue trusts. It has since [its conception], more broadly, been used to oppose the combination of entities that could *potentially* harm competition, such as monopolies or cartels," 1.

Table 2.7   **Professional job opportunities for male athletes in the United States[8]**

Leagues	Teams	Player Limits	Net Labor Prospects
National Basketball Association	30	15	450
National Football League	32	53	1600
Major League Baseball	30	25	750
National Hockey League	30	20	600
			3400

for at least three years are eligible to be drafted. This longer period compared to the requirement within the NBA reflects the factor of college play as a basis for labor within the NFL. Major League Baseball is less dependent on colleges for labor, so rules for eligibility for the draft differ slightly. Players are eligible if they have graduated from high school, and have not yet attended a college. Players who have started college are eligible for the draft after having completed either the junior year or senior and are 21 years old. Players from junior colleges (sometimes termed "community colleges") may be drafted regardless of the number of years of schooling completed. The National Hockey League is the least dependent on college labor, and because of the history of the sport in Canada, shows more openness to younger players than do the other leagues. Players must be 18 years old on September 15 and under 20 years old by December 31 within the particular draft year. If a college player, under NCAA rules, was drafted by a team that team retains rights to sign the player until 30 days have elapsed following his departure from college.

A Summary: But Also the Stage for Continuing Conflict over Resources

The historical accounts of hypocrisy, available in work by Shklar, Runciman, and Davidson, introduced in Chapter 1 alert us to its systemic features. As we know, a system is comprised of connected parts. When one part moves the other parts are affected. With Shklar, the parts of the cultural system which create higher or lower exigencies and add to the preoccupation with hypocrisy and the heightened chances of negative consequences vary in salience in time and different cultural settings. In Runciman, efforts to show a democratic spirit with politeness (as

8   These figures are consensual. Sources, in form and sponsorship vary. These sources for the four professional leagues are representative. For NBA: https://en.wikipedia.org/wiki/NBA_Collective_Bargaining_Agreement. For NFL: http://bleacherreport.com/articles/1640782-the-anatomy-of-a-53-man-roster-in-the-nfl. For Major League Baseball: https://en.wikepedia.org/wiki/Major_League_Baseball_rosters. For National Hockey League: http://www.nhl.com/ice/page.htm?id=26377.

opposed to abject sincerity that may insult others) may be accommodated to by subordinates with deference rather than protests or allegations of dishonesty. The politeness, though, may be a form of seduction.

These subordinates such as servants or women may be accommodating with acts themselves of politeness and deference, even though they hate or distrust the superior. But as these disenfranchised groups begin to press for opportunity, their politeness or deference may turn to sincere statement of disaffection from their culturally defined social superiors (note Mary Wollstonecraft as one important example: *A Vindication of the Rights of Women*, 2014 [1792]).

The NCAA which claims to provide structures of opportunity and to support material chances for 120,000 athletes a year, who receive scholarships, remains polite to the press, athletes, and colleges. Critics from the point of origin in 1906 point out the growing wealth and power and arrogance of the organization, which are masked by the NCAA's claims to beneficence.

This organization is now being challenged in US courts by a group which demands—sincerely—more rewards. They betray in the process similar strategies that the NCAA has used since its point of origin to protect its own privileges. Specifically, the legal cases come from a class of plaintiffs representing 0.29 percent of the US college population. Appreciation can be mustered for their case. And success from legal channels is occurring. But the self-interest is obvious and indeed a self-interest of a very small percentage of university students. In the interest of winning redress for their complaints, existing benefits are left to the background and no effort exists yet to assure there will not be losses to students in general or other scholarship athletes and to athletes participating but not on scholarship.

Does masking information in making a self-interested argument connect with the features of hypocrisy? The prospect clearly exists here. The NCAA and college sport administrations have over the years been accused of hypocrisy. In the courts, the term is not used, but the concealments and disputed promises of the NCAA—components of hypocrisy—are being designated for the defendants of these legal cases, the NCAA and college sport departments. The plaintiffs themselves are masking self-interest, and claiming moral superiority in their own arguments against the defendants.

Like eighteenth-century instances of mixtures of politeness and sincerity and the Victorian uneasy balances between these sentiments, the contest between the overseers of college sport and some who claim to have been disenfranchised execute compromises of information and mask clear self-interest. The ambiguities now, as with the eighteenth and nineteenth centuries in the descriptions of Shklar, Runciman, and Davidson, have to be acknowledged even if they cannot always be resolved.

Returning to the programmatic goals of the book, hypocrisy in context can show differences in appearance and salience. This may allow disinterest by researchers on the basis of a potential commonness. Now, as legal processes are in view the temptation may occur again to diminish the importance of hypocrisy for this possible lack of uniqueness from other types of exchanges intended to increase advantage at the expense of other actors.

But the other aspects of the book program remain: the damaging role of institutions which, themselves, may be complicit in hypocrisy through stylized inattention and concealment. Also, negative consequences do continue for individuals and institutions for forms of concealment and fabrication (dissimulation and simulation). The exact measurement-fix on a line of concealment and pretense may be hard clearly to establish. But the movement from smaller to larger levels of concealment and lesser and greater levels of fabrication draws individuals, institutions, and researchers into the openings into the persistence of patterns that compromise trust, the focus of Chapter 6. The presence of essential features of social arrangements that foster different levels of trust, now in a different, legal, context, point to three different approaches to sociological theory. Continuing the introduction of theoretical implications of hypocrisy in Chapter 1, and denoted as goal five of the book's sociological program, these three alternatives receive further attention in Chapter 7.

In brief, the 2014 instances of self-interested, minority groups challenging the NCAA add to an appreciation of the uniqueness of sport in the United States. The fact that the features of the system of hypocrisy now are moving into a legal context illustrates once more the significance of context for describing hypocrisy. The essentials of a system with the exigencies affecting levels of hypocrisy are occurring in the US legal system in substance, although the terminology of claim and counter-claim of moral superiority now lie within a context governed by legal discourse.

Criticism of the NCAA for potential compromises of higher education (Savage, 1929 for an early example) and for claims about services which are overstated persists. Part of the challenge by the very small group of students contesting the NCAA on legal grounds is occurring by accusing the NCAA of improprieties which in turn have been masked and for falsely promising benefits which have been overstated—attributions of hypocrisy, that is. Part of the response of the NCAA to the legal challenges includes efforts which appear to extend largess more broadly to other entities—universities themselves. But in doing so, a long-standing goal of the NCAA (expressed as ensuring competitive balance) has been undercut by now allowing a select group of schools (members of the "super conferences") to spend more money on their student athletes and sport programs than other institutions are allowed to do.

The choice of language for circuiting prospects of culpability and for making false fabrications are part of the many contributions Runciman, Shklar, and Davidson make to this project. Lakoff (e.g., 2002), appreciatively used as well in the book discussions, emphasizes how certain words may assume strong moral valence. Scott and Lyman (1968) describe procedures for neutralizing charges of wrongful acts, through justifications and excuses. But the success of these accounts depends on accurately making one's linguistic strategies accord with appropriate contexts where the accounts will be understood and can be judged meritorious.

The United States is a society where use of legal means to gain personal and group advantage is prominent (Lieberman, 1981). It is not surprising, thus, that law language and the courts are now being exploited to hide, or at least not make evident, selfish goals, and to make claims that are dubious—the very features of hypocrisy—as debates described here over rights and rewards within US sport have evolved.

The Old Context Defines the New Legal Challenges to the NCAA

Background
Three recent legal actions in the United States illustrate usefully the special character of the organization of sport in the United States contrasted with countries like France and Iceland. The cases, now unfolding, illustrate the social and cultural conditions of hypocrisy described in the book. Individuals and institutions are induced to hypocritical acts when some cultural good is valued highly, competed over, has some scarcity, and whose possession carries high regard among peers in a society. The combination, with high levels of saliency, creates the situation Shklar has termed with helpful efficiency, exigency. As the prototype cases in the book illustrate when the social expectations for success and possession of the good are high, and there is certainty of some blockage, then individuals or institutions may be induced to deny some act of failure, termed dissimulation, or fabricate some false accomplishment, termed simulation. These forms of non-genuine claims, indeed lying, constitute hypocrisy within most cultures. Hypocrisy is considered bad, and the appellation is often used to criticize others. Despite the negative connotation of hypocrisy the acts do occur commonly within many institutions. If the strength of social opprobrium is really consequential, there should be demonstrable limits of hypocrisy in institutions whose principles clearly show antagonism against dishonesty. The two institutions in view are sports and religion, both in principle strongly opposing acts of dishonesty, including hypocrisy. These, as introduced, are the ideal typical cases in view in the program to consider aspects of hypocrisy.

Individuals criticized the tie between sports and higher education from the beginning of the official connection, perhaps using 1906 as the institution of Intercollegiate Athletic Association of the United States as a starting-point (named NCAA in 1910). The criticisms remain, and the substance of the negative judgments remains. But in the last year, a specific form of legal challenge has occurred, with potential beneficiaries highly selective within the population of students in higher education, and within the population of student athletes at US institutions of higher education.

As the discussion of sport in the United States shows, the connection of sports and athletics is unique in the world with only Canada and perhaps one or two other countries offering scholarship support to athletes. So the first criticism is about the connection itself, claiming as the case in the rest of the world that sport may compromise the quality of education, or at least that they are distinct enough enterprises that they should not be connected as they are in the United States.

A mission of the NCAA among other ostensive ones has been since its establishment to smooth the connection, and to try to demonstrate that sports can have a place in higher education and not compromise the education of the sport participants and not dilute the integrity of an educational environment for all students.

Important changes in the insertion of the NCAA have included efforts to demonstrate that participation was not out of balance on the basis of the sex of the athletes. This led to the passage of Title IX of the United States Education Amendments of 1972, Public Law No. 92-318, 86 Stat. 235 on June 23, 1972. The mandate reads: "No person in the United States shall, on the basis of sex, be excluded from participation in, be denied the benefits of, or be subjected to discrimination under any education program or activity receiving federal financial assistance." A primary consequence of the law for sports participation within institutions of higher education was the increase of women within sports. The practical application of the law has not yielded proportional representation in sports for women relative to school enrolment. A qualifier in practice has been that while an effort to approach this proportionality should be attempted, schools cannot provide participation slots beyond what the eligibility and interest of women in those sports will allow. The proportion of women in universities is now 57 percent. Estimates place participation at the three divisions of the NCAA at 450,000. Divisions I and II, alone offer scholarship aid, with 119,864 scholarships available at these levels, with 55.07 percent being extended to males and 44.93 percent extended to females. Despite the law, then, women are underrepresented in sport and under-represented in scholarship aid.

African Americans, since the civil rights period of the 1960s, have been overrepresented in what are called the "revenue-producing sports," which are American football and men's basketball. Because of general underrepresentation of Blacks in higher education compared to Whites in the US, and because of lower graduation rates of Blacks relative to Whites, the NCAA has attempted recently to make the case for athletes, Black and White, being supported so that athletic participation does not compromise their educational opportunities. These forms of educational support do demonstrate positive results in graduation successes of athletes. Graduation rates comparing athletes regardless of race to non-athletes show higher rates for both Black and White athletes relative to non-athlete peers. Part of this comes from money invested in counseling and tutoring for athletes. Part of this comes from the way in which rates are now documented by the NCAA, giving athletes six years to graduate through a common four-year curriculum.

Recent legal challenges of the NCAA

Three lines of legal argument within the last two years against policies of the NCAA display the latest criticisms of the philosophies of the NCAA which, as noted, have historically intended to sustain a productive connection between sports and learning within colleges and universities.

All three legal challenges focus on issues of material reward for males participating in football and basketball. All three attempt to make their cases in ways that give alternative meanings for sport within higher education than was originally the case in the definition of "sport" through the NCAA tradition. And the three legal challenges clearly give different meanings to the essentials of "sport" used as the core definition used in the book (physical, rule governed, intrinsic, and consummative). All three exclude attention to implications of their claims for material advantage for all other sport participation in higher education. All three omit attention to implications of their separate and individualistic claims for material advantage for potential losses for schools' overall athletic programs, for donations to schools, and for both student and community consumption of the amateur sport products of football and basketball. The claim of exclusive individual rights to material rewards from sport with potential diminution of valuable resources of others suggests a weakness for moral legitimacy in the ways in which sport is employed in US society. The moral claims oriented to individual aggrandizement over potential losses to millions of students and sport spectators brings these three lines of legal argument into the discussion of sport and hypocrisy in the US. Table 2.8 provides summary information on sport and sex rates of participation and access to scholarship resources within universities in the US. Table 2.8 summarizes several contradictions within the claimed moral consistency of the individualistic claims being made by male members of collegiate football and basketball programs within universities.

Table 2.8   Scholarships by sport and division[9]

	I		I(AA)	II	
Football	20145		7563	5904	
	M	**W**		**M**	**W**
Baseball	3428	–		2259	–
Basketball	4381	5025		2960	2980
Bowling	170			105	
Cross Country	3868.2	5994		3150	3477.6
Equestrian	270			75	
Fencing	90	103.5		9	13.5
Field Hockey	–	948		–	163.8
Golf	1314	1494		784.8	831.6
Gymnastics	100.8	756		–	30
Hockey	1044	630		81	36
Lacrosse	756	1080		442.8	603.9

9   http://scholarshipforathletes.com.

	Men	Women	[Men (IAA)]	Men	Women
Rifle	10.8	–		–	–
Rowing	1700	–		320	–
Skiing	81.9	105		50.4	56.7
Soccer	1989.9	4410		1656	2326.5
Softball	–	3396		–	1972.8
Swimming	1346.4	2716		542.7	680.4
Tennis	1152	2512		774	1362
Track and Field	3452.4	5616		2116.8	2293.2
Volleyball	103.5	3852		72	2288
Water Polo	99	264		27	64
Wrestling	792			477	
Totals	41986.7	38901.5	7563	21626.5	19166.5

Some aggregate totals:
Number of athletes in divisions I and II—450,000
Number of athletes receiving scholarships—119,864
Men—71,176
Women—58,068
[Dual eligibility (bowling and equestrian)—620]

Table 2.9   Issues in the challenges to the NCAA

i.   The three lines of challenge.
   A. Kain Colter/Northwestern unionization case NLRB ruling on 3/26/14)
   B. O'Bannon v. NCAA (ruling released on 8/8/2014)
   C. Jeffrey Kessler-led case (filing on 3/17/14)
ii. Not covered, so far as understanding the role of intercollegiate athletics.
   A. Only football and basketball programs yield profits. Only a small proportion of those yield profits. The net is that the beneficiaries of the supposed revenues are those sports and those few schools.
iii. Only a small proportion of all university enrolments get to participate in sports.
iv. Revenues from football and basketball go to support other supports.
v.   All other sports do not receive the same scholarship aid as football and basketball.
vi. Scholarships for football may be for six years. This is related somewhat to the higher graduation rate for student athletes.
vii. Performance of the revenue generating sports affects fan support and giving to the respective universities.
viii. The competitive balance would be affected. Will students and spectators support sports that are not competitive?

ix. Revenues go to academic resources used for athletes, leading to higher graduation rates.
x.   Students attribute to schools that are good in sports, the prospect that they are good.

The three cases carry similar arguments by the respective plaintiffs, and proceedings that are recent serve here to illustrate what the plaintiffs want from the NCAA and select conferences within the NCAA.

Essentials in the first case lie in a Federal Court holding written by Claudia Wilken, a United States District Judge for the Northern District of California, on August 8, 2014. The holding principally agrees with a case begun in 2009 by Edward O'Bannon, and other plaintiffs, against the NCAA, Electronic Arts, Inc; and Collegiate Licensing Company. "The Plaintiffs seek to challenge the set of rules that basically bar student-athletes from receiving a share of the revenue that the NCAA and its member schools earn from the sale of licenses to use the student-athletes names, images, and likenesses in videogames, life game telecasts, and other footage" ("In the United States District Court for the Northern District of California, No. C 09-3329 CW, Findings of Fact and Conclusions of Law," 2014: 1). The primary reference for the arguments made by the student-athlete class (now, still football players, but also male basketball players) as in the third case described is that the rules violate the Sherman Anti-trust Act. This is the primary reference for argument, as with the Kessler case. The primary criterion for discrimination in these cases, as with the Kessler case, is "the rule of reason." The judge ruled in favor of the plaintiffs, against the NCAA and against vendors like the two defendants listed in gaining money from sales from the names, likenesses and images, in broadcasts, games, and rebroadcasts of the athletic contests.

In this new domain of complaint and defense, the courts do not use the word "hypocrisy." But the substance of hypocrisy of dissimulation and simulation take the linguistic form of legal language. The substance of the argument shows hypocrisy, the reference is not integrity and morality. The argot is conformity to legal precedent, and in the cases invokes reference to the Sherman Anti-trust Act (1890 in the United States). As in other substantive examples of hypocrisy, when relationships show violation of moral codes of concealment and fabrication the coin and argot of the critic (plaintiff) adapts to the rules of one accused of dishonesty (defendant).

The wording by the judge, in ruling in favor of the athletes not to be restricted in benefitting from revenues of sale of their names, likenesses, and images in rebroadcasts, is the same as the ruling favoring the athletes' request regarding live broadcasts and the sale of videogames. "Based on [the evidence], the Court finds that, absent the NCAA's challenged rules, there would be a demand among television networks, third-party licensing companies, and advertisers for group licenses to use student-athletes in game re-broadcasts, advertisements, and other archival footage" (ibid., 2014: 19). This accords with her ruling with respect to the market for selling names likenesses, and images. The judge stated that the intentions for restricting access to the revenues from the three markets which are: maintaining amateurism, maintaining competitive balance, insuring integration for the athletes with the education experience of being a student, and increasing output of the athletic product all were not convincing. The grounds for rejection by the judge for the claim of amateurism were that the NCAA has a record of changing its own rules, thus their claim of preservation of the status of amateur is considered not to be genuine. The claim about assuring competitive balance among teams is dismissed by the judge on grounds that the NCAA has in the past, and just recently, taken steps to give some conferences more money and privileges, thus giving the teams of those conferences competitive advantages (contradicting the NCAA's own claim). The claim that the athletes' case would prevent them from integrating athletics and education was judged not supportable by the facts, since the scholarship to begin with has increased the chances of athletes taking part in class activities, and the difference of athletes from the student body is no different from other groups with unusual wealth being separated as well.

The judge rejected, on the evidence in court, the idea that consumption of the events would decrease with athletes more fulsomely compensated. And the claim of a blunted expansion of football and men's basketball by the existence of players earning more money belied the fact that schools' support of these sporting events has been growing, not contracting.[10]

The arguments and consequences of the second case lie in a ruling by the National Labor Relations Board (Region 13) delivered on March 26, 2014. The statement responds by an appeal by a group of athletes (football players in this case) at Northwestern University to be treated as employees of that university, having the right to unionize as employees, and by extension bargain with the employer, Northwestern University, for salaries consistent with their market worth. The case between the College Athletic Players Association (Petitioner) and Northwestern University (Employer) was decided in favor of what the players requested. The decision reads: "For the reasons discussed in detail below [i.e, the evaluation of evidence by the two sides and the resulting conclusions], I [Peter Sung Ohr, Regional Director of National Labor Relations Board, Region 13] find that players

---

10 A very recent change in NCAA organization of the conferences coincides with the judge's reasoning that the NCAA is contradictory, if not misleading, in their claim of favoring competitive balance. Recently they have designated five conferences, known colloquially as the "power conferences," which will have greater discretion in setting their own rules about scheduling, internal organization, and compensation. The net of the designation gives considerable advantage to these conferences and the schools within the conferences. Speculation is volatile about the possible levels of discretion allowed to these conferences, and their constitutive schools. The athletic director of the University of Texas claims they may pay athletes $10,000 per year, which would be in addition to the customary scholarship award (Lindenberger, 2014). The NCAA itself has a draft document, of 86 pages, enumerating prospective changes (Proposal Number 2014-2, October 21, 2014.)

receiving scholarships from the Employer are 'employees' under Section 2 (3) of the Act [referring to National Labor Relations Act of 1935, (49 Stat. 449, 29, U.S.C)]. Accordingly, it is hereby ordered that an election be conducted under the direction of the Regional Director for Region 13 in the following appropriate bargaining unit:

Eligible to vote are all football players receiving football grant-in-aid scholarship and not having exhausted their playing eligibility employed by the Employer located at 1501 Central Street, Evanston, Illinois, but excluding office clerical employees and guards, professional employees and supervisors as defined in the Act" ("United States Government before the National Labor Relations Board, Region 13," Case 13-RC-121359: 2).

The goal of this action was to give football players the right to unionize and in turn to be able to bargain, as a unit of employees of Northwestern University, for salaries and benefits available in a competitive market. Effectively, the group did not want to be limited by the benefits provided by the NCAA guidelines, and possibly be controlled by one of the five "power conferences," a group that includes the Big Ten Conference of which Northwestern is a member.

The third case, "Complaint and Jury Demand Class Action Seeking Injunction and Individual Damages" was filed in United States District Court, District of New Jersey on March 17, 2014 ("United States District Court, District of New Jersey, Complaint and Jury Demand—Class Action Seeking Injunction and Individual Damages," 2014). The legal representation for Martin Jenkins, a former Clemson University football player, three others, and a class (made up of football players and men's basketball players) was led by Jeffrey L Kessler of the law firm of Winston & Strawn LLP. Defendants are the NCAA and five athletic conferences. The athletic conferences of the Atlantic Coast Conference, the Big 12 Conference, the Big Ten Conference, the Pac-12 Conference, and the Southeastern Conference were singled out because they recently had been awarded special and exclusive new discretionary rights for administration and economic bargaining by the NCAA.

The heart of the legal argument of plaintiffs in this case, and central in the preceding two, was that the NCAA and now in special degree these five conferences restrict economic freedom of the players. The reference was the Sherman Anti-trust Act of 1890. Arguments from the plaintiffs the courts are accepting, the courts principally using the "rule of reason" as their criterion, have concluded that the defendants were violating the Anti-trust laws of the United States. Based on the amount of money the conferences, through the performance of their football teams and men's basketball teams, are making, and the associated return from sales of products enhanced by the athletes' competition, the case was being made that the football players and male basketball players should not be prevented from sharing in these profits.

From the beginning of the NCAA (1905 conception; 1910 formal naming) proponents and opponents of mixing higher education and athletics have made their cases. Debaters argue over who controls athletics (faculty, students, separate administrations, alumni); money (funding and also discretion over revenues from some sports such as football); benefits for the school (student entertainment; reputation and source of general revenue); benefits and liabilities for participants (recreation, health benefits and risks, material reward, addition to and detractions from academic learning).

This statement, from a 1929 publication of a general review of college athletics, could have come from statements at the moment of origin of the NCAA:

> No one who is familiar with the history and aspirations of higher education expects that the administration of college athletics should be entirely logical, or that it should wholly serve the ideals to which so much lip service is rendered. We talk much of sportsmanship, fair play, and the moral values inherent in games, but we act as if we believed that an ornamental gateway to these ends must be provided before the ends themselves can be served. Much of the work of administering our college games, therefore, rests upon expediency. The notion is that the first essential to the execution of any athletic policy is money, and plenty of it. This attitude is accounted to be hard-headed and practical, and such it is, but it is also short-sighted in that it leaves out of consideration the fact that athletics are grounded in human relationships that are at least as much spiritual as physical or financial (Savage et al., 1929).

Twenty of the 189 allegations of hypocrisy by commentators in *The New York Times* from 2002–2011 (Tables 2.1 and 2.2) identify the NCAA as the target of the judgments about either dissimulation or simulation. The claims of concealment and dishonesty in substance continue. The claims of attention by the NCAA to injuries are challenged. Concealment of information about revenues from merchandizing player and event products are criticized. The magnitude and growth of football and men's basketball coaches are circuited. NCAA claims to emphasize competitive balance in college athletics, juxtaposed by the NCAA willingness differentially to allow some conferences unequally to enrich themselves show fundamental contradictions within the NCAA. (The latest demonstration of NCAA lack of genuineness occurs in the extension of favored status for five specific conferences, which will further compromise the competitive balance the NCAA espouses.)

The three legal actions described here illustrate the continuation of patterns of hypocrisy within US college sports. The cases also represent again the durability of the systemic components of hypocrisy which have been shown in Chapter 1 and in this chapter. The nature of the language now becomes judicial rather than ethical or moral as has occurred in previous hypocritical processes. The language and forms of attribution and re-attribution are now legalistic. The strategies of plaintiffs and defendants, and the ruling of the deciding judge in one of these cases, the O'Bannon case, serve as illustration of the stakes and the strategies of competing parties over the stakes, and the respective efforts at self-justification and other-vilification.

The O'Bannon case comes from 20 present and former football players and male basketball players. The stakes in this case lie with the claims of NCAA about three markets where sales of names, likenesses, and images of players are sold (with no benefit to the student-athlete). Also contested were claims of the NCAA over maintaining amateur status, maintaining competitive balance of school competitions, promoting alignment of athletics and academics, and maintaining present and future levels of consumption by spectators. Judge Claudia Wilkin presiding of the United States District Court for the Northern District of California ruled against the NCAA and for the plaintiffs on all of these counts. The substance of the ruling—from facts assessed, and using the standard for evaluating contests of the Sherman Anti-trust Law, "rule of reason," the NCAA displays hypocrisy as defined here, although not used with such language. The context here, a judiciary setting, has its own dominant language form, not using "hypocrisy."

The O'Bannon case will be appealed by the NCAA. It will also be followed by resolution of the case brought by the New Jersey firm, and continuing appeals and new cases by similar plaintiffs. The character of the standing of the plaintiffs does not need to be shown clearly here, because their obligation and their strategies within effective legal practice is contest and defeat the opposition on matters of legal precedent and principle. To charge others with a disingenuous posture, as the plaintiffs have done, generally requires some concealment and claims, at least by intimation, of morally superior status relative to the opposition and a pretense to a more supportable general interest. How the plaintiffs in these three cases will be judged as the cases continue is a matter of both practical importance of the progression of collegiate sport within the United States, and of considerable importance for the five goals of the book—again, the sociological program on hypocrisy.

Religion in the United States: Belief with Capital Letters

The strong condemnation of hypocrisy by religions illuminates a dynamic that the extent of censure may insure preoccupation with it; and in ideological conflicts may lead to preoccupation with hypocrisy. Judith Shklar notes this dynamic within politics, as recorded in Chapter 1. Religions whose essence stresses moral purity are a more extreme example of an institution in which fear of hypocrisy is escalated and charges are used as a tool against opponents; a description, again, which Shklar provides and is included in Chapter 1. Shklar's observations add an issue of context to the interpretation of acts as hypocritical and the responses to these hypocrisies. One dimension to assess the context is within the US culture through time. This is done by an examination of a population of instances of "hypocrisy and sport" and "hypocrisy and religion" through a population of 50 years of treatment within *The New York Times*.

Hypocrisy leads to bad consequences for individuals, close associations, and institutions that can be sometimes devastating. Describing some of these, with efforts to illuminate the chain of steps that lead from acts of deception through dissimulation (hiding something) or simulation (professing something that is not true) is one task of this project.

The persons and the deeds we can call hypocritical are not bad without qualification. This qualification, often a degree of complexity or ambiguity hampers clarifying the beginning point and the series of steps leading to costly consequences. Hypocrisy in its frequency, intensity, and consequences is conditioned by contexts. Again, Shklar has lead us to acknowledge this.

In this and the following chapters the goal is to examine, by at least illustration, the import of context within culture and through time, as here, and then across the cultures of the United States, France, and Iceland. Both through time and across cultures, major chances of identifying variability at least lie with these following factors.

1. Contexts that have high valuation for performance, particularly evaluated in relative terms create exigencies for hypocrisy in institutions, such as in sport and religion.
2. Some individuals have a distinct willingness to assure accomplishment, and proceed to seek it without reservation of effort or expense.
3. The individuals on the path to accomplishment have the cognitive capability and are structurally situated in institutions where they can compartmentalize promised or claimed achievement and documented, objective achievement.
4. Individuals and the surrounding institutions have the resources to control how publically available information is framed and accessed by publics.
5. Individuals and the surrounding institutions have the resources to persist in the maintenance of the putative valorized performance even as evidence and outside knowledge about its falsity grows.

With these factors in view attention now turns to distinctive features of religious history in the United States that display constancy across time and do contrast with Iceland and France (which will be discussed in Chapter 3).

Puritanism, Morality, and the Great Awakenings in the United States

Puritanism does not completely define religion in the United States, but the unique placement of Puritans being among the first settlers on the East Coast of the US, and the pattern that some central tenets of Puritan theology and experience re-erupt periodically affirm the centrality of the religious tradition for Americans and American institutions. Because a common characteristic of the Puritan's experience was to refine one's behavior in the interest of greater perfection (often creating invidious distinctions with other believers and non-believers, has left Puritanism in common parlance with and often aligned with hypocrisy.

A succession of moral and behavioral renewals within the United States tied to essentials of Puritanism convey the long-lasting strain of this religious system in US culture. The First Amendment to the United States Constitution states: "Congress shall make no law respecting an establishment of religion, or prohibiting the free exercise thereof or abridging the freedom of speech, of the press; or the right of the people peaceably to assemble, and to petition the Government for a redress of grievances." An openness to religious choice so distinctive of the United States in contrast to states where religion is supported at national levels, or at least receives state acknowledgement as in Iceland and France (Chapter 3), does not mean a disinterest in religion. Quite the contrary. The democratization of choice of religion displays how important religion is seen to be in the United States. The "Pledge of Allegiance" affirms loyalty of citizens to "one nation under God." US currency includes the epigraph: "In God we trust."

Religious censuses of denominations cite more than 200 such separate listings for Protestants themselves, which in net make up 51.3 percent of the US population. Catholics number 23.9 percent, and relatively highly visible denominations such as Jews (1.7 percent) and members of the Church of Jesus Christ of Latter-Day Saints (colloquially, "Mormons") number 1.7 percent as well. There is a range of non-affiliated persons between 16 and 20 percent. In 50 years, the number of persons claiming they are Christians has dropped from 90 percent to, in Pew surveys, 78.4 percent. Among developed countries, though, the importance of religion for persons in the United States remains relatively strong. "According to a 2002 survey by the Pew forum, nearly 6 in 10 Americans said that religion plays an important role in their lives, compared to 33 percent in Great Britain, 27 percent in Italy, and 21 percent in Germany" ("Religion in the United States," 2014).

Demonstrating the strong cultural characteristic of America's "belief in belief," the denominations that advocate the most stringent ethical and ideological purity in belief are the ones that are growing the most rapidly. Evangelical churches, which are known within the Protestant wing, are distinguished by their twin stipulations of being born again (having an individual religious conversion experience as an adult), and subscribing to the confidence in the literal truth of the Christian Bible, usually the King James Version.

The American ethos advocates success and moral fidelity. These contextual factors, laudable in the abstract, create the exigency for hypocrisy: denial of past mistakes and exaggerating present accomplishments. The persistence of the ideal of morality manifested in religion continues through periodic renewals of religious fervor, sometimes identified as "Awakenings." The First Great Awakening occurred both in the UK and in America over the years of the 1730s and 1740s. Components of this revival, or awakening, included appeal to a variety of constituencies, including Blacks, but distinctively an emphasis on emotional aspects of conversion and religious experience. The Second Great Awakening emerged in the United States toward the end of the eighteenth century and continued with interest and conversions into the middle of the nineteenth century. Spread of the message included broader appeal to groups of a varying social class and educational-levels. The Third Great Awakening, occurring from the late 1850s through the early years of the twentieth century, has been associated with the Social Gospel and with the emergence of several new denominations in the United States such as Christian Science and the Salvation Army.

Table 2.10   Religious interest in the United States (percentages)

	Religion Very Important	Scripture is Word of God	At Least Once a Week Attendance	Formal Membership
Total	56	63	39	61
Protestant	70	75	50	72
Evangelical	79	89	58	74
Mainline	52	61	34	64
Historical				
Black Churches	85	62	59	83
Catholic	56	62	42	67
Jewish	31	37	16	55

From *U.S. Religious Landscape Survey: Religious Beliefs and Practices.* June 2008. Washington, D.C.: Pew Forum on Religion & Public Life.

The 1960s in the United States saw several examples of interest groups to which have sometimes been attached the term "movement." Civil rights activity which had started in the 1950s continued, efforts to extend formal legal rights to females were visible, the involvement of the United States in military conflict in Southeast Asia prompted protests against the involvement and conscription. General ideological ferment of the 1960s include also apparent movement away from the centuries-old trajectory of religious conservatism in the United States. *Time* magazine on its cover of April 8, 1966 asked the question, "Is God Dead"? This sought to engage a controversial theological trend in the period. Liberal theologians such as John A. T. Robinson and Thomas J. J. Altizer wrote provocative books arguing that the language of a material God was perhaps dated; the ideas posed led to very serious discussions in the seminaries within the United States. Could potential believers, whose experience with life and scientific substance in many fields be expected still to profess the literal meaning of a deity such as that represented in Christian teachings?

The Persistence of American Religion in Altered Forms

Some commentators on American religion through the 1970s emphasized the downturns in sales of religious items such as Bibles, reduction in attendance of church services (and membership), and decreases in giving to religious institutions. The up-surge in religious sensibility captured by the "Fourth" Great Awakening with the rise in strength of Evangelical churches and the modified, but vibrant, beliefs and practices in some religious expressions of the youth, contested the overall conclusion on the decline of religious interest.

An enduring remnant of Puritanism and the Awakenings contains five key elements of Evangelical religion. These are the requirement of being born again (as an adult) with a recognizable experience; the belief in the plenary (word by word) inspiration of scripture; the consequent belief in creationism, as it is so stipulated in the Bible; often an enhanced preoccupation with sin and purity; and a sense of obligation to evangelize (Figure 2.1 shows lines of influence on these features). Religious censuses of religious affiliations of the religious in the United States support the continuity of these themes, and continuity strength of membership in churches that emphasize these features. The Pew Foundation's determination of membership yields figures of 78.4 percent who are Christian. This 78.4 percent is made up of 51.3 percent who are Protestants and 23.9 percent who are Roman Catholics. The Protestant 51.3 percent is comprised of 26.3 percent from Evangelical churches, 18.1 percent from mainline churches such as Presbyterian, Lutheran, and Methodist, and 6.9 percent from historically Black churches.

Figure 2.1   Protestant traditions and Evangelicalism in the United States

Protestant Reformation

Luther (1483–1546)

Pietism (Jakob Spener, 1635–1705)

Calvin (1509–1564)   Anglicanism (Henry VIII, 1491–1547;
(Puritanism)   Elizabethan Religious Settlement, 1559)

Anabaptists (Thomas Münzter, 1490–1525)
(Amish, Hutterites, Mennonites)

The Methodists, John (1703–1791),
Charles (1707–1788) Wesley

Baptists (Roger Miller, 1603–1683)

Fundamentalism (1910–1915)

Elements of Evangelicalism	Disputes over Contradictions
– Adult baptism	– Pretended or real conversion
– Literal interpretation of scripture	– Creationism but avoidance of social welfare messages in the Bible
– Church-state separation	– Political support for Republican candidates; religious incursions into privacy
– Ethical, moral refinement	– Personal ethical errors despite claims to piety and ethical rigor
– Conveying the gospel (εὐαγγέλιον)	– Massive media use for messages; combined with restrictions on school curricula

Associations of Puritan and Evangelical Religion with Sport

The association of religion in the United States with athletics has assumed institutional form in organizations such as the Fellowship of Christian Athletes and Promise Keepers. The Fellowship of Christian Athletes was founded in 1954 by Don McLanen who at the time was the basketball coach at Eastern Oklahoma A&M University. The mission is "to present to athletes and coaches, and all whom they influence, the challenge and adventure of receiving Jesus Christ as Savior and Lord, serving Him in their relationships and in the fellowship of the church" ("Fellowship of Christian Athletes," 1: 2014). Promise Keepers was founded in 1990 by Bill McCartney, at the time the head football coach at the University of Colorado. This is a Christian organization for males. The first three of its seven core beliefs suggests the group's priorities:

1. "A Promise Keeper is committed to honoring Jesus Christ through worship, prayer and obedience to God's Word in the power of the Holy Spirit.
2. A Promise Keeper is committed to pursuing vital relationship with a few other men, understanding that he needs brothers to help him keep his promises.
3. A Promise Keeper is committed to practicing spiritual, moral, ethical and sexual purity" ("Promise Keepers," 2012).[11]

---

11   The close connection between sport and religion, each pursued with intensity, occurs in the late nineteenth and early twentieth centuries in the United States with a movement termed "Muscular Christianity." The movement emphasized a life-style associated with physical and distinctively male attributes. Investment in physical exercise was stressed, and specifically activity within amateur sports could be seen as a marker of a "masculine" Christianity. Clifford Putney draws the time-span between 1880 and 1920 in the United States. A similar movement occurred with an earlier beginning in Britain, which holds some differences but did influence the American trends. The highly regarded movie "Chariots of Fire" (1981) centering on events of the 1924 Olympic Games displayed some elements from the British movement.

Within the United States, Putney notes key elements as dissatisfaction with a certain feminist cast to the Victorian era, opposition to the Puritan disinterest in sports, and stultifying desk-work coming with a more urban concentration of workers (as opposed to the work-hardened males from farms). "Convinced that the archetypal buttoned-down Victorian gentleman was ill-equipped to handle the challenges posed by modernity, many progressives proposed a new model for manhood, one that stressed action rather than reflection and aggression rather than gentility" (Putney, 2001). The movement was strongly aligned with White males and with Protestant denominations—even in particular evangelical ones. But the movement was neither exclusively Anglo-Saxon nor exclusively evangelical Christian. Some male members of Black churches supported the movement, as an adjunct to civil rights efforts. The Roman Catholic Church showed support but further into the twentieth century.

The data show the continuity of Evangelical memberships and support for representative doctrines of this branch of Christianity. Spokespersons do debate how much of the inconsistencies of belief and practice, opened up here as hypocrisy, occur more or less regularly within the Evangelical ethos. Despite the popular conception of Puritanism as containing teachings that counsel against physical pleasures and wasting of time not spent on purer activities, both censorious ideas aligned with sports in the history of church and athletics in the US. An alternative view of Puritanism exists as well (Daniels, 1995).

Trends of Church Interest and Durability of the Evangelical Tradition

Robert Wuthnow in a series of studies over the past decade has carefully used large surveys and focused interviews to piece together a picture of modification of religious trends over the recent two decades, but suggests a picture with considerable constancy. A common argument for the decline of religious interest in the US comes from ideas about secularization, with mention of several key social changes that combine to deter people from religious commitment and the institutional support of religion. The increase of women in the labor force and the divorce rate, which rose until 1978, compromise the time and energy that women and family groups invest in religion. The loss of a sense of community diminishes the confidence church-goers have for the replenishment of these feelings through church attendance. The uncertainties people feel about religion, as a marker of secularization, provides an additional basis for expecting religious interest and attendance to drop. Wuthnow uses a variety of surveys to conclude, though, that: "The persistence of Americans' commitment to organized religion over the past few decades had been striking, especially since [these] major social trends have been working against this commitment" (Wuthnow, 2003: 75).

The characteristics of Evangelical expressions of Protestantism: of rigid attention to the words of the Bible, determination to retain moral purity, and admonitions to bring their religious views to bear on public policies, make Evangelicals susceptible to the charges of hypocrisy. The very complex character of such forms of deceit allow competing interpretations by writers, and open contrasting judgments from readers of the evaluative literature. One exemplar cites the inconsistencies in the emphases of Evangelicals (Balmer, 2006). Professor Balmer is a historian of religion in the United States who has produced extraordinary visual programs on religious traditions within the United States. He has written carefully about the positive essentials and the contemporary liabilities of Evangelical thought and practice over the last 50 years. In *Thy Kingdom Come* (Balmer, 2005), he notes the salience of opposition to abortion, opposition to gay rights, and the advocation of public funding of religious schools as based on selective reading of scripture as support. Additionally, he observes that many of those advocating steps to move into policy-making corridors within various governmental layers (with an eye to promoting Christian values within government policies) say they are Baptists. This systematic effort to bring their religious values into policy formation stands sharply in contradiction to the historical stand of Baptists against the State establishment of any particular religion, and certainly one strand of Protestant belief.

The title of Professor Bradley Wright's book conveys his message of contesting negative valuations of Evangelicals, by carefully using available survey evidence to redress mistakes in such judgments: *Christians are Hate-Filled Hypocrites ... and Other Lies You've Been Told* (Wright, 2010). Within surveys he identifies as recent and qualitatively sound, Wright notes "Evangelical Christian" comes from one of three markers: professing within a church that is grouped as Evangelical (as opposed to Mainline Protestant or historically Black denomination); self-identification as Evangelical; or ranking in response to a series of tests of Evangelical authenticity. Born-again Christians (a generally assigned marker by Balmer and others) must specifically agree to these nine criteria. "(1) They have made a personal commitment to Jesus Christ; and (2) believe they will go to heaven because of having confessed their sins and accepted Jesus Christ as Savior. Among born-again Christians, Evangelicals are those who agree with seven more theological points: (1) Their faith is very important, (2) they have a responsibility to share their faith with non-Christians, (3) Satan exists, (4) salvation is gained through faith alone, (5) Jesus lived a sinless life, (6) the Bible is accurate in all that it teaches, and (7) God is the perfect and powerful Creator of the World" (Wright, 2010: 225).

While Balmer calls attention to inconsistencies in the selective use of scripture to condemn or advocate policies, and contradictions in Evangelicals' adoption and exploitation of its historical roots, Wright argues for what can be considered personal successes of Evangelical believers compared to other Christians and the public at large in the United States. Hence the aspirations of Evangelicalism having been comparatively realized gives evidence of superiority and takes accuracy out of the labels of "Hypocrisy" sometimes addressed toward them. As one summary vehicle for his argument, Wright gives letter-grades to performances of Evangelicals in terms of frequently identified personal accomplishments within American culture. In his evaluation, Evangelicals receive an A or A- grade on these features: "Considerable growth since the American Revolution [;] Beliefs and practices get stronger with more education [;] Prayer Bible reading, and evangelism are up [;] Prayer, evangelism, and probably church attendance are up in recent decades (among young Evangelicals) [;] Relatively low rates of adultery, premarital sex, porn; these decrease with attendance [;] Low Rates [of drugs], but no consistent changes with attendance. Need better data [;] Relatively high levels (of interacting with neighbors), goes up with attendance [;] Selfless, empathetic toward others" (Wright, 2010: 212, 213).

Roman Catholicism within the Prevailing US Protestant Culture

Within the framework of the five programmatic goals of the book, a final word here clarifies the focus on the claims of pedophilia and assault within the Roman Catholic Church introduced in Chapter 1. There are publicized instances of such examples of hypocrisy in Protestant denominations, include the Episcopal Church in the United States. The programmatic goals of the book—not to do everything but to invite research into important sociological topics—emphasize goal number 2 on ideal typical cases and goal number 3 about the contributions of organizations to the persistence of hypocrisy. The information now available about the Roman Catholic Church provides relatively ready access to journalistic coverage and intentionally created archives tracking priest and organizational violations (described in Chapter 1). The Roman Catholic Church is organized along hierarchical or episcopal lines. The origin and now the main focus of criticism, and now legal action, cites not just the priests but higher levels of Church administrators such as bishops and even cardinals. So this is another reason for the strategic selection of the Roman Catholic Church. The choice, to be specific, follows the programmatic goals of the book and does not exclude the prospect that instances of such hypocrisy and administrative concealments and protections from other church bodies will not be documented and analyzed by future researchers.[12]

Continuing the Program

The program underway includes: attending to contexts, identifying strategic cases for study of the topic of hypocrisy, considering organizational factors in the

---

12   By way of an outside bracket for this overview of distinctive features of American religion, I include this bibliographic note. For distinctiveness of the contributions of Martin Luther, I use the still canonical volume by Ronald Bainton, *Here I Stand: a Life of Martin Luther* (1995). The distinctiveness of Jean Calvin's thought lies in Edward Dowey (1994) and E. David Willis (1987; 2002).

Randall Balmer, a historian of American religion, provides a combined set of resources for tracing the strands of Protestant thought into what is now American Evangelicalism (1999; 2002; 2006). In the latter of the three, he addresses with examples contradictions that lie within writing and political actions of those that claim to be Evangelicals. For example: Charles Colson's, among other persons, claim to conversion has been questioned. "Creationism" or "Intelligent Design" both claim to be scientific alternatives to Darwin's *Origin of Species* (1859), but from the standpoint of both general science and law, such claims have not been supported. The alliance of the New Christian Right with the Republican Party in the United States starting in the late 1970s contradicts the strong history within the Baptist tradition (Roger Williams and following) of separation of church and state. Instances of both personal and financial irregularities of Evangelicals, claiming moral superiority, are documented in Balmer (2006), as is the exploitation on the part of Evangelicals of the US First Amendment allowance for free marketing of religious ideas through aggressive use of modern communication media. At the same time, they have sought to impose on individual privacies and individual life-style choices, such as divorce, contraception, abortion, access to teaching about evolution, through use of their own religious values. The work of Robert Wuthnow (2003, 2007, 2012), who skillfully uses regular survey results from the Pew Foundation, provides the best overview of Americans' religious alliances and preferences.

origin and management of hypocrisy, identifying consequences of hypocrisy, and suggesting theoretical options for the study of hypocrisy.

The origins of the word "hypocrisy" and its sequences of meaning through time and place carry consistently degrees of dishonesty or at least artifice. This is why religious texts condemn hypocrites (given the incompatibility of religion and compromises of truth). Sport carries in its special ingredients adherence to rule, a component of this ideal-typical institution which suggests attention to hypocrisy as well as religion as test cases. If hypocrisy should be resisted at all, at least this should happen in sport and religion—reasons being stressed thus far about the selection of these two institutions among others.

The history of writing on hypocrisy being followed, though, describes the history of the word usage and its meaning to vary since the eighteenth century with social and cultural contexts. Chapter 2 has attended to this documented history by looking at sport and religion within the historical context of the United States to establish a reference point for examining some variation of uses, meanings, appearances, and consequences of hypocrisy depending on cultural context.

Chapter 2, thus, has progressed toward the first two goals of the program by considering hypocrisy in religion and sport in one strategic location, the United States. The idea of variation of contextual influences now needs some comparison, which includes the contexts of Iceland and France. The requirement to compare within sociology depends on factors that make a comparison possible and fruitful. These include sufficient likeness to allow some control in the comparison, cultural characteristics that potentially show differences that matter (here patterns of salience and exigencies within sport and religion in the two countries selected to compare with the United States), and meet practical demands for information access and information which will allow useful comparisons.

The selection of sport and religion, and attention to the United States follows the guidelines of goal number two of the program: strategic selection. Sociology considers the import of context on behaviors and meanings, and special ones within the United States context exist here. Regarding hypocrisy, from the consideration of the words and usages of "hypocrisy," the weight or valence or importance of hypocrisy can diminish with its ubiquity. From the work on eighteenth-century appearances of hypocrites, variations on the initially apparent negative valuation emerge. Hypocrisy—from within the case of the United States—prospers when heightened emphasis on success (here in sports and religion) exists. Success gives assurance of goodness, both moral and from a status standpoint. These are the conditions of exigency Shklar perceptively emphasizes. All by the realities of life cannot succeed at maximal levels, so the denials and posturing enter as dissimulation and simulation. Other settings provide different magnitudes of these exigencies, leading to varied displays of hypocrisy. Iceland and France, strategic alternatives for comparison with the United States, allow consideration of variations of settings and the resulting differences of appearances and consequences of hypocrisy—now viewed in the next chapter.

Chapter 3

Some Aspects of Sport and Religion in Iceland and France

Introduction: Exigency and the Contexts of Hypocrisy

The following letter from the Bishop of Iceland intending to deal with a clergy problem opens Halldór Laxness' book on the Icelandic church, *Under the Glacier* (Laxness, 1990).[1] The cast of the letter provides a fruitful entry-point into religion in the country. While Chapter 2 explored the meaning of hypocrisy in sport and religious institutions within the United States, Chapter 3 will add geographic expanse to the generality of the argument about hypocrisy within the institutions of religion and sport, and associated implications for trust in societies, by examining instances and contexts of hypocrisy in Iceland and France.

> The bishop handed me a dog-eared scrap of paper which could barely have come through the post; it looked as if it had been carried from farm to farm and shuffled from pocket to pocket through many districts.
>
> Nonetheless, the letter evinced a mental attitude, if you could call it that, which has more to it than meets the eye and which expresses the logic of the place where it belongs, but has little validity elsewhere, perhaps. The bishop rattled on while I ran my eyes over the letter:
>
> And then he's said to have allowed anglers and foreigners to knock up some monstrosity of a building practically on top of the church—tell him from me to have it pulled down at once! Moreover, he must get around to divorcing his wife. I've heard he's been married for more than thirty years, since long before I became bishop, and hasn't got round to divorcing his wife yet, even though

---

1   Halldór Kiljan Laxness (1902–1998) won the Nobel Prize in Literature in 1955, the only Icelander to win a Nobel Prize. He earlier had won the World Peace Council Literary Prize (1953). His novels (denoted here with the dates of English-language publication) document major moments in the history of the people of Iceland: *Independent People* (1934); *Salka Valka* (1936); *Independent People* (1934); *World Light* (1937); *Iceland's Bell* (1943); and *The Atom Station*. Most follow traditions of realistic fiction, though the last publication satires the existence of the US military base in Keflavík. *Under the Glacier* represents durable traditions of Christianity in Iceland, though there are elements of criticism of the contemporary church. The book appeared first as *Kristnihald Undir Jökli* (1968) and in English, *Christianity at Glacier* (1972). Biographical materials come from: Gudmundsson, 2004; Sigurjónsson, 1986; and Hallberg, 1971a; 1971b.

it's a known fact that she has never shared bed nor board with him. Instead, he
seems to have got mixed up with a woman they call Pestle-Thora, of all things!
Is Christianity being tampered with or what? (Laxness, 1990: 12).

The clergyman to be located and sanctioned has compromised the church and
his clerical duties. In the famous play by Molière, a family sets up the famous
hypocrite, Tartuffe, and encourages him to try to seduce the wife of his friend and
host Orgon. Tartuffe's presentation of religious purity and exemplary intentions
lose veracity when his hosts observe his attempted seduction. Inconsistent
claims and actions by clergymen figure within fiction in the United States. For
example, these characterizations occur in John Updike's *A Month of Sundays*. In
the mid-nineteenth-century novel by Nathaniel Hawthorne (discussed in Chapter
2), depictions of duplicity within early Puritan settlers to America provide an
important baseline to literary depictions of religion and hypocrisy in the United
States. The novel from US culture which is perhaps most apt in introducing the
varied features of hypocrisy in the United States, relative to religion and hypocrisy
in Iceland and France, is Sinclair Lewis' *Elmer Gantry* (Lewis, 1970).

Central analytical steps in sociology include comparisons. Max Weber
emphasizes this in his writing on methodology and embodies the priority in
what are now his classic studies, such as *The Protestant Ethic and the Spirit of
Capitalism*. Émile Durkheim in his methodological writing (for example, *Rules of
Sociological Method* (1982 [1895]) and in his classic substantive reports such as
Suicide and *Elementary Forms of Religion* gives a central position to comparisons
of societies and cultures.

Comparison, to continue methodological canons, must be strategic. In the
process efforts should be made to exclude factors that are not key to the questions
being asked. Terminology now refers to this as getting rid of excess variance in
comparisons, at whatever level of analysis that is occurring. John Stuart Mill
discusses logical methods in his classic, *A System of Logic, Ratiocinative and
Inductive: Being a Connected View of the Principles of Evidence and the Methods
of Scientific Investigation* (original, 1843). A range of practical options now used
throughout the social sciences lie in Donald T. Campbell and Julian Stanley's
inventory, *Experimental and Quasi-Experimental Designs for Research* (1963).
A classical embodiment of both comparison and excluding excess variance occurs
in the minimal form of a true experiment, which must include randomization and
at least two groups which receive different treatments or variable manipulations.

Excess variance also can be reduced when random sampling (or a suitable
alternative, conditioned on practical requirements) occurs from populations where
surveys are distributed, such as in the work of sociologists of religion who study
national populations and draw samples from these populations (used in Chapter 2).

In the same way that a condition in a true experiment comes from priorities
of the research existing in a researcher's theoretical interests, Weber discusses
the import of making special kinds of theoretically relevant comparisons between
cultures. One wants to compare ideal types of two or more societies, the ideal types

being a distillation of the most salient features of those societies, respectively. The criterion of salience for him is *significance*. When Shklar discusses hypocrisy, as reported in Chapter 1, she stresses a set of cultural conditions that make the stakes in hypocritical acts (seriousness, for example) and levels of preoccupation over hypocrisy as conditions of exigency. The different contexts where hypocrisy differs in meaning somewhat in Shklar's illustrations (and also in discussions by Runciman and Davidson) commonly hinge on these cultural characteristics (that is, seriousness and pre-occupation) that lead to exigency. So, following Weber (and Durkheim as well) in selecting cases that are useful in comparison, the attention to Iceland and France allow degrees of the extent of exigency that affect levels and consequences of hypocrisy.

A representative statement from Weber (1949) comes from his essay *Objectivity in Social Science*: "Accordingly, cultural science in our sense involves 'subjective' presuppositions insofar as it concerns itself only with those components of reality which have some relationship however indirect, to events to which we attach cultural significance" [here, *cultural Bedeutung*].

This chapter, which lengthens the geographic range and culture of the context for hypocrisy, again examines dissimulation and simulation but here within the Lutheran country of Iceland and the strongly Catholic country of France. Exigency, Shklar's (2004) evocative term, means there are particular cultural and social conditions that predispose or perhaps one can say "tempt" individuals and institutions to hypocrisy. In turn, the conditions elevate the importance of hypocrisy for people in such a society.

These conditions include: the strong moral valuation associated with success; some religious and secular norms that mandate such success for its adherents; a system of evaluation that is vertical leading to invidious distinctions of performance on the scale; the real prospects that everybody cannot succeed as demanded—all of which means accounts of accomplishment must be manufactured from hopes and desires as well as factual results.

Shklar's point and the specific mention of Puritanism as a contextual factor, that may elevate the stakes with hypocrisy, suggests an inclusion of some cross-cultural/cross-geographical comparisons as well. For this comparison, news appearances of "hypocrisy" in *Morgunblaðið* and *Le Monde* are in view as well as within *The New York Times* (Chapter 2). These combine with representations of Icelandic and French sporting traditions and notable sporting events in the two countries. These two countries are defensible for this comparison because they offer some variance, but they allow access to media comparable to *The New York Times*, and they do not carry excessive variation as nation-states. The three countries are all Christian, but they differ in the strains of Christianity that are dominant in each case. France has a long history of institutionalized Roman Catholicism; Iceland's national church is Lutheran (hence, a product of the Lutheran Reformation); the United States has a special historical association with the Reformed theology (Calvinistic Reformation) carried to the US East Coast in the seventeenth century as Puritanism. (The strains of Protestantism appear in Figure 2.1 in Chapter 2.)

The social and cultural conditions of sport and religion in the United States, France, and Iceland differ. These contexts—the sources of different valences of exigency—do not determine patterns of deceit. But the uniqueness of the contexts, both singly and in comparison, give unavoidable clues to the strength of exigencies in the three countries, and the clues accord suggestively with the frequency and quality of displays of hypocrisy in the three settings. Table 2.3 in the previous chapter summarizes a group of representative features and manifestations of sport and religion in the United States, France, and Iceland; and Iceland and France receive attention now.

Special Features of Sport in Iceland: "A Deed Not Done Needs No Reward" (Icelandic Proverb)

Examples of sport during the earliest periods of Icelandic history appear in Figure 3.1. The approach to sport and the priorities of types of sport profit from noting these early accounts in the saga record.

Figure 3.1   Icelandic saga sources for sports and contests

For general ease of access, a concentrated source for English translations is noted below from The *Complete Sagas of Icelanders* (General Editor, Vidar Hreinsson. 1997. Reykjavík: Leifur Eiríksson Publishing), with volume numbers within the series noted. The volume locations are also provided for access within *Íslendinga sögur* (Jonsson, Editor, 1981). Two references to the Icelandic text are to *Íslenzk Fornrit*. The identification of the event or reference to a game, sport, contest, or amusement within each of the sagas is by a parenthetical number, which refers to a section demarcation in the printed versions of the sagas.

1. *Bandamanna saga* (Vol. V, in *Complete Sagas of Icelanders*); "The Saga of the Confederates," Vol. V in *Íslendinga sögur*.
   — None.

2. *Bjarnar saga Hitdaelakappa* (Vol. I.); The Saga of Bjorn, Champion of the Hitardal People," Vol. III in *Íslendinga sögur*.
   — (3) Note poem contests.
   — (4) Duel [*Holmgánga*].
   — (23) Thord and Bjorn have horse fight.
   — Poem contests.
   — (29) Contests with recitations.

3. *Droplaugarsona saga* (Vol. IV); "The Saga of Droplaug's Sons," Vol. X in *Íslendinga sögur*.
   — (13) Board game with a Norwegian.

— (14) The Norwegian came to the games (*leik*) at Krossavik.
— (15) Duel [*Holmgánga*].

4. *Egil's Saga* (Vol. II); "Egil's Saga," Vol. II in *Íslendinga sögur*.
Period of events: c. 858–990 (Egil's death).
— (40) "Skallagrim took a great delight in trials of strength and games, and liked talking about them. Ball-games were common in those days, and there were plenty of strong men in the district at this time."
— (40) "Egil was a keen wrestler ... ."
— (40) "A ball-game was arranged early in winter on the plains by the river Hvita, and crowds of people came to it from all over the district."
— (65) Duel [*Holmgánga*. Extensive treatment; comment on rules of dueling.].
— (66) "What Egil said was law too, under the ancient custom that every man had the right to challenge another to a duel, whether to prosecute a care or defend it."

5. *Eyrbyggja saga* (Vol. V): "The Saga of the People of Eyri," Vol. III in *Íslendinga sögur*.
Period of events: Ends in 1031 when Snorri Thorgrimsson dies.
— (8) Ulfar is challenged by Thorolf to a duel over property.
— (18) "Thorarin had a good fighting stallion which he grazed up on the mountain."
— (31) "Relations between them and Arankel soured to the point where they did not even plan games together any more, whereas before that had often held matches."
— (43) "Around the Winter Nights it was the custom of the people of Breidavik to hold ball-games under Oxl mountain of Knorr." [Additional discussion of meaning and role of games.]
— (43) "That same autumn the Thorbrandssons told their slave Egil to go to the ball-games and find some way to kill one of the Breidavik men, either Bjorn ... ."

6. *Fosbraedra saga* (Vol. II); "The Saga of the Sworn Brothers," Vol. V in *Íslendinga sögur.*
Period of events: written late thirteenth century.
— (15) "One day, they [Eyolf and Thorgeir] were wrestling on the floor and making a great row, and they kept bumping into the woman [Thordis] and trampling on the work she was doing."
— (18) Fighters "amused themselves" with head of victim.
— (22) "Skin throwing games" [*skinnleikum*].

7. *Gisla saga* (Vol. II); "Gisli Sursson's Saga," Vol. V in *Íslendinga sögur*.
— (1) Duel [*Holmgánga*].
— (2) Duel [*Holmgánga*].

— (15) Ball game on ice; Gisli throws Thorgrim.

— (18, 19) Winter games; ball with bat; ends in fight.

8. *Grettis saga* (Vol. II); "The Saga of Grettir the Strong," Vol. VI in *Íslendinga sögur*.
Period of events: Grettir killed between 1030–1040.

— (15) Winter ball game; ball bat, acrimony, some wrestling.

— (19) Norwegian king bans duels [Both kinds].

— (22) Grettis and Bjorn duel [*Einvíga*]; it continues if is unequal; continues
for several chapters.

— (28) On the basis of the earlier disagreements over sport at Midfiardarvatn,
Gretti's provokes Audun into a fight; they wrestle; use term "having
some sport."

— (29) Horse fight.

— (30) Reference to previous horse fight.

— (31) Duel [*Einvíga*].

— (35) Wrestling with Glam.

— (40) A challenge provided a farmer by criminals to fight for the women;
Grettir steps in as a proxy.

— (65) Wrestled with troll.

— (70) A board game (*hneftafl*) played by Thorbjorn Ongul.

— (72) Wrestling and games at the assembly [Note different terms here: Glíma
is used but *skemmtun* for games, which means in the dictionary, amusement].

9. *Gunnlaugs saga ormstrungu* (Vol. I); "The Saga of Gunnlaug Serpent-Tongue,"
Vol. II in *Íslendnga sögur*.

— None.

10. *Hallfredar saga* (Vol. I); "The Saga of Hallfred the Troublesome Poet," Vol.
VII in *Íslendinga sögur*.

— (2) "An autumn feast was held at Grimstunger together with ball games"
[woman hides ball].

— (3) Games were over.

— (4) Duel [*Holmgánga*].

— (10) Duel mentioned [*Holmgánga*].

11. *Heidarviga saga* (Vol. IV); "The Saga of the Slayings on the Heath," Vol. VII
Íslendinga sögur.

— (11) Games and wrestling mentioned [But at Constantinople in
Varingin Guard].

— (15] Duel [*Holmgánga*].

12. *Haensa-Thoris saga* (Vol. V); "Hen Thorir's Saga," Vol. III in *Íslenzk fornrit*.

— None.

13. *Hrafnkels saga* (Vol. I): "The Saga of Hrafnkel's Freys' Godi," Vol. X in *Íslendinga sögur*.
Period of events: Early 10th.
— (2) Mention of duel [*Einvíga*].

14. *Kormak's saga* (Vol. I); "Kormak's Saga," Vol. VI in *Íslendinga sögur*.
Period of events: Kormak probably lives between 945 and 975.
— (3) Game of "tables."
— (10) *Holmgánga* rules [Note: two forms of duel existed. Single combat, or *einvíga* was a less stylized fight; *Holmgánga* reflected an elaborate set of rules].
— (12) *Holmgánga* rules.
— (14) Duel [*Holmgánga*].
— (21) Duel [*Holmgánga*].
— (22) Duel [*Holmgánga*].
— (23) Duel [*Holmgánga*].

15. *Laxdaela saga* (Vol. V); "The Saga of the People of Laxardal," Vol. IV in *Íslendinga sögur*.
— (33) "Olaf followed him [Gest] a short distance along his onward journey, down to the river Laxa. The two foster-brothers had been swimming in the river that day, a sport in which the Olafssons took the lead."
— (36) "Kotkel and his family then left, taking no possessions except a stud of four horses with them. The stallion was black, large and powerful and had proven his fighting prowess."
— (40) "Kjartan then dived out into the river and swam over to the man who was such a strong swimmer, pushed him underwater and held him down for some time, before letting him come up again." [Note: This is the contest between Kjartan, and what turned out to be Olaf Tryggvason, in Trondheim.]
— (45) "Bolli had a stud of horses regarded as the finest of animals. The stallion was large and handsome and had never been known to give way in a fight."
— (45) "Hall [son of Gudmund the Powerful] gave Kjartan a very warm welcome, and organized games as Asbjarnarnes to which people from nay parts of the surrounding region were invited." [May have been a ball-game played on ice, with a combination of skill, strength, and resiliency—as the text describes an event that lasted over multiple days.]
— (71) "That winter the brothers met regularly, spending their time talking privately to one another and showing little interest in games or other entertainment."

16. *Ljosvetninga saga* (Vol. IV); "The Saga of the People of Ljosvatn," Vol. IV in *Íslendinga sögur*.
   — (9) "A short time later, games were organized there." [Ends in loser injuring victor.]
   — (11) Single combat duel [*Einvíga*].
   — (12) Horse fight.
   — (16, 17) Two duels [*Holmgánga*].
   — "Came there to participate in games."

17. *Njal's saga* (Vol. III); "Njal's Saga," Vol. XII in *Íslenzk Fornrit*.
Period of events: Njal born in 930; the burning of Bergthorsknoll and death of Njal in 1011.
   — (19) "He [Gunnar] could swim like a seal, and there was no sport in which there was any point in competing with him. It was said that no man was his match."
   — (24) Duel [*Holmgánga*].
   — (58) Extended commentary on horse fighting.
   — (109) "Skarphedin had a dark-horse, four years old, big and handsome. It was a stallion and had not yet fought another horse."

18. *Reykdaela saga* (Vol. IV); "The Saga of the People of Reykjadal and of Killer-Skuta," Vol. IV in *Íslendinga sögur*.
   — (1) Duel [*Holmgánga*].
   — (12) Horse fight.
   — (13) Reference to games.
   — (19) Duel [*Holmgánga*].
   — (23) Horse fight.

19. *Thorstein's saga stangarhoggs* (Vol. IV); "The Tale of Thorstein Staff-struck," Vol. X in *Íslendinga sögur*. [Uncertain authorship date; no chapter headings, hence page references are to Viking Classics translation.]
   — (p. 335 in Viking Classics) Horse fight.
   — (p. 338) Duel [*Einvíga* or single combat].

20. *Thorstein's saga hvita* (Vol. IV); "The Saga of Thorstein the White," Vol. X in *Íslendinga sögur*.
   — (8) Informal "bull fight." [Man adds spurs to his own bull to afford an advantage.]

21. *Valla-Ljot's saga* (Vol. IV); "Valla-Ljot's Saga," Vol. VIII in *Íslendinga sögur*.
   — (4, 5) Laws of dueling abolished [*Holmgánga*].

22. *Varnfirdinga saga* (Vol. IV); "The Saga of the People of Vopnafjord," Vol. X in *Íslendinga sögur*.
— (4) Reference to winter games (note term used here was *leik*).

23. *Vatnsdaela saga* (Vol. IV); "The Saga of the People in Vatnsdal," Vol. VII in *Íslsendinga sögur*.
— (7) "He [Ingimund] was talented in all games."
— (14) Played games.
— (24) Went to the games.
— (25) "In the morning Thorstein said to his brothers, 'you will play at a board game today and I shall talk with Geirmund.'"
— (27) "He had the sword with him at games meetings and horse-fights, and Thorstein carried it at autumn meetings and law meetings, because this was the way that Jokul wanted it."
— (33) Three duels mentioned [Holmgánga].

24. *Viga-glum's saga* (Vol. II); "Killer Glum's Saga," Vol. VIII in *Íslendinga sögur*.
— (4) Duel (with explicit rules) [*Holmgánga*].
— (6) "When he [Glum] got to the farm he saw a great crowd of people there, with games and amusements of all kinds, and it seemed clear to him that everything there was done in the grand manner."
— (13) "It happened one summer at the Althing that teams of men were competing at wrestling ... ."
— (13) Horse fighting contest.
— (14) Duel threatened [*Holmgánga*].
— (18) Horse fighting [Note whole set of rules].

The sources here represent a set arranged by Icelanders (and international scholarship) as *Íslendinga sögur*. This particular population of sagas (N=24) follows the selection of Theodore M. Anderson (The Icelandic Family Saga Origins. New Haven, CT: Yale University Press). One from his list of 25 has been dropped due to the judgment from assessments that *Hávardar saga Ísfirdings* ("Howard the Halt") may have originated in different production contexts: viz. the date of writing of the saga is considerably later than that of the other 24, and it may be a parody rather than the kind of stylized history represented by the others. The sagas refer to events taking place in the first two centuries of the Early Commonwealth which lasted from 930–1262. By current scholarly consent, the sagas were written in the thirteenth and fourteenth centuries, a period when the Commonwealth was breaking down, perhaps prompting authors to celebrate in the writing the honored history of the early years of the Commonwealth. The critical position adopted here is to use these sources as a credible basis of constitutive norms of the Early Commonwealth period. A systematic argument for such use is provided in Stephen G. Wieting and Thórólfur Thórlindsson, "Divorce in the Old

Icelandic Commonwealth: an Interactionist Approach to the Past." 1990. *Studies in Symbolic Interaction* 11: 163–89.[2]

One example of how Iceland has continued a tradition of sport lies with this account of the national sport of Iceland: Glíma, a form of wrestling still practiced in the country. As contemporary sport in the United States displays a continuous line of integrity from the seventeenth century, and the contemporary expressions of French sport contain elements of earlier cultural traditions, specific sports and styles of play currently in Iceland represent continuity as well. In addition to the anticipations of Glíma in the early saga record, descriptions of contests of strength, and early ball games within the saga sources identify a context in Iceland where success and popularity of strength competitions and team handball exists currently.

Glíma and Wrestling History

Glíma is the national sport of Iceland. Iceland treasures, as shown in Figure 3.1, a group of 24 books called *Íslindinga sögur* which recount the years of settlement from 870–930 and the years Iceland was a free republic from 930–1262. There are 88 references to sports and games in these volumes, including duels, horse fights, turf throwing, ball games, and duration staying under water. There are nine references to wrestling. Glíma wrestling continues through the period when Iceland was an independent country from 930 to 1262, the long period of being a colony of first Norway and then Denmark until full independence in 1944, to the present day where all ages of men and women participate.

Many forms of wrestling existed before these Icelandic records. Wrestling was introduced in the Ancient Olympics in 708 BC. In the modern Olympics starting in 1896, a form of wrestling designed to approximate the original form entered and is known now as Greco-Roman in the Olympic schedule. This wrestling was omitted in 1900 and 1904 but has been continuous since 1908. What we know as freestyle wrestling entered the Olympics in 1904 and has been continuous since then. Glíma was a demonstration sport in the 1908 Olympics. Many forms of wrestling with Celtic influences occurred during the settlement years in Iceland, and several were practiced there in the early years. The special wrestling form now known

---

2   There are two purposes for the recovery of this population of sport episodes from this canonical set of documents. One is substantive, since themes of the conduct and meaning of sport currently are anticipated in the early sources: these include the emphasis on activities of physical strength, which occur now with Icelandic men and women engaged successfully in contests of strength (latter in the chapter). The sport contests also focus on matters of honor and often occur over debates and need to demonstrate fidelity to rules of fairness. These latter two substantive themes figure in current character of sport activity in Iceland. Sampling, always a problem with variable populations, becomes acute with the distance in time in the origin of documents. Methodologically here I follow the guidelines of Robert Darnton in his study of clandestine and forbidden literature of late eighteenth-century France. Rather than try to sample, he advocates an attempt to reproduce a population of documents (Darnton, 1982; 1995; 1996).

as Glíma was practiced by the twelfth century with: a fixed grip on the waistband and trouser leg of the opponent; upright position of the opponents; the clockwise rotation of the wrestlers; and the reliance of stylized throws or "tricks" to dominate an opponent. Glíma persisted after independence was lost first to Norway in 1262 and then to Denmark in 1380.

Glíma was part of early nineteenth-century school physical education at the two bishopric schools of Hólar and Skáholt and then in schools in Reykjavík. Rules were formalized by the Icelandic Sports Federation in 1916 and amended in 1951. A recent version of the rules of Glíma, nine single-spaced pages in English, went into effect on March 21, 2003.

Glíma as a special form of wrestling

Some of the alternative forms of wrestling were oriented to military skill, others to recreation. Glíma was a recreational sport within a group of wrestling types called "trouser grip." It now is practiced fairly exclusively in Iceland, though competitions do occur in Canada, other Nordic countries, and in the United States today. The term "Glíma" has been associated with a Faroese term for wrestling. Also, the term has been linked to a term of a sudden light, which captures an element in the practice of the sport of sudden, unexpected throws. A fairly common meaning is now for joyous or gleeful (related to the Anglo-Saxon term "glee"). This identifies the sport as essentially for amusement and entertainment as well as recreation.

Historically Glíma was practiced in large, outdoor spaces and often occurred at national celebrations such as *Thingvellir*, a dramatic outdoor historical site 50 km east of Reykjavík where the national assembly was held each spring, and where national independence day, June 17, is celebrated (*Þjóðhatídardagurinn*). The sport was also practiced in the small confines of homes, some of which were merely sod huts. Writers on Glíma believe the compact competitive style of the sport accommodated itself to these small indoor residences. Now all age groups 17 and older, males and females, mostly compete on floor courts such as modern gymnasia.

A competition begins civilly with a hand shake; competitors face each other and grasp the other on a special belt at the waist with the right and on an extended loop of the belt at the thigh with the left hand (originally these reciprocal grips being made were of trousers, but in 1905 the special belts were added as equipment). At the referee's prompt, competitors begin to circle clockwise; there are 8–10 special techniques or throws a competitor can use to get the opponent off balance; the throws use a combination of feet and legs as leverage and the attached hands as fulcrum and leverage to throw the other; a victory comes when a body part above the knee, above the elbow, the back, or the head of the opponent touches the floor; if opponents both fall simultaneously a draw is in effect, and the match resumes; periods of one-and-a-half minute continue until a successful throw occurs (two minutes for athletes 17 and older); in traditional Glíma, no weight classifications existed.

Glíma today[3]

The national organization of Glíma is the Icelandic Glíma Federation (*Glímu-samband Íslands*, www.glima.is) located within a large array of national Icelandic sport offices situated in Reykjavík. Another international Glíma organization known as the Viking Glíma Federation has been developed and directed by Lars Magnar Enoksen. There is also an international organization that governs international competitions, the International Glíma Association (www.internationalglima.com).[4]

World Strongman and Related Contests for Women

The self-description by Icelanders of their sport lies in the *Íslendinga sögur*, and they continue their self-identified sense of uniqueness with their special form of wrestling. From the standpoint of world sport, Iceland's uniqueness perhaps lies in the World's Strongest Man contest which began in 1977 and continues to this day. As of the 2013 competition, the Icelandic competitors Magnús Ver Magnússon and Jón Páll Sigmarsson each have won four times.

Icelandic women appear in similar strength contests as well. The most direct analog to the World's Strongest Man contest is now the United Strongmen Women's World Championships, which has appeared under other titles since 1997. Gemma

---

3   Soccer is the most popular sport in Iceland for both young men and women, followed by handball for both young men under 16 and young women. Basketball, track and field, and golf are popular along with Glíma. Golf for all ages in Iceland has grown recently in popularity; between 1996 and 2004, golf for males under 16 grew 117 percent, and for older males, 138 percent, making it now the most popular sport for males 16 and over. For young females, golf grew 99 percent and for older females there was a 186 percent change from 1996–2004 making golf the most popular sport for older females (16 and older). Glíma participation has been modest but stable compared to these five other sports popular among Icelanders, with participation rising for young males by 10 percent from 1996–2004 and by 31 percent for females aged 16 and over during this period; rates reduced by 6 percent for older males and by 14 percent for younger females in this time segment.

4   Basic books and articles on Glíma are available in the National Wrestling Hall of Fame, Dan Gable Museum by: Kjartan Bergmann Gudjonsson, *Islensk Glima og Glimumenn*, 1993, a major documentary source of the sport's history and famous competitors from an Icelandic publisher; Johannes Josefsson, *Icelandic Wrestling*, 1908 (this is the oldest book in English on Glíma, now out of print); Thorsteinn Einarsson, *Glíma: the Icelandic Wrestling*, 1988 [1984] (this is material circulated by a long-time Icelandic proponent of the sport); M. Bennett Nichols, *Glíma: Icelandic Wrestling*, 1999 (the one book on Glíma by a North American writer, now out of print); Lars Magnar Enoksen, *The Secret Art of Glíma*, 2008 (Mr. Enoksen [Viking Glíma Federation]), Swedish, has sought to broaden understanding of the sport. He now presents demonstrations and clinics in the United States]; Lars Magnar Enoksen, *Glíma Fighting Techniques*, 2010. Similarities between Glíma and other nations' traditional sports appear in Stephen G. Wieting, Simona Ionescu, Felix Sinitean-Singer, "Romanian Oina and Icelandic Glíma: Preserving Traditional Sports within the 21st Century Global Marketplace," pp. 208–17 in Tomaz Pavlin, ed., *Sport, Nation, Nationalism*, published in 2009.

Taylor-Magnússon, who married Benedikt Magnússon in 2008, was a runner up in 2011 (when the contest was named "World's Strongest Lady") and, as Gemma Taylor from Thirst, North Yorkshire, also came second in 2005 (entitled at that time, "World Strongwoman Championships").

Contests of strength, shown in reports from the early sagas, appear commonly in Icelandic history. Now, for both men and women, Icelandic athletes in world strength contests, appear with unusual frequency. Icelandic male contestants follow only the United States in winning the "World's Strongest Man" contests. Started in 1977, this contest through to the summer of 2014 shows the United States with nine winners followed by Iceland with eight (for reference, note that the population of Iceland is 1/1000 the size of the population of the United States). An analogous competition in which women participate, the Cross-Fit Games, started in 2007. Annie Mist Thórisdóttir, an Icelandic athlete, won the contest in 2011, 2012, and was second, following an injury that kept her out of the 2013 competition, in 2014. She is the only female multi-year winner.

Team Handball in Iceland

Iceland is known additionally within international sport circles for their success in team handball. Iceland's winning the silver medal in the 2008 Olympic Games makes them the smallest country ever to win a medal in a team sport. They were a favorite to win a medal in the 2012 Olympics in London, though they lost to Hungary in the quarter finals and did not receive a medal. Viðar Halldórsson and Thórólfur Thórlindsson have written productively about the cultural and social conditions undergirding the remarkable success of Icelandic team handball (2013). Joined with American sociologist, Michael Katovich (2014), the analysis continues, with potential for comparison with research on the contexts of the origin and perpetuation of particular sports.[5] Team handball is an important sport in France as well as in Iceland, but not in the United States. France was the team which defeated Iceland in the 2008 Olympic Games. Halldórsson, Thórlindsson, and Katovich raise the question of whether there are characteristics of prominence in sport and also quality of sport performance that show associations with national culture. The prospective is a provocative one in this analysis of ways in which a culture creates conditions that foster (or at least do not constrain) dissembling and simulating of athletic success. In ideal-typical terms, sport as referred to here is: physical, intrinsic, rule-governed, and consummative. The coverage of the development of international sports clearly brings into play tests over

---

5   Some examples include: Wooden (1997), Axthelm, (1970) and Carril (1997) for basketball. Continuing collegiate examples, wrestling can be included with Nolan Zavoral's description of The University of Iowa and Dan Gable's program (Zavoral, 1998), swimming (Chambliss, 1988; 2006), tennis (Carlson, 1988), Kenyan running (Bale and Sang, 1996; and also Wieting, 2005), and soccer (Lever, 1983). This research complements similar traditions of research on specific contexts of success in science and in the creative arts.

the conception of intrinsic reward and in the fidelity of players and entire sport systems to rules.

But the authors noted above, and in focus here the work on culture and athletic culture, allow the prospects of cultural expectations contributing to the way a particular sport is played in a particular society, as here Iceland. Halldórsson and Thórlindsson note a special nationalism associated with the history of small but significant victories within the national team's history (for example, over Denmark in 1969) (Halldórsson and Thórlindson, 2013). The authors mention also characteristics of a democratic team structure, a craft approach to preparation and conduct in playing, strong social bonds among players, intrinsic motivation as opposed to lucrative financial support, sacrifice, and minimum of arrogance (elaborated as well in Halldórsson, Thórlindsson, and Katovich, 2014). Elements of intrinsic enjoyment, craft as opposed to expediency in quality of play, modesty, sacrifice, and mutual trust contrast importantly with characteristics associated with concealment of pasts and questionable claims of current prominence emphasized in cases where hypocrisy can be acknowledged.

> Specifically, Icelanders trust that the ambition to do well translates into the development of character. Beyond outcomes, the play itself, the excitement of competition, and the demonstration of skill and mastery under difficult circumstances served as primary rewards. The emphasis on intrinsic motivation, skill and craftsmanship in Icelandic culture demonstrates an even broader trust in the Icelandic society itself. Whatever the specific outcome of any particular game, the broader outcome will involve the development of internally directed participants who, nevertheless have a great appreciation for the external 'rules of the game.' Thus, the local culture may promote some of the values fostered through informal sport (Halldórsson, Thórlindsson, and Katovich, 2014: 20, 21).

The Icelandic Church

Christianity in the Development of a Republic

The newspaper in Iceland that is closest to type and circulation of *The New York Times* and *Le Monde* is *Morganblaðið*. The ease of access for so long a period as the United States and French sources may be somewhat less, but there is a search mechanism for a reasonably long history of publication of this newspaper. As above in the recovery of long traditions of Icelandic sport, internally and in hands of outside commentators the self-defined import of the old sagas for recounting religious history in the country exists. Attention to these volumes suggests that from this earliest set of documents, that record the settlement period and early Commonwealth period of Iceland from 870–1262, there is a special meaning of lying and trust that is different from the essentials of hypocrisy with Puritanism in the United States.

When Norwegians migrated West toward more opportunity for land, the tailing wind of their ships carried them to the coast of present-day Iceland, and they landed for the first time in the Southwest part of the country, where Reykjavík is located. Religious sentiments were defined by belief in the gods, Thor and Freya, and these entities were spoken of in their mythical sagas. From 870–930 settlement took place on this southwest coast, and in 930 a commonwealth was defined with a designated central decision-making site now located about 50 km East from Reykjavík, called *Thingvellir*.

In 1000, a controversy emerged over religious commitments of Icelanders. Christianity had arrived with some settlers from the British Islands and through contact by Vikings in touch with fighters associated with the Eastern Church. Olaf Tryggvason, King of Norway, mandated Christianity in that country and sought to spread the faith to the other Nordic countries as well. Conflict between followers of Freya, Thor, and Odin, and the Christians grew intense at the end of the tenth century. Unity then (and often, now) was uppermost in the thinking of the people, and they gave over the decision of what to do about the controversy to Thorgeir Thorkelsson, the representative to the national assembly (*Althing*) who was then the elected spokesperson of the 32-person legislature. The account in *Njal's Saga* records that he meditated for a day and night under a cloak, and in the morning he conveyed his judgment: "It appears to me that our affairs will be hopeless if we don't all have the same law, for if the law is split then peace will be split, and we can't live with that. Now I want to ask the heathens and Christians whether they are willing to accept the law that I proclaim."

"They all assented to this. Thorgeir said that he wanted oaths from them and pledges that they would stick by them. 'This will be the foundation of our law,' he said, 'that all men in this land are to be Christians and believe in one God—Father, Son and Holy Spirit—and give up all worship of false idols, the exposure of children, and the eating of horse meat. Three years' outlawry will be the penalty for open violations, but if these things are practiced in secret there shall be no punishment'" (*Njal's Saga*, Chapters 100–105). In practical terms, the country, in the interest of unity became Christian in the year 1000.

The organization of the Church (Roman Catholic) surrounded two bishoprics, Hólar and Skálholt. The external influences on the history of the Church, and the corresponding type of resistance by Icelanders to this external influence, occurred in the Protestant Reformation that came to Iceland between 1538 and 1550. The Reformation entered Denmark in 1536–7, and the Danish King, Christian III (Denmark having gained control of both Norway and Iceland in 1380) sought to extend his existing rule over Iceland by mandating religious change in the dependent country. The bishop at Skálholt, Ogmundur Pálsson, accepted the Reformation, but Jón Arnason the bishop at Hólar did not. He was beheaded on November 1550 as a step in the total country change to Lutheranism; his actions have made him a hero in Iceland for his opposition to external rule.

Contemporary Religion in Iceland

Iceland continues today as officially Lutheran, with state support of clergy and churches. Pétur Pétursson describes the role of the Icelandic church in the period of modernization and official statehood. During the control by Denmark of Iceland from 1380 until final recognition of the status of a republic in 1944, the administrative levels sent by Denmark to Iceland meant that government and civil offices were run by Danish functionaries and used Danish as an official language (Pétursson, 1983: *Church and Social Change: a Study of the Secularization Process in Iceland, 1830–1930*). The Danish King did annex church lands after the Reformation signaling growing interest by Danish leaders in Iceland. Pétursson asserts that the Lutheran Church, by contrast to governmental offices, was staffed by native clergy and administered largely by Icelanders. This allowed some continuity of Icelandic culture through the Church. The administrative sites for the Church (officially Lutheran from 1552) at Skálholt and then at Hólar were abolished successively in 1785 and 1801 and in turn amalgamated with the Diocese of Reykjavík, site of the Bishop's offices.

Today the State Church, The Evangelical Lutheran Church of Iceland, commands 77.6 percent of the national population (in 2011, 247,245 out of 318,452), with small representations of other denominations, including other branches of Lutheranism (5.5 percent), Roman Catholicism (3.2 percent); and the aggregate of Roman Catholicism and other denominations comprising 6.5 percent of the population. Despite the large, official membership in the national church, attendance is low, with 10 percent reporting attendance at least once a month in a 2004 Gallup Poll.

A scandal within the Evangelical Lutheran Church in 2010 led some members (estimated at as many as 10,000 by *The Reykjavík Grapevine* [2013]) to de-register. The scandal lies within a succession of acts and claimed cover-ups within the Bishopric. The current Bishop, Agnes M. Sigurðardóttir, has had to deal with the controversy. "Serious trouble began for the state church when it was brought to light that former Bishop Karl Sigurbjörnsson was involved in a sex scandal concerning the previous bishop—the late Olafur Skúlasson—whom several women, including his own daughter, have accused of sexual abuse. Karl [Sigurbjörnsson], who was a priest at the time of the abuse, concealed evidence of this bishop's crimes. Public outcry prompted Karl [Sigurbjörnsson] to step down" (*The Reykjavík Grapevine*, 2013).

Sport in France

Three sporting traditions serve to illuminate the history of sport and France; their features connect closely with the themes of contradictions and hypocrisy in the book: the origins of the Modern Olympic Games, the history and development of the Tour de France, and the success and lingering controversies of the recent success of France's World Cup Soccer Victory in 1998.

France and the Modern Olympic Games

John MacAloon's definition of cultural factors (MacAloon, 1981) associated with the Modern Olympic Games and how Pierre de Coubertin both continued and transformed the ancient Games (represented in Finley and Pleket, 1976 and Miller, 2004), puts the Olympics forward with several epochs where issues of contradiction existed, such as the class homogeneity of the Games, disputes over amateurism, intense nationalisms varying from the express definitions of Olympianism, and drug violations.

France and the Origins of the Tour de France

The very origins of the Tour de France as a commercial vehicle introduces the prospects of the event compromising our conception of sport here. The prominence of hypocrisy in the event, from at least 2005, signals the importance of this sporting institution for general themes addressed as well as representing French sport. The Tour began in France in 1903, and continues as a type of provenance of the French. Directors of the Tour all have been French: Henri Desgrange (1903–1939), Jacques Goddet (1947–1961), Jacques Goddet and Felix Levian together (1962–1986), Jean-François Naquet-Radiguet (1987–1988), Jean-Pierre Courcol (1988–1989), Jean-Marie Leblanc (1989–2005), and Christian Proudhomme (2005–present). The governing body for professional cycling is the Union Cycliste Internationale (UCI). The organization started in Paris in 1900, though it is now located in Aigle, Switzerland. Power struggles between leadership within the UCI and specific teams and riders from North America, such as Lance Armstrong and the teams of which he was a member, figure prominently in accounts of drug use and attempts to control drug use reported throughout this book.

The Tour de France is now organized by the Amaury Sport Organization (ASO), a part of Editions Philippe Amaury, a French media group. French national spectatorship continues to be huge, though the success of French riders has dwindled notably in the past two decades. The last French rider to win the event was Bernard Hinault in 1985. Members of French teams, as would be anticipated, featured prominently as winners early in the event and varied in success over the history of the Tour, until being shut out recently. Of 36 French winners their success by decade ranges as follows: 1900s (6), 1910s (2), 1920s (1), 1930s (7), 1940s with the event held three years in the decade (0), 1950s (5), 1960s (6), 1970s (4), 1980s (5), since (0).

France and International Soccer

France's soccer team won the World Cup in 1998, an outcome exceedingly popular in that country and also a result used productively by writers to describe essential characteristics of sport in French society. Lindsay Sarah Krasnoff's account (2012) and the array of post-event perspectives in Dauncey and Hare's *France and the 1998 World Cup* (1999) illustrate the importance of France's victory for the History of the World Cup itself. The books also serve as useful vehicles for understanding patterns of participation, fan interest, and the place of sport within the politics of France.

Sport in France has a long history of being supported with national resources and incorporated into education as a vehicle of health and national identity. Both soccer and basketball have served as major sport institutions in these purposes. Lindsay Sarah Krasnoff records the perceived failure of France in the international contests of the summer Olympics in Rome in 1960 as a source of national reflection and increased attention to the development of youth sport. France's victory in the 1998 World Cup of soccer served for governmental figures and broadly through French society to be a reward for the efforts of society in the development of sport among the youth of society.

Success in international football since then for France has not been linear, with consequent public criticisms of French developmental programs and public recriminations about the failure of national teams in their responsibility to carry national prominence as a world-renowned civilization. The men's national team played its first official match in 1904. Evidence of France's longevity within European football comes from being in the first World Cup in 1930 and from entry into 13 FIFA World Cups. They did not qualify in 1962, 1970, 1974, 1990, and 1994. They qualified but withdrew in 1950. The men's team won the UEFA European Championship in 1984 (following four events of non-qualification in 1964, 1968, 1972, 1976, and 1980). They won a gold medal at the 1984 Olympics and won the FIFA Confederations Cup in 2001 and 2003.

The national women's football team in France qualified for its first FIFA Women's World Cup in 2003; in the 2011 World Cup they finished fourth. The history of the development of the women's program shows minimal success at the beginning of its competition on the international level and improvement recently. The team did not qualify for the World Cup in 1991, 1995, 1999, and 2007 but did, as mentioned, accomplish a fourth place finish in 2011.

Following the 9/11 (2001) attack on the US, combined with a history of support of the United States, some events in sport lifted the cover on some antipathetic sentiments within Moslem society. France played Algeria in a friendly football match later that fall in the Paris suburb of Saint Denis. Fans booed the playing of "La Marseillaise" prior to the game, and with the French Les Bleus leading 4–1 toward the end of the game, fans of the Algerian team rushed the field. Threats to France's international prestige (so much a matter of pride in 1998) came as well from the French electorate's opposition to the EU; lack of success in its bid to host the 2012 Olympics; and a highly publicized attack on youths in a *banlieue* of Paris, Clichy-sous-Bois (2005).

The work of Krasnoff and combined judgments of an international group of commentators on the 1998 football victory (Dauncy and Hare, 1999) draw several lessons about the meaning of the event for French sport and French society. These editors of this post-event set of perspectives note two particularly visible implications. "Debate in the French Press following the victory endlessly rehearsed the basic issue: *une France Fracturée* needed a *prétexte fédérateur*, and the football celebrations were celebrations of national unity ... A second cultural and psychological effect of the victory seems to be that the French have discovered that the world loves them and they are not eternal losers. France has discovered the reality of 'Une France qui gagne,' as well as the reality of 'Une France multiraciale'" (Dauncy and Hare, 1999: 217; their emphases).

Religion in France

The Separation of the Roman Catholic Church from the State in Early French Republicanism

France has traditionally been associated with Roman Catholicism. Between 1975 and 2010, Catholic representation within the French population has ranged from 86 percent to 75 percent (current). This compares with Italy (99 percent to 95 percent in the same periods) and 98 percent to 93 percent in Spain. The high proportion of formal association with a dominant religion is similar to the US, where 51.3 percent are listed by organizations and 72 percent self-identify as Protestants and Iceland, where, as noted, 77.6 percent of Icelanders are associated with the Evangelical Lutheran Church. Despite evidence of similarity of association between the countries, there are important characteristics in the Roman Catholic history of France that contrast with church and state relationships in Spain and Italy. And there are large differences in levels of participation between France, the two peer Roman Catholic countries, and the United States (with participation rates in France being closer to those in Iceland).

The Peace of Westphalia in 1648 was a pivotal point in the long, tendentious history of church-state relations across Europe and in the contests over religious identities of particular states. A baseline for the historical trajectory may be the Concordat of Worms (9/23/1122) where, in an agreement between Pope Calixtus II and Holy Roman Emperor Henry V, kings claimed the right of control over the secular authority of bishops, while the Pope retained the right of investing religious authorities their Church rights. The Peace of Westphalia, bringing to an end the Thirty Years' War, strengthened the sovereign rights of states, particularly the right to govern internal affairs.

During the French Revolution, citizens' groups prompted the secularization of Church authority by making Church property part of the civil order. In the

Concordat of 1801, between Napoleon and Pope Pius, independent rights of the State over the Church were further strengthened. Religious freedom for Protestants was noted, by designating Catholicism as the religion of the majority of the French people, but not a State religion, and the Catholic Church gave up claims to Church lands. The control by the civil sector of the Church ended in 1905, with the end of the 1801 Concordat. Based on a principle of *laïcité* the prerogatives of church and State over each other were reduced.[6]

France and the Protestants

Signal dates for religion in Iceland and France, two countries in the group of three undergoing comparison, are Martin Luther's proclamation of his stance toward the Church in 1517 (articulation publically of his 95 Theses, i.e., *Disputatio pro declaration virtutis indulgentarum*) and Jean Calvin's first edition of *Institutes of the Christian Religion*, 1536). Embedded in both were criticism of errors in the Church, concern over excessive temporal control on nations by the Papacy, and appreciation of the effect of humanism in opening up access to lay people of religious texts. Evidence of all three of these key components of what became the Protestant Reformation existed at the time in France. The kings of France were trying to diminish control by the Pope over France. Reformers were appearing within the Church to refine theology, to counter the selfishness of clergy, and to stop the use of the Church to sell ways to heaven in the form of indulgences. Desiderius Erasmus (1466–1536) was at the forefront of a wave of scholarship that emphasized learning the languages in which important documents were written, giving both secular readers and religious scholars the mandate *ad fonts.*

The history of efforts to maintain the strength of the Roman Catholic Church occurs in a series of oppositions to the activities of Protestants, especially Reformed Protestants such as the Huguenots. The Huguenots looked to the theology, Church organization, and idealized relations with the State of Jean Calvin in Geneva. At first informal groups appeared meeting in homes. By the time Henry II had succeeded Francis I in 1547, churches began to form and organizations of clergy appeared, such as the Company of Pastors in 1555 (Treasure, 2014: 99). While Francis had been relatively tolerant of Protestants, Henry II saw them as a threat and combined with the more visible opposition of the Queen Consort (Catherine de' Medici) encouraged repression. Repression both reduced numbers in some

6 The term *laïcité* refers to a situation where religion does not become involved in secular affairs; and there is an absence of State institutional interference within religious organizations. Dates, sequences of political rule, and key treaties come from public-access sources: http://en.wikipedia.org/wiki/List_of_French_monarchs; http://en.wikipedia.org/wiki/Charlemagne; http://en.wikipedia.org/wiki/Charles_V,_Holy_Roman_Emperor; http://en.wikipedia.org/wiki/Francis_I_of_France; http://en.wikipedia.org/wiki/French_Third_Republic; http://en.wikipedia.org/wiki/Edict_of_Nantes; http://en.wikipedia.org/wiki/1905_French_law_on_the_Separation_of_the_Churches_and_State.

municipal settings where Huguenots lived (comprised principally of urban, bourgeois members) and practiced their religion and also pushed membership through the persecutions. Treasure notes conservatively a peak in 1572 of 1,200 churches and 1.8 million members (approximately 10 percent of the French population of the time). From 1562 until the Edict of Nantes (1598), nine wars occurred between Catholics and Huguenots. The most costly conflict for the Protestants was on St Bartholomew's Day, in 1572. "[This] massacre that started in Paris in the early hours of St Bartholomew's day, 24 August 1572, continued for three days and was then repeated in a dozen other towns, has a special place in Huguenot history. The effect on so many families; the horrors revealed in individual stories; the psychological impact; the apparent ascendance of sectarian passion over human feeling; for Huguenots the sense of betrayal; for some of them the loss of confidence in a righteous cause; the crippling blow to the leadership—all contribute to the unhappy distinction" (Treasure, 2014:167).[7]

France and Rome

While Roman Catholicism remains the dominant religion in France, the relationships between the Roman Catholic Church and the state apparatuses of France have evidenced a general pattern of separation. Charles I (742–814) united Western Europe by 800, becoming Charles the Great. He was crowned by Pope Leo III on Christmas Day, thereby assuming control over the area which became modern France, and holding the authority of the Church and a monarch. Charles V (1500–1558) ruled as Holy Roman Emperor from 1519 until 1556 and as King of Spain (1516–1556, Charles I, of Spain), again representing a unity of the Church and the secular authorities. He opposed the Protestant Church, which as noted above, had begun appearing through first Lutheranism and then from Reformed groups (influenced from the Swiss Reformation).

Francis I (1494–1547) was king of France from 1515 until 1547. He provided guarded support to the Protestants, and fought Charles V over control of France by himself or the Holy Roman Emperor. Not receiving requested help from Henry VIII of England, Francis allied himself with Suleiman the Magnificent. Germany at the same time was having similar conflicts with Rome and with Charles V. Those conflicts, allowing some autonomy of Germany to support its own religious traditions, were partially resolved in the Peace of Augsburg in 1555.

Henry IV of France (who followed in line from Francis I, Henry II, Francis II, Charles IX, and Henry III), issued the Edict of Nantes in 1598 which granted Reformed Protestants of France (known as Huguenots) some rights in France. While officially a Catholic country, the intent of the Edict was to advance national

---

7   Information on reformation influences within France, the appearance of Lutherans, and the appearance of Reformed groups such as the Huguenots comes from: Augeron, Poton and Van Ruymbeke, 2009, 2012; Butler, 1992; and Treasure, 2014; and http://en.wikipedia.org/wiki/Desiderius_Erasmus.

unity because of the presence of the Protestants. (Henry IV himself was baptized a Catholic, fought with the Huguenots in the Wars of Religion, but renounced Protestantism in 1593.) The Edict was revoked in 1685 by Louis XIV. This prompted the exodus of Protestants (notably the Huguenots), or compliance within that country to requirements within France to convert to Catholicism. Estimates of departures of the Huguenots to neighboring countries, and to the United States, among further destinations, hover around 500,000 total departures over the next half century. France remained largely Catholic until the French Revolution at which time Church property was taken and clergy privileges were ended. Napoleon Bonaparte reconciled with the Church with the 1801 Concordat, providing some subsidization of Catholicism, Judaism, Lutheranism, and Reformed Protestantism. The formal separation of the church and the state occurred in 1905 (*Loi du 9 décembre 1905 concernant la séparation des Églises et de l'État*).

Contemporary Religious Involvement within France[8]

France remains predominantly a Roman Catholic country as far as religious culture is concerned. As such it is different from the United States and Iceland. France shows a heritage of trying to separate its government and political institutions from the Roman Catholic Church. In this respect France shows similarity with the United States, which has sought at the Federal level to separate religion and politics. This formally is done with the First Amendment to the US Constitution. It is different from Iceland, where, as noted, the government plays a role in religion with hiring priests, the Evangelical Lutheran Church being a form of State church.

France is similar to Iceland with low religious saliency, and both are different compared to the United States, on the basis of the expressed importance of religion, giving, beliefs, and attendance at religious meetings. In the terminology of the conditions underlying hypocrisy, religion in France is not part of the condition of exigency (religious purity, accommodation to standard doctrine, behavior expectations that are refined, and looking for distinction to be made in comparison to other actors).

This special history of religion in France locates the country separately from both religion in the United States and in Iceland. In the United States, as noted, strong influences of migration to North America and formation of early political units in the territory came from Calvinism and other Protestant traditions. The Constitution severs the formal ties between church and state, with, especially, the First Amendment. In practice, though, the traditions of belief, commitment, and participation within Christianity, and in particular within Evangelical segments of Protestantism, remain uniquely powerful within the United States. Over several centuries, the state support of religion in general, and the Roman Catholic

---

8   Information on recent religious patterns with France comes from: Pew Foundation; Roman Catholic Church, 2014; World Council of Churches, 2014; http://en.wikipedia.org/wiki/Roman_Catholicism_in_France.

Church specifically, has varied in France. Membership now is estimated as high as 88 percent (*CIA World Factbook*). But the principal of separation of church and state has been firmly established, and resembles the United States more than Iceland, as noted. Again, participation in services and religious activities in France is low, however, and much closer to participation in Iceland than in the United States (commonly measured as at least once a month attendance at a service or communion).

The low levels of religious commitment in France appear in the following summary table from recent Pew survey results from responses by individuals who identify themselves as Catholic. Today, Protestants number about 2 percent among the French. An indication of the diminution of Protestant influence lies in the recent joining of Lutherans and Reformed Church members into a new church. The Reformed Church of France and the Evangelical Lutheran Church of France, both founding members of the World Council of Churches, merged into the United Protestant Church of France with 400,000 members and 500 pastors.[9] Numbers of Moslems now are growing faster than numbers of Christians in France (Kern, 2014).

Table 3.1 **Importance of religion in select European countries (percentages)[10]**

	France		Germany		Italy	
	2002	**2011**	**2002**	**2011**	**2002**	**2011**
Religion is very important	12	13	36	34	29	25
Daily prayer	14	14	35	27	30	31
Weekly mass attendance		9		16		

Table 3.2 **Baptisms and priests in French Roman Catholic Church[11]**

	Baptisms	**Priests**
1990	472,130	32,267
1995	424,829	28,694
2001	391,665	24,251
2005	349,075	21,187
2008	334,664	19,640
2010	302,941	–

9 http://www.oikoumene.org/en/member-churches/united-protestant-church-of-france.

10 Pew Research Center, March 5, 2013.

11 Annuaire statistique de l'Eglise jusque' en 2003, puis conférence des évéques de France.

Continuing the Program

The contexts of sport and religion in Iceland and France have been looked at as strategic points of comparison with the context of sport and religion within the United States. Control of some variation, and allowance of contrasts of variation where a "difference can make a difference" underscore the utility of Iceland and France. They differ importantly in the degrees of exigency associated with interest, performance, and criteria of success with sport and religion. Iceland, for example, illustrates specifically how sport emphasizes physicality, but also how sport in its definitional essence gives deference to rule compliance.

In Chapter 5, the potency of organizational influences on the appearance and maintenance of hypocrisy in sport will continue with concentration on two visible and strategic cases: the Tour de France and an incident of error and concealment that began in the UK in 1989 (the Hillsborough Tragedy). So, item three of the combination of five goals assumes the center of attention. In the case of the Tour de France, instances of rule violation, even to the point of commonness within the event, become apparent. Individuals and then surrounding institutions start a long and forceful process of concealment and attempted neutralization—essentials of hypocrisy (dissimulation and simulation). In the Hillsborough Tragedy, action or non-action of officials at a sporting event become associated with many injuries and 96 deaths. The event is followed by over a decade of efforts of officials and various judicatories to conceal and neutralize the culpability—dissimulation and simulation again.

Organizational influence—indeed what may become an organizational imperative depends on the control of information. Hypocrisy as dissimulation (concealment) or simulation (manufacture) becomes necessary to the degree that the falsehoods are available to various publics. As a bridge to describing the role of organizations in the management of hypocritical information which becomes very visible in the cases of the Tour de France and the Hillsborough incident, an overview of how levels of technology may alternatively allow concealment or detection by interested parties must occur. This topic receives attention now, in Chapter 4.

Chapter 4

Hypocrisy and Information: Technologies Used in Detection and in Concealment

Introduction: the Good and Bad of Information Technologies

"My internet hunt for heroin took five minutes—less time than lacing up my shoes and backing out of the driveway. I was spoiled for choice: 121 options for opioids, 243 for ecstasy, 339 varieties of weed, 45 dissociatives. Stimulants, downers, psychedelics—a global network of sellers stood ready to ship them all to my door in 'discreet packaging' that might arrive from Switzerland, Germany, the United Kingdom, the United States, or even India" (Anderson, 2013: 229). Thus, Nate Anderson provides the outer frame in his concluding material in *Internet Police*.

He provides the inner frame, a line of constraints on access, as it were, by noting a stalemate in a test case brought by music producers against a user who distributed the products from the original sources through the email. "Without comment, the US Supreme Court declined Thomas-Rasset's final appeal on March 28, 2013. She owes the record labels $220,000 and continues to say that she cannot pay" (Anderson, 2013: 247). The Supreme Court proceeding, had it occurred, would have been the third layer of appeal (and legal investment by the record industry) by Ms Thomas-Rasset, a single mother from Minnesota, since her first conviction in 2007. The record companies, after finding barriers to catching and retrieving losses from pirates, have identified select targets and pour in huge sums to gain returns, but also to set their targets up as examples: a traditional sociological deterrent theory of crime prevention.

The items of contention in the chapters of the book are objects sometimes, and consistently they are items of information. To be judged deceitful the information must be identified by consumers, and for the pretenders with dissimulation and simulation the misinformation must be concealed or at least mitigated in some way. The issues Anderson raises concern the role of technology in the service of the opposing sides in this contest. The complexity and number of players in the exchange elaborate when he observes that the security for the purchase of illegal products uses a mechanism originally produced by the US Navy to allow sign-ons to hide their identity and therefor prevent recognition and punishment from the "police" (Anderson, 2013: 232).

Technological refinement holds mixed outcomes: "Life is a messy business on the Internet as it is everywhere else, and we're never going to engineer the mess out of it … To do that, we need public and private actors who can police the Internet's chaos—and who also recognize that such chaos comes in two forms. The first is productive, allowing new and disruptive innovations to launch without permission and letting free speech thrive; productive chaos is the fertile soil in which the future grows. The second is unproductive, more crime and anarchy, spam and spyware and child pornography and credit card theft" (Anderson, 2013: 241, 242).

When the sociological yield from aspects of hypocrisy are lightly attended to, issues of concealment and discovery assume associated modest treatment as well. But as the instances of these deceits appear, with potential consequences, then technologies available to the hider, the consumer, the one who detects, and, if relevant, the ones who sanction grow in import and as topics of interest. Each of the foci of the project can be open to such technological resources: the definitions and distribution of hypocrisy through time and geography; special conditions of salience and seriousness (exigency); organizational expediency; and social consequences.

The beginning objective of the project from Chapter 1 is an inventory of meanings of "hypocrisy," with special attention given to contexts of use and interpretation. Since meanings can reflect interpretive alternatives of authors, representative interpretations intrude within this first objective as well. Variable usages, including definitions by scholarship, may affect presumed seriousness of hypocritical events. As noted, the expansion of meanings that lie in national inventories, particularly the heavy usage noted over 50 years in *The New York Times* can lead to conclusions of irrelevance from this ambiguity alone—despite the ubiquity of occurrences of the uses of the term and its synonyms.

But variability of meaning can show potential for different social consequences. George Lakoff's studies of the stakes in the metaphoric load in lexical items for how people think and how these metaphors structure and align with political and social causes is an example of concerted attention to words like "hypocrisy" (Lakoff, 1987, 2002; Lakoff and Johnson, 2003). This is a level of attentiveness, if reviewed, which gives clues to positions held by significant public figures and significant social positions advocated. The roots of "hypocrisy" in drama (and hence potential artifice) and interpretation make large parts of its meaning, and certainly with wide expanse of allusions, metaphoric. Rhetoric by public figures that is described and possibly criticized as hypocritical carries the meaning, with the metaphor load, of play acting.

"Hypocrisy" is a word of reference, but it is also a word of intended pragmatics. A scholarship evident in such carefully chosen steps of word selection in political endeavors such as by individuals like Frank Luntz (Luntz, 2007) adds another research-oriented example that wishes to take specific words—ours, here, "hypocrisy"—with great seriousness. (The words in the title of Masha Gessen's recent book describing young radicals in Russia provide another, and very contemporary, example of actors and commentators interested in the pragmatics of word use: viz., *Words Will Break Cement: the Passion of Pussy Riot* [Gessen, 2014].)

The inventory of uses of hypocrisy over 50 years in *The New York Times* (Tables 2.1 and 2.2), as well as the comment on the term within religious texts (Chapter 1) yields a nearly universal view of the act as negative. (One, from the *Times* with a satirical cast, does say at least a promised, productive act, though unlikely to occur, may carry laudable goals to which aspiration should be made [Ehrenhalt,

2001].) A contradiction in actions often yields the hypocritical epithet. This could be an inconsistency between a true motive and the *appearance* of intent in the action. A worthy appearance may mask a selfish or even highly destructive motive.

William Ian Miller is a legal scholar of note in the history of Icelandic jurisprudence as referenced in the book. His acumen and care appear even more directly on topics in the project when he analyzes carefully the several ways a spokesperson, technically a hypocrite, may engage in the deceits of dissimulation and simulation. He also surgically slices contradictions in historical periods which sometimes give hypocrisy a positive valence, or at least combined positive and negative valences in combination (Miller, 2003).

Coining the term "antihypocrisy," Miller describes actions which try to show lack of ostentation, such as fasting or acting cross and self-absorbed, when engaging in secret acts of philanthropy. The discovery—often designed—may itself allow suspicion that the anti-hypocrite's motives are mixed. The choice (he mentions St Thomas a Becket and St Thomas More) to use hidden corrosive undergarments supposedly to remind them of the wrongs of ostentation may prompt forms of real hypocrisy to self, as in: "Look what I am doing?" The wearer considers his superior virtue magnified because he experiences the discomfort when he does not need to. Considering the evaluation of others, the hope could be that their sentiments of respect for my humility would be elevated as well. The wearer of the items, the historical hair-shirt, knows his uncomfortable attire eventually will be discovered (Miller, 2003: 20, 21).

An act eventually judged courageous by observers may have been prompted by fear, worry of censure by one's peers, or compromised awareness of what the real risks were that actually prevailed. The reflective person here may worry after the event that the public adulation makes him or her hypocritical because the act was really not prodded by pure motives. But Miller notes that whether the act was preceded by boastful claim or some kind of incipient and unintended chance, the consequences for self and others are still honorable (Miller, 2003: 31–5).

In similar ways, politeness which extends honor and respect to another through compliments and deference may not be technically representative of one's true feelings—hence symptomatic of the inconsistencies hypocrisy focuses on. But the consequences which may induce good feelings and confidence in the object of the politeness, and the dependence and trust now potentially available to the other who receives the politeness, renders the formal inconsistency moot. Here the meaning of the act (perhaps named "hypocritical" in form) must be in the consequence, which is positive. Jenny Davidson in a careful analysis of philosophical writing, manner-literatures, and fiction from the eighteenth and nineteenth centuries provides an extended analysis of the use of technically dishonest (read, hypocritical) behaviors in the form of self-control, civility, and politeness. The techniques were used earlier in the period by the gentry to cement their positions with one another and toward the under-classes. But gradually, structurally defined lower layers of society such as women and servants, adopted these techniques of civility and politeness in their self-interest (Davidson, 2004).

As discussed in Chapter 1, and in further examples here, contexts affect the meaning of hypocrisy. Contexts, too, affect the importance people vest in the seriousness of violations of fidelity of information when they occur, as in dissimulation or simulation of information. Hypocrisy refers to acts which hide untoward information (dissimulation) or acts that claim, falsely, information that enhances one's worth (simulation). The program outlined in Chapter 1 stresses that these acts (particularly with respect to contexts, organizational influences, and consequences) must be seen in relationship to what other people do, cultural settings, institutional influences, and what can happen when the dishonesty occurs. As illustrated in Chapter 1, and as stipulated in Chapter 2, hypocrisy should be recognized as a system of duplicity. Peter Gay, to cite one additional scholar who has commented on the influence of contexts on hypocrisy, details this for nineteenth century America, and for Britain and parts of Europe (Gay, 1984). Standards of conduct for the bourgeois are high and restrictive as referred to in the term "Victorian." Accomplishment often does not meet claims, so artifice occurs—a sequence common within all the chapters here. He provides good additional examples within the operative system. Mechanisms of maintenance of one's positive image (and, of course, the system as a whole) include blaming others for their hypocrisy. Also, the deceits compound when editors intervene with exclusions when the substance of novelists and other writers approaches levels of provocation or excess. Reputation-minded autobiographers or relatives and later biographers may carefully select and reject documents such as letters and diaries to assure the resulting product may give the life recorded the most luminous hue, and make no offense to conservative readers (Gay, 1980: 408–15).

The point here is that a falsehood may begin as an intended accurate item of information. A writer of realist fiction may intend to recount actions faithfully, but an editor as part of a productive system may limit the report on the basis of assessments of receptivity of an audience. A testimony about a life to an autobiographer may seek for unqualified accuracy, but the autobiographer (with concerns about the object's reputation or implications for the object's family) may select portions from the testimony. A reporter charged with uncovering malfeasance of a government agency, as described later in the chapter, may be unhesitating in describing dark secrets of the Central Intelligence Agency's running of prisons. But layers of selectivity by oversight groups within the United States Senate may edit—or in the operable terminology, "redact" the reports with claims to be protecting some constituency, which is not divulged in the process of redaction.[1]

---

1 Considering the variables of timeliness, identification of scapegoats or underlings to blame for organizational conduct, and level of acceptance of responsibility by high officials within an organization, a recurring question of military and intelligence agencies' running of prisons outside the United States appears later in the chapter along with organizational treatment of lies in the Penn State Case and within the Roman Catholic Church. To anticipate, information about US management of prisons is added to material from the cases on sport and religion partly to extend the generality about organizational response to malfeasance.

Michel Montaigne and the political philosophers, Judith Shklar, and David Runciman, who aid this project, speak of "Ordinary Vices." These differ from the objectionable infractions known to Christian theology as the "seven deadly sins;" wrath, greed, sloth, pride, lust, envy, and gluttony. The ordinary vices share the characteristics that they all have both personal and social implications. They are ordinary because of their commonness, commonness that includes general repulsiveness toward acts and persons who display the vices. They are vices in particular because each in turn poses intractable difficulties in containing them, even as attempts to do so can know few limits.

Lists of ordinary vices may include hypocrisy, cruelty, snobbery, betrayal, and misanthropy (Shklar's list) with hypocrisy vying with cruelty as the most serious in its consequences to society. As the project thus far has shown, several large negative consequences for persons and institutions can occur within both dissimulative and simulative hypocritical acts, acutely in the institutions in focus because of the special demands sport and religion require in their essence for fidelity, and the consequent special harm that occurs where trust is high where deceits such as hypocrisies do occur.

The commonness captured in the descriptor "ordinary" may lead to disinterest and inattention to hypocrisy at the individual and institutional levels. But the other side of the terminology, "Vice," remains in a general opposition to hypocrisy.[2] The existence of extraordinary efforts to conceal it by the offenders and to discover it on the part of self-designated persons and institutions who want to control hypocrisy, occur within sport, religion, and other institutions. This contest over the control of information appears in the history of lies, concealment, and efforts to detect malfeasance by parties within the Tour de France (cyclists, coaches, promoters, organizational commission, and oversight groups) emerges in coverage of this event in Chapter 5. The history of the National Collegiate Athletic Association treated in Chapters 1 and 2 exists thus far as an illustration of this pattern of contestation over information.[3] The contest of concealment and discovery shows variable uses of information technologies over time. But these years of the early twenty-first century present a moment of expanding and ponderous technological efforts both to conceal effectively and to discovery efficiently acts of dissimulation

---

2 Hypocrisy is consistently characterized negatively in religious texts and in popular media in the United States, France, and Iceland. Examples exist in Chapters 1 and 2.

3 One of the central dimensions of contest over control of information in the development of university athletics has occurred between the NCAA and the efforts of an alternative organizational group, the Association for Intercollegiate Athletics for Women to equalize treatment of women following the passage of Title IX in the United States. Efficient access to this particular exchange occurs through juxtaposing the Wikipedia summaries of the NCAA (http://en.wikipedia.org/wiki/National_Collegiate_Athletic_Association) and the AIAW, the acronym for the competing organization (http://en.wikipedia.org/wiki/Association_for_Intercollegiate_Athletics_for_Women).

or simulation. As "ordinary vices" conveys, again, the stakes here are serious, and they are now being contested with a withering array of technological armaments.

Hypocrisy carries a dynamic of concealment and potential detection of information. The individual or institution hiding a bad past or manufacturing an unwarranted present image of goodness must protect against detections. Beneficiaries and constituents who want to guard against such deceptions would like to know how to find out about the lies. And those charged by statute to protect publics from hypocritical institutions and individuals want ways to determine occurrences of dishonesty as well. This dynamic of concealment and detection has both old and current dimensions; the continuation of the conflict, in different forms and with varying types of technological aids used by both parties, illustrates the centrality of the conflict in how hypocrisy plays out in past and current situations.

Earlier Players

The literacy rate for men and women in France in the eighteenth century was, respectively, 48 percent and 27 percent. This meant information in printed form was not available to a majority of French citizens then. This information, a knowledge "coin" as it were, was denied to them. If a person in the church or representative of an earlier sport or leisure business wrote something factually false, making a claim worth something, the majority of the population could not evaluate the claim. This could be denying a charge of doing something bad or, as per words used here, a "simulation," a fabrication claiming something about a person or the institution was true even though it was not true. Here as an extreme case, hypocrisy, which depends both on the initial false claims and subsequently on the publically available unmasking, is not available to these non-readers.

Access to incidents of printed records of hypocritical deceits were even more limited in the seventeenth century where the literacy rates for men and women in France were 29 percent and 14 percent. In seventeenth century in England, the literacy rate for men was 30 percent and a rate not even regularly recorded for women. The majority of citizens, then, depended on non-written forms of information. This lack of access to certain kinds of information encourages our appreciation of plays that Shakespeare (1564–1616) wrote and performed, and plays by Molière (1622–1673) as well which featured hypocrisy as a topic. We still enjoy seeing "The Merchant of Venice" and "Twelfth Night" from Shakespeare. And Molière's "Tartuffe" continues as an important vehicle for defining hypocrisy. For the non-literate, again, the majority in each country, through viewing the plays audiences could be exposed to illustrations and usually the vilifications of the hypocrite.

Audiences in France were advantaged or disadvantaged further depending on their literacy or non-literacy when political literature was provided. Also, early written ideas of science were variably available to publics depending upon levels of literacy. As with hypocrisy and the effectiveness of a non-literary medium for communication, ideas about science came through alternative means. The substance of the information could be accurate, or totally false, or it could be speculative. But not being able to read meant citizens never had the chance to evaluate nor the choice to use the printed form of information. The non-reader lacked the "coin" of scientific information, a deficit of cultural capital.

However, as Robert Darnton shows in his study of Franz Mesmer (1734–1815) (Darnton, 1968), consumers could be alerted to his sensational demonstrations via large posters affixed to buildings. Excited audiences then could attend the events and consume whatever entertainment value or "pop" science became available in the expositions. Darnton additionally illuminated the eighteenth-century marketplace for ideas through books by focusing on a market that was rather more available to the upper tiers of society, both through the possession of reading skills and the ability to access the materials through known procedures and economic resources. This was the market for forbidden books.

French law, from between 1765–1789, identified 720 books that were forbidden (Darnton, 1995b). The books were, however, available from distributors in other countries, notably in Switzerland. Literacy and economy of resources limited use by potential consumers, but those with both could access this informational capital. Thirty-five of these appear in his data to be best sellers (Darnton, 1995b: 63, 64). So we might say consumers had restricted access to scarce information, but money and ingenuity allowed purchases, and patterns of purchasing emerged.

With this baseline of the association of information production, dissemination, and consumption, we can turn to the import of those factors which operate similarly today in the creation, distribution, and consumption of what may become news reports of hypocritical activities of individuals and institutions. Moving a clock forward to the moment, the dynamic between access and concealment occupy Bruce Schneier's (Schneier, 2012) and Nate Anderson's (Anderson, 2013) informed and provocative assessments. If a person or an institution wants to conceal information then the ability to do so represents a type of control over cultural capital. Similarly, if a person wants to contrive an image or fact that has elements of falseness, their ability to do so represents control over capital again.

People who do not have access to the concealment nor have enough information to evaluate the deceitful artifice are potentially disadvantaged. So, starting with reading increments of consumer access to information increases the access to information produced by hypocrites. Printed books and newspapers are followed by the radio, television, computers, and now the world-wide-web, and social networking sites.

In the baseline condition, there are other parties along the pathway to access by potential consumers, of course. To create a false message the producer requires printers and sales forces, and eventually experts to protect the secrecy of the information, and when threats emerge legal help to forestall efforts at detection. The consumer depends on the printing and sale, and may also depend on a journalistic introduction of potentially hidden information or suspicions of dubious claims.

The consumers, in their turn, tend to want detection devices and also with available resources want to gain legal support to access the hypocritical information.

With the computer, internet, and social networking sites, the exchange between a producer that wants to conceal a bad image or produce a false one, and the consumer that wants protection from these deceits becomes very complex. The success of both sides can be seen as dependent on respective tools of knowledge creation, knowledge protection, knowledge access, and knowledge evaluation.

Modern Players

Even moderately conversant use of the existing information technologies would suggest both that hiding information or sculpting information to one's advantage might allow concealment with no little effort today. Michael Wines writes just recently in *The New York Times* (November 10, 2012) about the David Petraeus affair which was discovered: "There would seem to be nothing new about the weakness of otherwise powerful Washington figures in the fact of temptation. But that is not precisely true: the difference these days is that it is virtually impossible to get away with it."

Despite this easy judgment about the spread of news concerning the affair once it had been discovered, the long *periods* of discovery within the public in the illustrative cases in this book are impressive. Rather than suggesting ready transparency, the record illustrates how powerful people and strong institutions can keep news about questionable behavior hidden for long periods of time. In the Penn State situation, the events that in retrospective review first were problematic occurred in the 1990s; and the particular event that was seen to trigger the arrest of Sandusky and then the dismantling of the athletic department occurred in 2003. When finally in the past two years, Lance Armstrong was formally stripped of his seven victories in the Tour de France (2012), one must appreciate that information had been hidden or shielded since just after his first victory in 1999. Documents that are just now being accessed about Roman Catholic priests refer to events, and cover-ups, going back to the early 1960s. The provocative yet intransigent question is then: with the availability of ever-developing technological aids of detection, how have hypocritical acts and lies remained hidden for such long periods of time?

How the Sides are Drawn in History

Puritanism holds an important place in the book's characterization of hypocrisy as showing a dynamic tension between high expectations and self- and community-censure when expectations fall short of claims. Knowledge about such a distance would seem to begin with an individual, but of course self-censure may be resisted and errors glossed over and performances continuously overblown. More likely, others knowing of the dark past or being in a position to evaluate a false claim vary with access to relevant information. What are the technologies of such information display and detection?

The moveable type printing press in principle made printed material available from the middle of the fifteenth century. But the cost of paper and books did not allow general readership in industrialized countries until the mid-nineteenth century. So in the seventeenth and eighteenth centuries one cannot assume people learned of tarnished reputations from some print medium. From this period on, knowing or not knowing of a dissimulation or a simulated identity could influence the personal and institutional consequences of hypocrisy.

The world illiteracy rate has declined from nearly 40 percent in 1970 to 17 percent today, so during periods of the coverage of cases, here, access by various publics to the alleged hypocrisies would be conditioned by the reading capacity of potential beneficiaries, constituents, and critics. In the United States now, literacy is virtually universal, though some educators and policy makers have warned that it has slipped in the last ten years. In France, Iceland, and most of Western Europe literacy is almost universal. In the early part of the eighteenth century (a period important in Runciman and Shklar's discussion of hypocrisy), illiteracy was as high as 65 percent.

Television, an evolving product from the end of the nineteenth century and the Internet, based on computer technology and growing from initial military use to unrestricted commercial use in 1995, add to the communication technologies that can carry information (and in turn which create domains that are competed over by actors who want to control information and increase access to information). The rapidity of the spread of the expansiveness of the Internet suggests the pace of information technology development will be rapid, elevating the stakes existing for both the side of the concealers and the side of the detectors. One overview statement about this pace highlights these stakes: "The Internet's takeover of the global communication landscape was almost instant in historical terms: it only communicated 1% of the information flowing through two-way telecommunication networks in the year 1993, already 51% by 2000, and more than 97% of the telecommunicated information by 2007."[4] Television is virtually universal now, with the number of sets per household in France in 2000 being 1.4 and 1.99 in 2012; and in the United States 2.43 per household in 2000 and 3.01 in 2012. The number of internet users is an even more telling information-access marker for developed countries. In 2003, users in Iceland totaled 195,000 in 2003 and 301, 600 in 2012; in France 21.9 million persons used the internet, and 45.3 million did so in 2009; in the United States the figures have grown from 159 million in 2002 to 245 million in 2009.

The general point here is that the creation of a lie may occur independently by an individual or institution, who have in their official or non-official rounds

---

4   From Hilbert and Lopez, 2011; reported in http://en.wikipedia.org/wiki/History_ of_the_Internet.

of activity perpetrated the deceit. Though not obviously assured, they may then with conjectured probabilities further hide the deceit, or conversely they may assume some responsibility for fault. However, for a hypocritical act to have consequences, in all the cases highlighted in the cross-temporal and cross-cultural inventories in Chapters 2, 3 and 5, an audience becomes aware and responds to the knowledge in some way. Knowledge of hypocrisy still can show some variation in response. Not everybody watches or cares about news shows. Not everyone reads religion news or back-story sports news. So, with these qualifications in view, the balance of concealment and detection we are pairing now considers—with TV, computers, print media—that once a story is out then access is nearly universal in the three countries foregrounded. (Though certainly not in many other countries of the world, with illiteracy overall of 17 percent and considerably lower in some underdeveloped countries.) But, again, consumption and reaction to such conditions of access may vary.

So, now we return to the possible contradictions between claimed standards and behavior. Wide information access and rich detection resources suggest immediate discovery. But the several highly consequential cases described in Chapters 2, 3, and 5 show concealment may last for many years. It is true, of course, that once a trail to the ostensive hypocrisy becomes even slightly visible, then (but perhaps only then) the detection and distribution from sophisticated information technologies can rapidly go into effect. What follows are arrays of steps and artifices that concealers can use and resources that detectors and publicizers can use.

Resources of Concealment

1. Separation of individuals from institutional control and separation of institutions from external oversight.
2. Use of professional staffs specifically to hide and to reframe acts of hypocrisy. (Note Lakoff, 2002 and Luntz, 2007 for different prospects.)
3. Use of lawyers to exploit existing guarantees of privacy of certain kinds of information.
4. Outright rule breaking such as destruction of records, flight, libeling the accusers, and perjury.

Resources of Detection

1. Various oversight groups with subpoena power and power to fine, suspend, and disqualify (Tour de France).
2. Legal challenges using Freedom of Information Acts.
3. Appeal to public through news media.
4. Use of New Detection Tools (noted below).

Today, as the progression of cases described illustrates, hypocrisy can be costly to institutions. Illustrations exist within the cases of the Roman Catholic Church and within Penn State University. And, again, it is in the character of hypocrisy for watchpersons to look for it and guard its circulation by one's own institutional members, and at the same time to try to detect it and to try to guard against it in other institutions—particularly others who might be competitors. Contenders to discovery, containment, and penalization of deceivers, including hypocrites, are many and serious. The intensity of the efforts exists in the vigor and sophistication of technical aids to identify, document, and if not assure penalties, at least start processes toward censure in the "court of public opinion."

Some Examples of Institutional Efforts at Oversight[5]

Transparency International. Transparency International was founded in 1993 with the mission: "… to stop corruption and promote transparency, accountability and integrity at all levels and across all sectors of society. Our Core Values are: transparency, accountability, integrity, solidarity, courage, justice, and democracy" (www.transparency.org). The headquarters of this organization are in Berlin, with 70 national chapters.

One of the most concrete products of the work of the organization is to publish a regular "Corruption Perceptions Index," which started in 1996. The 2012 index uses an aggregate of measures (a minimum of three per country) to yield a score of perceived corruption in respective countries, with standardized scores combined

---

5   The very nature of the contest over concealment and detection makes provision of the most current work on both "sides" of the contest dated by definition. I use Schneier (2012) and Anderson (2013) for their recency and richness of examples. The institutionalized detection efforts mentioned here are illustrative for the sport and religion cases discussed in the book. The title of Schneier's book, *Liars & Outliers: Enabling the Trust that Society Needs to Strive* conveys the continuing dynamic between those who lie and conceal and those who detect in the interest of protecting information fidelity. The title of Anderson's concluding chapter, "Productive Chaos," serves to illustrate an emphasis of both books on how to maximize the fidelity of information dissemination within new technologies against the risks of lies and frauds that can simultaneously come with the new technologies. The problems they address are not new. Adam Zamoyski in *Phantom Terror: the Threat of Evolution and the Repression of Liberty 1789–1848* argues that the rise of freedoms in democratization efforts of the late eighteenth century create the seed-bed for repressions that develop in the beginning of the nineteenth century: "In this book, his main focus is on how European governments came to develop the tools and methods of repression. As [Zamoyski] says, today's security services, anti-terrorism measures, spy networks and systems of policing all have their roots in Europe during the first half of the 19th century" (*The Economist*, November 15, 2014: 84; reviewer comments on Adam Zamoyski [2015 publication in US].) It is not surprising, given this competitive process of control of information, that opposition to what may be considered extremes of "transparency" may eventually appear (*The Economist*, December 13–19, 2014: 63, 64).

into an index with 0 at the bottom and 100 at the top of a continuum of most to least perceived corruption.

The 2012 distribution of 176 countries lists Denmark at the top with a score of 90, Iceland 11th with a score of 82, the United States tied with Japan for 17th with scores of 73, and France 22nd with a score of 71 (Afghanistan, North Korea and Somalia lie at the bottom of the list with scores of 8). Transparency International broadly addresses corruption in the public sector; and recently they have begun to include in yearly news items attention to corruption in sport institutions.

BishopAccountability.org was established in 2003 intent on: "Documenting the Abuse Crisis in the Roman Catholic Church" (www.bishop-accountability.org). The timeline addressed starts in the 1940s and is updated to the moment. A variety of services are provided with the most continuous being an "Abusetracker" listing instances of reported priest abuse by name of priest, US diocese, or state. These are neither determinations of criminal guilt nor persons liable for civil claims; they are allegations only. One hundred seventy-five dioceses exist in the United States. To illustrate the array of information available from one of these categorizations, Iowa, a middle-America state, lists four dioceses with records of abuse distributed: Diocese of Davenport (36); Archdiocese of Dubuque (25); Diocese of Des Moines (8); and Diocese of Sioux City (6).

Politifact.com started in 2007 within the *Tampa Bay Times* Washington news office in conjunction with the United States *Congressional Quarterly*. A visible product of the organization is the "Truth-O-Meter" that lists current statements by visible figures and assesses their veracity. Most of the statements archived and evaluated are political, but there are 155 listed that could provide statements to be evaluated. "Religion," in one listing on March 19 2013 provides 107 "test" statements. "Sport" is included as an inclusive issue category, but reflecting the importance of "Baseball" with American culture, this particular sport is separately examined. Relative to the salience of religion in the web-page assessments, on March 19, 2013 there were 20 "Sports" statements and 13 "Baseball" statements.

A Project of the Annenberg Public Policy Center is **FactCheck.org** and was started in December 2003. The focus is on the correctness of political advertising. Their self-definition and mission includes the following: "We are a nonpartisan, nonprofit 'consumer advocate' for voters that aims to reduce the level of deception and confusion in U.S. politics. We monitor the factual accuracy of what is said by major U.S. political players in the form of TV ads, debates, speeches, interviews and news releases. Our goal is to apply the best practices of both journalism and scholarship, and to increase public knowledge and understanding" (Fact.Check. org web site).

Fullfact.org is an analogous organization and service within the UK. "Full Fact is an independent fact-checking organization. We make it easier to see the facts and context behind the claims made by the key players in British political debate and press those who make misleading claims to correct the record" (fullfact. org/about: 1).

The Sunlight Foundation was founded in 2006 "with the goal of increasing transparency and accountability in the United States government" (Wikipedia. org: 1).

Do Refined Technical Resources of Detection Constrain Lying and Limit Its Consequences?

Hypocrisy is lying. As a lie, the acts and actors yield censure generally, and the incidents of hypocrisy either as hiding a wrong or pretending a false attribute elicits wide and serious negative reaction. But the hypocrite may move to the edge of falsity from sincere and intense aspiration. The tendency of those in the West heavily to self-evaluate by comparison with others (the invidious distinction phenomenon!) may prompt us with special acuity to find hypocrisy in others. These features of this special form of deceit have been described in the project to this point. But the inescapable reality is that hypocrisy can have large individual and social consequences. The character of the deceit may propel the individual or institution to take extraordinary steps to continue the façade. But as the record shows in the progression of this project hypocrisy may lead to the perpetrator harming himself or herself, victims compromised by the hypocrisy committing suicide or otherwise harming themselves, organizations found culpable fined large sums, and individuals and institutions judged by civil and criminal courts to be culpable penalized severely. Hence, attention to social order questions requires that the difficulties in defining and detecting hypocrisy cannot ultimately deter efforts to at least gain leverage on detection and control—with an eye to reducing negative consequences.

With an appreciative eye to the group of technologies fairly recently developed (and their surrounding organizations) for dealing with public deceits, what has aided detection and constraint and perhaps reduced negative consequences? As the attached accounting scheme illustrates (Table 4.1), gains here pose formidable challenges. As both Schneier (2012) and Anderson (2013) describe (and as summarized in Note 1), the level of technology can benefit both concealers and detectors. But even with the goals of detection of falsehoods and security of accurate information, consumers may be reticent or ambivalent about knowing. There is a production side of the equation, those generating the initial falsehoods and the intermediate component of the detectors and publicizers. Though some audiences may be hyper-interested in hypocrisy, the consumers so to speak, others may not know or not care. So the receptivity side of the exchange of deception and disclosure cannot assume a ready and receptive public. The actors and resources prominent in this chapter are the "Intermediate Players."

Table 4.1   Factors in determining consequences of hypocrisy

The "Hypocrite"	Intermediate Players	Consumers
Self-criticism (as Puritan)	Damage control people	Interest as readers or victims
Power of Institution	Journalists	Access to information
Isolation/ Compartmentalization	Advisors and superiors	Ability to evaluate
Control of media to conceal	Laws	Action plan (flee, copy, and replicate)
Control of media to publicize	Lawyers	
	Jealous third parties	

In this chapter the processes of information management and control in the cases of the Roman Catholic Church, the Church in Iceland and Penn State are analyzed. In Chapter 5 after the introduction of the more ambiguous cases of deceit are described, the analysis will address those. The stakes now that lie in these endeavors are profound. Loss of trust, which is endemic in depictions of institutions throughout much of the world, includes minimally the perception by publics that actors and institutions in sport and religion are not truthful. So, the question of whether and how effective refined technological steps to identify, constrain, and punish liars matters. Thus, the results of these analyses of the processes of concealment and discovery occurring now will inform material in Chapter 6.

The Sequence of Management of Hypocrisy

Fidelity as Normal in Sport and the Church

A useful definition of religion in use here that shows its central role in culture is this famous one by Clifford Geertz, introduced earlier: "Religion is (1) a system of symbols which acts to (2) establish powerful, pervasive, and long-lasting moods and motivations in men [and women and children] by (3) formulating conceptions of a general order of existence …"

Sport, as defined from the beginning of this sociological program, essentially is physical, intrinsic, rule governed, and consummative. It is a moral preserve because it requires, to maintain its venerated status as a means of cultural memory (along with appealing to all the senses and being a source of common conversation topics), preserving intact rules that define practices and outcomes. The fundamental presupposition is one of fidelity on the part of clergy and the Church; in ways similar to the presumptions about normalcy in sport.[6]

These special characteristics of religion and sport—namely that their identity rests on fidelity—prompts the attention to these two institutions as limiting cases while evaluating the consequences of hypocrisy. Consistent in the cases viewed here as exemplars is the overwhelming sense of order and normalcy within the sport examples and the church examples. Of course, there is a great deal of published criticism of sports within higher education in the United States (illustrative are Sperber, 1990, 1998, 2000; Bowen and Levine, 2003; Shulman and Bowen, 2001; and Zimbalist, 1999). Educational critics, sports journalism, social scientific studies of sport, all have written voluminously about inconsistencies in the fit between sport and education. Despite this, the presumption at the start of a progression that took 14 years to begin to approach resolution at Penn State was of these people, this program, and this school as being the best of the best. Joe Posnanski (2012) has written of the end of life of Joe Paterno, describing carefully the events of the discovery of Sandusky's assaults on children, and the acquiescence of layers of administrations to what appears to have been known for years. But the account of these events are woven into a decades-long sequence of excellence on the part of the football program, a balance of fire and modesty and of intellectualism and athletic competitiveness of the coach, and a depiction of an institution often the model of resisting the excesses of big-time collegiate sport in the United States.

Surprise and Marginalization by the Institution

Vagaries or moral lapses tend to be treated as anomalies. A useful comparison point here is the existence of anomalies and the usually-occurring normal science in Kuhn's work: *The Structure of Scientific Revolutions* (1996). Since the initial "violations" of hypocrisy are often revered figures, with productive histories, but who have been able to compartmentalize their lapses, the institution feels obligated to protect them. Within a scientific discipline, as Thomas Kuhn has written when unusual facts and findings appear, initially the discipline follows procedures to

---

6   Note the Vatican pronouncement that it was in the interest of the stability of the church not to pursue prosecution of accusations against priests, mentioned later in the chapter. Regarding the timeliness in the institutional reaction to mistakes of institutional members, if an organization identifies a problem early and either changes policy or excises the "anomaly," that organization sustains much less long-term damage than those institutions which ignore or try to hide the problem. A pivotal item of Federal legislation prompting corporate responsibility (which includes early detection of violations, and corporation resolution) is the "Corporate and Auditing Accountability and Responsibility Act" or Sarbanes-Oxley (enacted on July 30, 2002). Research examples include: "Corporate Compliance Programs in the Aftermath of Sarbanes-Oxley (2003); Chandler, 2005; and "Blowing the Whistle on Workplace Misconduct," 2009.

determine what went wrong in the research process that yielded such anomalies or "non-normal" findings. The accuracy of research methods may be faulted, an odd blip within the distribution of expected findings can be named an "outlier" on either end of a distribution.

Within a science the number of discordant findings needed to begin change in a discipline varies a great deal, as can be appreciated. Kuhn's durable study notes after an initial effort to characterize the anomalies as unimportant outliers, more drastic steps must be adopted. Within science, sanctions toward those who challenge the normative order may occur—some, as the history of science shows, were extreme. If there is power among the marginal group there may be efforts among normative science to incorporate the new data by incorporating into a dominant theory new conditions or a minor theoretical appendage to the main body of established knowledge that can accommodate the new, discrepant findings.

The judgments of the Penn State athletic department and the Roman Catholic Church were similar. A janitor claimed he saw Jerry Sandusky in a comprising position with a young boy in a shower in 1998. He evidently was reluctant to describe his sight to a superior. A boy told his mother that Sandusky had acted improperly toward him. When told of the accusation, Sandusky, the highly regarded assistant football coach, apologized and the discussion of impropriety ended there.

Establishment figures externalize the moral vagaries either by ignoring them or acquiescing in institutional acts that marginalize them. Following claims by an ostensive victim of Sandusky's unwelcome advances, a victim claiming offense over several years brought the prosecutor's office into investigating Sandusky in 2009. In the process, Michael McQueary gave testimony about what he had seen in 2002 (later documented to have occurred in 2001). The administrative layers above the football program, which included the athletic director, the vice president in charge of athletics, and the president of the university all claimed that the 2009 testimony of McQueary about what he witnessed in 2001 and reported to Coach Paterno was not what he originally reported. Their stakes in the factual matters were that the more explicit and serious report of 2009 dwarfed the ambiguous report in 2001. Had they known in 2001 of what McQueary later claimed in 2009, of course, they would have acted forcefully to deal with Sandusky's infractions. Together these three administrators "dealt" with the report of McQueary by challenging his credibility.

By 2012, after the report of the independent panel designated culpability of these three administrators, they themselves were marginalized by either being fired or placed on administrative leave pending the outcome of criminal actions against them.

Evidence of charges of assault and pedophilia go back in the Bishops webpage to 1949. How did the various layers of the church deal with these charges? As outliers, as exceptions. If you have such a person in your charge, an administrator of several priests should simply move the priest quietly to another parish. This became a standard procedure taken by bishops for priests who had been accused.

Joseph Aloisius Ratzinger, Pope Benedict XVI, resigned from the papacy on February 13, 2013. Along with being a stunning precedent, the first such resignation in 600 years, his eight years as leader of the Catholic Church has left a legacy of unfinished business regarding the number of abuse claims throughout the population of priests and bishops. The record is even more provocative for the history of abuse, and the Church's response, since his role as a cardinal before becoming pope existed in an office charged with adjudicating doctrinal and behavioral claims against clergy in the Church. A debated pattern of Cardinal Ratzinger's style administration is the slowness of dealing with cases recommended to the office for review, censure, or removal from the leadership of the church.

Discovery, Broadcast, and Institutional Outrage

An "outsider" presses an inquiry and gains public notoriety. It is conceivable that an offender, or one overseeing him, may on the basis of principle identify the deceitful person and offending act. The prevailing pattern in the cases used as exemplars here and many other similar instances of hypocrisy is that discovery and the process toward correction does not come from within the sport or religious institution. The strength of "normalcy" is simply too pervasive and protective. The journalistic institution may be thought to be a likely critical audience and potential discoverer and broadcaster. Again, though, the industry itself often profits from the continuity of the normalized sport or religious institution; in some cases, as included in Chapter 5, a journalistic company may be a primary benefactor of a sport practice which itself is compromised with dishonesty.

The dominant pattern is for either a victim to seek a legal agent to make the case of a discovery, for a writer on the fringes of journalism to take the risk of "spitting in the soup," as terminology shows, or a legal investigator accidentally stumbles on the dishonesty or is prompted by an ostensive victim.

Some in the institution try to neutralize, but the body reacts strongly, often excessively to display moral outrage at the anomaly. Within the Penn State setting, such groups would be those of students currently enrolled and groups of alumni of the university.

Leaving the Scene when Lapses are Revealed

Various parties attempt to separate themselves from the institution by legal means or by their own independent appeal to the "court of public opinion." Those people who are identified and at least within public media charged with an infraction or a lie of simulation or dissimulation commonly take steps, within economic and practical realities available to them, to redefine their position within a once-normal sphere of activity. Self-condemnation may occur. As noted in Chapter 1 some may feel the diminution of the normal state of affairs and their changed position within it and may literally attempt to extricate themselves by an attempted suicide. Cases where this happened in business have been noted in Chapter 1. A priest who was confronted with an illegal habit of using pornography in Kansas City attempted suicide by driving a motorcycle into a barrier. Others associated with the exposed person may take or attempt to take their own life, as the father-in-law of Floyd Landis did.

A more common strategy—once having had the state of normalcy, and one's place in it compromised—is to use media resources to make an appeal to the "court of public opinion." This is the strategy used by the family of Joe Paterno, in an effort to contest and counteract the negative fallout from the Freeh Report which had been commissioned by Penn State University.

A third alternative is to make use of courts of law and lawyers to reduce damages either of a material nature or with respect to a compromised reputation. One example would by the steps taken by Mr McQueary. One of the early instances of an "anomaly" within the routine of the Penn State Program occurred when Mike McQueary, then a graduate assistant in the football program, believed he saw Jerry Sandusky showering and possibly having sexual contact with a minor male child. Within a presumptive system of "normalcy," and being a figure low in the institutional hierarchy order he asked his father what to do and then reported it to Joe Paterno. By 2012, at the time of the arrest of Sandusky and the subsequent trial, McQueary had become an important and permanent coach on the Penn Staff. After his testimony and the trial and conviction of Sandusky of 405 of 409 criminal counts, McQueary was placed on administrative leave on November 11, 2012, and his contract was not renewed. McQueary had testified in 2010 about the event, and indicated he had told Paterno that sexual congress had taken place with the boy facing the shower wall, and Sandusky embracing him from the rear. Following McQueary's testimony, the athletic director, the vice-president, and the school president all had disputed this latter-day testimony saying that at the time (first represented as 2002, and later specified as 2001) the description was not of an act as explicitly sexual as the 2010 testimony had shown. The three effectively contested McQueary's honesty. In McQueary's law suit, he requests damages for defamation; specifically, distress, anxiety, humiliation and embarrassment, a sum to cover specific yearly salary and future earnings of several million dollars.

The use of the courts was also attempted by Tom Corbett, the governor of the state of Pennsylvania who is trying through a suit against the governing body of major college athletics in the US, the National Collegiate Athletic Association. He requests return of some or all of the $600 million the NCAA exacted as an initial penalty against Penn State for the infractions. The school itself has levied law suits against its insurance carriers, claiming their liability for payment of some of the loss within the fine. The school does not appear to have a case in making such claims for payment.

If the "new technologies" are exploited, they will enter most regularly at step three for institutions who want to protect themselves, or they may (and likely will continue to) be used by outside, independent moral entrepreneurs who want to "catch" a person or institution in hypocrisy.[7]

Continuing the Program

The public appearance, maintenance, and eventually consequences of hypocrisy rely on resources and activities of the organizations surrounding those who dissimulate or simulate information. Chapter 4 illustrates the role of mechanisms of information storage, dissemination, and sometimes concealment within these organizations. As the chapter suggests, the technology may aid both the concealer and the investigator intent on discovering the information.

Chapter 5 examines the activities of these organizations in handling initially deviant acts within two kinds of sport event: the Tour de France and an important playoff event in international football in Hillsborough, UK. In the Tour de France, discoveries of rule violation started a long process of accounting activity (excuses and justification) of those accused of cheating. Their rhetorical efforts display both dissimulation and simulation. In the soccer event in 1989, the record (as available some years after the event) charges authorities who were responsible for maintaining order and safety of spectators with errors. The errors led at least partially to the death of 96 persons at the scene.

The activities of the surrounding organization in each case—over more than ten years—further illustrates the seriousness of hypocrisy. Agencies in each instance persistently used information control mechanisms to conceal and then for attempts to claim non-culpability for the original cheating and the initial mistakes of police officers. Both dissimulation and simulation, constitutive factors of hypocrisy, occur over a long period of time among the organizations overseeing the Tour and the conduct of service groups at the soccer event.

Goal 3 of the program is central within Chapter 5, the organizational imperative. The interests within Goal 1, where contexts matter, additionally receives illustration in the next chapter. The availability of multiple kinds of information over more

---

7   Within the Tour drug use seems still common as evident by the huge list of violations inventoried. The winners of the Tour since the disqualification of Floyd Landis have appeared clean from drug use, with minor exceptions. Oscar Pereiro replaced Landis as the official 2006 winner. The victories of Alberto Contador (2007), Carlos Sastre (2008), Alberto Contador (2009), Cadel Evans (2011), Bradley Wiggins (2012), and Chris Froome (2013) have remained intact; but Alberto Contador was disqualified in 2010 and the win given to Andy Schleck. To illustrate the fine line between acceptable and non-acceptable training and performance behaviors, Andy Schleck's brother, Frank, was disqualified from the 2012 Tour for use of a banned substance. The role of external agents in the person of Travis Tygert and the steps of the USDA against Armstrong and several of his associates suggest some success of the control side of the equation.

than a decade (a duration needed to illustrate with some durability the role of the organizations) allows accountability to Goal 2, attending to strategic sites.

Goal 4 of the program is to note some consequences of hypocrisy. These can occur for the individual, close associates of the hypocrite, or for the organizations housing the actor who has dissimulated (concealment) or simulated (falsely fabricated) information. The examples of such dishonesty from Chapter 1, 2, and 3 show that consequences are not benign. There are general consequences from individual acts which become institutionally sustained over many years. Trust in the specific institutions, here, first, with sport and religion can be affected. Too, the consequences of lost trust can add to the general pattern of attenuated trust in all institutions, a loss documented consistently from other research resources. This costliness for trust from violations of honesty expectations central to sport and religion, as anticipated from the table of contents and Chapter 1, appear in Chapter 6.

Earlier in this chapter material addressed the principle of early attentiveness to malfeasance within an organization by law and organizational practices. This early attention holds the prospect for minimizing occurrences of dishonesty and costs of dishonesty and others types of malfeasance. In four of the main cases under scrutiny in the book, varieties of timeliness after publicity of the problems support the durability of the central principle and also add some nuances.

With Penn State, once acknowledged (after a long period of time of inattention, which the university personnel were deemed responsible for) outside judicatories such as the NCAA considered that the response to the personnel faults was prompt and effective. Hence, some of the original penalties were reduced. George Mitchell, an appointed independent monitor, recommended the restriction on bowl appearances be ended, making the school eligible for post-season events following the 2014 football season. The NCAA accepted this recommendation and also upon Mitchell's recommendation returned all 85 football scholarships to the school beginning in the 2015–16 season.

As the discussion recounts in Chapter 1 (schematized in Figure 1.2), Penn State acted relatively quickly and strongly to the penalties and accusations. In addition to distancing themselves from Sandusky and firing a person relatively low in the administrative hierarchy, they fired the coach, Joe Paterno, the athletic director, the Vice President overseeing athletics, and the university President. While late in the overall timeline of development of the case, oversight bodies did provide some acknowledgement for the severity of the response and the quickness of the timing: the sanction regarding post-season play was lifted and the restriction on numbers of scholarships was reduced in length of time. Revenue from direct payouts from bowl participation in bowls from 2013 figures range from $325,000 to $18 million. After team expenses for participation, members of the Big Ten pool proceeds for even distributions through the conference. Penn State on the basis of the reduction of the penalty on bowl participation will play in the Pinstripe Bowl in New York City on December 27, 2014: a bowl with payout in 2013 of $1,800,000.

The case of the Roman Catholic Church discussed thus far shows a slower pattern of response, and, in turn, gives evidence of a less effective movement toward resolution of negative consequences of the priest abuses and the administrative handling of the abuses. As the complementary timeline for the Roman Catholic Church shows (Figure 1.1), a long period of time passed before a recognition appeared and organizational correctives started. The timeliness and severity of sanctions against potentially culpable people is less clear-cut than with the Penn State case. While priest acts now are known to have been occurring for a long period of time, public awareness and organizational response occurred with accusations such as those by the Boston newspapers (January 6, 2001) against bishops for their concealment and non-action over the priest acts. This delay (from priest transgressions to recognition of mid-level administrators' lack of action) has meant difficulties in penalizing priests, either for prior deaths or inability to punish due to statutes of limitations on trials. Priests have been jailed and removed from offices. The acceptance of responsibility—and in turn the sanctions—for higher levels of church administrators has been relatively slow (compared to the Penn State situation). Bishops' organizations have acted preemptively, with statements censuring the priest acts and conveying some censoriousness to the public. The church now claims Cardinal Ratzinger, who became Pope Benedict, wrote a letter in 1988 condemning abusive acts of priests. As Pope Benedict XVI, he acknowledged some organizational responsibility: "Faced with a church sexual abuse scandal spreading across Europe Pope Benedict XVI on Saturday apologized directly to victims and their families in Ireland, expressing 'shame and remorse' for what he called 'sinful and criminal' acts committed by members of the clergy. But the pope did not require that Roman Catholic leaders be disciplined for past mistakes as some victims were hoping nor did he clarify what critics see as contradictory Vatican rules that they fear allow abuse to continue unpunished" (*The New York Times*, March 20, 2010).

Reports of Pope Francis' response to the allegations about priest misconduct show a modicum of shared responsibility compared to Pope Benedict XVI's stand-point, but critics still see a persistence of lack of direct action toward those accused. In CNN reporting of Pope Francis' homily directed at six victims: "I beg your forgiveness, too, for the sins of omission on the part of Church leaders who did not respond adequately to reports of abuse made by family members, as well as by abuse victims themselves" (Pearson, Burke, Yan, 2014). The authors of the report add, though: "Despite the strong words, a victims advocacy group, the Survivors Network of those Abused by Priests, or SNAP, said Monday's session [July 7, 2014] failed to advance the cause of preventing molestation by priests, arguing that 'no child on earth is safer today because of this meeting'" (ibid., 2).[8]

---

8   BishopsAccountability.com similarly has criticized the sudden "discovery" of Archbishop Ratzinger's letter of 1988 as a public relations ploy to claim early administrative attention to the problem, and to deflect criticisms of the continuation of abuses by priests.

Individual acts contain culpability. They are done within organizational contexts which can conceal, aid, or eventually sanction the individual acts of hypocrisy. The organization may tacitly accept the act and then conceal it in the interests of organizational self-preservation. Priests and personnel within the Penn State situation have been discussed. In Chapter 5, commentary on individual acts within organizational contexts continues, there within the Tour de France. Riders know rule violations are happening. While aware of the wrong-doing, the system norms dictate silence—the code of *omertà*. Some riders become sufficiently despairing of the contradictions to leave professional cycling. For those who remain, they may attempt to sanction those who break the silence (while personally still engaging in the cycling rule violations). Or they may try pre-emptively to avoid eventual censure from sport-governing bodies by divulging their cheating in advance of being formally charged with violations. This can come with intended personal advantage. They may be forced to do so as witnesses against others, with clear hopes of personal gains such as Floyd Landis has been doing with his "whistle-blowing" efforts. Or they may claim a higher good in saving the sport, while having lied until discovered (Hamilton and Coyle, 2012). Further to show the interplay of the system of personal acts of cheating, and then efforts to protect advantages, riders may accuse others in the sport, such as riders on other teams. Favor is curried with the new team by condemning former teammates on the team a rider has left.

Together, then, Chapters 4 and 5 create a setting from this interplay of individual acts and organizational constraints which cautions against optimism for general social trust. There are differences in the individual-organizational dynamics within the Penn State case and the Roman Catholic Church case, as noted. Further differences will appear when the cases of the Tour de France and Hillsborough are considered.

Though the intention of the book is to focus on the ideal-typical cases of sport and religion, the resiliency of conclusions from these cases should potentially extend to other social institutions. Some movement into these other institutions could occur with highly visible cases of rule violations within the American military in Iraq, which have recently been magnified by the United States Senate's recent reporting of Centralization Intelligence Agency conduct in running prisons. Fairness in looking at the sport and religion cases as limiting instances, and now, albeit only briefly, considering some additional institutional cases demands considerable reserve over generalizations.

But within the reserve about over-generalizations of commonalities, the record in the comparisons does lend to the book program goals about the use and misuse of information that will contribute to insights about social trust and elaboration of theoretical alternatives in dealing with hypocrisy—matters of consequences (Chapter 6) and theoretical development (Chapter 7): goals four and five from the program outlined from the start of the project.

With respect to the variables of timeliness, "throwing people under the bus," and acceptance of responsibility (or not) by superiors, the primary point will be a comparison between the Penn State case and the Roman Catholic Church case (the institutional themes foregrounded in the book). Added, however, is some material on Abu-Ghraib as another instance of variation on these three variables (again, timeliness, predisposition to punish underlings, and deflection by superiors of responsibility). One reason for doing so relates to the generality issues in Chapter 6 on trust. Too, given recent (12/9/2014) disclosure of the US Senate's long review of prison abuse, clearly the prison issue is still alive.[9]

The United States took control in 2003 of a prison in Abu Ghraib, 20 miles from Baghdad, for purposes of housing captured Iraqi troops. Control was passed to the Iraqis in 2006. By November 2003, some recognition of irregularities in handling prisoners occurred. Seymour M. Hersh's account in *The New Yorker* (Hersh, 2004) carried early news of abuses within the prison. Retrospective reviews of continuing problems occur in the film "Standard Operating Procedures" (2006) and other summaries (CNN, 2014). The lack of timeliness of attention further has been brought into question by the recent report by the United States Senate (December 2014) which has summarized abuses in prisons by the Central Intelligence Agency, as well as making references to the durable history of abuses in military prisons.

Eleven military personnel received some disciplinary action. Nobody above a staff sergeant (E-6) served prison time. Janis Karpinski, the officer in charge of the prison, was demoted from Brigadier General to Colonel (O-7 to O-6). The penalties appear to be oriented to lower-ranking personnel, rather than attending to levels of responsibility by higher-ranking military personnel. The internal military review by Major General Antonio M. Taguba (not originally for release, but commented on by Hersh) was very critical, but largely deflected by senior

---

9   Accessible and graphic information sources referred to here include Seymour M. Hersh's report in *The New Yorker* (2004); a CNN summary, updated in 2014, "Iraq Prison Abuse Scandal Fast Facts" (2014); and the film, "Standard Operating Procedure: the Scandal was a Coverup," which through interviews of several of the principals allows access to the subtleties of excuses and accounting (Lyman and Scott, 1968). With respect to the continuation of the issues of abuses in US-run prisons, there is a heavily redacted report now public released by the Senate. It is 524 pages in length, being, ostensibly a summary ("Senate Select Committee on Intelligence: Committee Study of the Central Intelligence Agency's Detention and Interrogation Program" [December 9, 2014]) of the original 6,700 report on "the CIA's detention and interrogation Programs under President George W. Bush" (this identification used from Moyers & Company, 2014). In the interest of not letting the prison issue stand alone as a movement away from sport and religion, I am going to anticipate here some treatment of the continuing discussion about information control made very visible by the new book on Eichmann. I am not going to pretend the sport issues and the religion issues are quantitatively akin to the Eichmann issues (Stangneth, 2014). But the kinds of lying occurring within the sport and religion cases in the book on hypocrisy in these institutions are qualitatively similar to what is now being written about Eichmann and his associates in Germany and Argentina. Again, there is a system of lying that becomes self-perpetuating. This point from the cases in Chapter 1–5 becomes critical to incorporate into the treatment.

military and political personnel (Hersh, 2004: 14, 15). "As the international furor grew, senior military officers, and President Bush, insisted that the actions of a few did not reflect the conduct of the military as a whole. Taguba's report, however, amounts to an unsparing study of collective wrongdoing and the failure of Army leadership at the highest levels. The picture he draws of Abu Ghraib is one in which Army regulations and the Geneva conventions were routinely violated, and in which much of the day-to-day management of the prisoners was abdicated to Army military-intelligence units and civilian contract employees. Interrogating prisoners and getting intelligence, including by intimidation and torture, was the priority" (ibid.).

Chapter 5
Hypocrisy and Related Deceits: When Lying becomes Normal

Introduction: Hypocrisy and Organizations

The Safari Simbaz cycling team and several hundred other riders rode through Nairobi as the 2013 Tour de France came to a close with Chris Froome leading. The Simbaz and the parade of riders was led by David Kinjah, the team's coach and a former mentor of Froome when Froome started cycling with the group as a 12-year-old on the roads in the village of Mai-I-Hii in the Kikuyu township north and west of Nairobi. The French Senate released a 918-page report on July 24 discussing drug use in sport, with commonly noted items on performance enhancing drugs detected from the 1998 Tour. Responses that followed quickly came from Lance Armstrong who said he was not surprised by the findings of the commission, the Italian Cycling Federation who criticized the report, and the International Cycling Union (UCI) which also criticized the report. Stuart O'Grady was banished from the Australian Olympic Committee for his acknowledgement of use of drugs in 1998 (having just been celebrated for most Tour entries). In the space of a few days, this composite of news related to international cycling foregrounds key ingredients of hypocrisy. Hypocrisy is organized; and hypocrisy is durable.[1]

The focal cases within the ideal-typical institutions of sport and religion in prior chapters come from real and attributed malfeasance of members of Penn State University and the Roman Catholic Church. Compromises of truth telling, hypocrisy, come over a relatively long period of time as individuals attempted to hide errors (dissimulation) and, falsely, attempted to claim acts not accomplished (simulation). The Tour de France, which started in 1903 as a promotional vehicle for a news medium, shows within the earliest races, instances of violation of rules.

---

1 Chris Froome's biography describes the personal and athletic history with the Safari Simbaz (*The Climb*, 2014). Other efforts at the grass-root level, and following lines of athletic success of Kenyans' success at distance running, exist in the efforts of Nicolas Leong to found a professional cycling team starting in 2006 (Kenyan Riders, 2015; Ingle, 2014). The goal of the team (located in Iten, in the Rift Valley) is to make the team eligible for the Tour de France. A top rider, John Njoroge Muya, died when a truck driving against the race competition (and having evaded traffic controls) hit him during the Tour de Matabungkay in the Philippines (Windsor, 2014). Froome had visited the team headquarters after his 2013 Tour victory.

In 1998, to acknowledge a highly visible recent instance, just prior to the start of the annual race, claims of cheating and news of associated disqualifications spread broadly through sport media available both to cycling participants and consumers of cycling events. The prospects of large-scale cheating existed in what is now called the Festina Affair.

Over the past eight years, locating the inner time period with the disqualification of Floyd Landis from the 2006 event, coverage of rule violations by journalists and efforts by various judicatories from specific teams through world anti-doping agencies such as WADA, have been highly visible. As the Penn State case and the Roman Catholic Church cases show, the consequences of cheating compound when offenders try to hide the offense or if they claim behaviors falsely. These are lies, and within the definitions of the book this is hypocrisy.

Two bodies of information from 2013 until the present consistently show that cheating in the Tour de France has been appreciably compounded by lying, and specifically hypocrisy. One of these bodies of information is the aggregate of careful reporting by journalists and others burdened with a felt obligation to document visually the dishonesty. The other body of information comes from a set of very recent biographies and autobiographies by present or former riders in the Tour de France.

The titles of two recent compilations of reporting on the Tour, one from personnel of *The New York Times* and one from a pair of reporters from the *Wall Street Journal*, show how the issues of lying within the Tour now are assuming centrality: Juliet Macur's *Cycle of Lies* (2014) not only focuses on the issues of violation of truth, the title and the substance evokes awareness that the features of arrangements of information exchange, which can be called hypocritical, have a systematic character. The book by Reed Albergotti and Vanessa O'Connell, *Wheelmen: Lance Armstrong, the Tour de France, and the Greatest Sports Conspiracy Ever* (2013), frames the events described in this chapter as matters of lying as well as cheating. Their terminology of "conspiracy," captures a system, as does Macur's book; and in the inner portion of the front cover Albergotti and O'Connell diagram such a system with 31 nodes or players who are mutually linked in the system of information distribution, concealment, and ultimately detection. One agrees, in conspiracy, to conceal a shared body of information from other onlookers. The complementary report, visual, comes from Alex Gibney's documentary, *The Armstrong Lie* (2014). The title and the cover blurb show what has become the explicit framing of the events in this chapter as dishonesty: "*The Armstrong Lie* picks up in 2013 after Armstrong was stripped of his 7 Tour de France titles, and presents a riveting, insider's view of the unraveling of the greatest deception in sports history" (Gibney, "The Armstrong Lie," 2014).

The second source comes from riders' biographical statements that make the whole system of deceit within the Tour de France a point of reference where they, in turn, seek justification for themselves, describe their efforts to leave the system, or self-interestedly use the Tour as a vehicle for their own gains. In brief, the deceptive Tour is objectified in ways that Macur, Albergotti and O'Connell, and

Gibney have described it. The Tour as an honest event may evoke excitement of participants and on-lookers. The Tour, with an accepted order of deceit, when threatened with detection, bears on judgments and actions of those who participate. Their stories frame the system as deceptive. But additionally their own rules magnify threats hypocritical systems hold for levels of trust in societies in general. Their own rules display deception, escape, continuing contradiction, and attempts at establishing innocence, a system that casts doubt on prospects of maintaining trust in a society as a whole (Chapter 6).

Riders, in acts and narratives about their actions and motivations, orient themselves toward the identified system of cheating, coupled with concealment. Some riders or support members of teams may leave. Some confess, attempting to justify their own involvement by claims that they were doing it and they needed to do so to remain competitive. Some confessed, and then used their ostensive openness to gain personal reward (Floyd Landis being an example). Some acknowledged they cheated and then argue they are providing revelations about the sport for the good of the sport, tacitly to justify their own cheating in the interest of a future clean sport. Some may resist telling of the system, but be forced to do so to save their own positions or to prevent criminal indictments. Recent autobiographies may write preemptively to claim they were not involved to assure that others not judge them as complicit.[2] Lance Armstrong represents a combination of concealment and use of his secrets for personal advantage. While speaking of the system of drug use and acknowledging some involvement, he has directly and with his lawyers worked behind the visible news scene to bargain his knowledge of his cheating and his cover-up for immunity from some penalties.

Once the system of the Tour as a sport shows efforts to depart from cheating, and there are outside entities like journalists and oversight groups investigating, then the prospect of an institutional entity where possible culpable actors try to protect themselves emerges. An institution with appearances of being honest and non-hypocritical creates a reference where efforts at possible concealment changes. That is, the object represented in discussions such as those of Albergotti and O'Connell and Macur, and the recognition by the riders that they had better begin to protect themselves from the parts of that system that now is starting to redefine itself conveys a new set of normalcy. Yes, there were rule violations and wholesale concealment and lies. But once the trend of the record and associated admissions becomes the new state of affairs formally (the body of knowledge and practice considered "normal science" again, Kuhn, 2012), then this system rapidly starts to sanction the deviants in efforts to justify the claim of a reformed sport to various audiences and constituencies.

There are characteristics of this system that carry, with warrant, cynicism about the prospects for general levels of trust. Formally, to participate one has to cheat. Then to assure one's own safety, one has to sustain the deception about cheating. When risks to knowledge about one's culpability rise from the prospects

2 For example, Froome, 2014; and Hushovd, 2014.

of other people divulging your cheating, or oversight groups appear to be gaining in uncovering the deception, then a variety of schemes by actors occur both to exculpate oneself and to give the best possible public image to the participation of cheating. As a social system a reflective actor would prefer, these characteristics seem very unpleasant (Chapter 6). But one of the theories addressing bases of social order in Chapter 1 and that is developed in Chapter 7 acquiesces in the prospect that this is the common state of affairs within societies.

The sequence of events reported from the Festina Affair in 1998, through the latest expansive coverages of the Tour, shows change in the fundamental displays of honesty and dishonesty: an institution where lying was common, turns, by the latter period, into an institution which at least attempts to be honest. Figure 5.1 schematizes the change.[3]

Figure 5.1   A dubious system of information vs. a credible system of information in the Tour

A Lying System 2004 and 2005	The Fulcrum 2012	System as Credible 2013 and 2014
a. omerta persists[4]	USADA, 6/12/2012	a. The presumption of "cycle" changes
b. Org, financial support		b. Writing accommodates the change
c. Oppositional journalism rejected		c. Supporters of previous system "jump"[5]

---

3   Illustrative biographical materials include the following: Millar, 2012; Hamilton and Coyle, 2012; Froome, 2014; Hincapie, 2014; and Hushovd, 2014. *L.A. Confidentiel: Les secrets de Lance Armstrong* (Ballester and Walsh, 2004) and Damien Ressiot's article in *L'Equipe* (August 23, 2005) represent the set of presumptions about the Tour at that time: the Tour was honest. Armstrong sued Walsh and *The Sunday Times* (who serialized the book in 2004) over claims of Armstrong cheating, and won a settlement of about $470,000. Ressiots's claims about positive drug tests for Armstrong going back to 1999 were commonly ignored by cycling governing bodies, or ignored by fellow journalists.

4   With an Italian-language origin, *omertà*, the term holds a traditional meaning among the Mafia of a code of silence. One effort to capture the use and meaning within the Tour by Ian Moynihan (2013: 1): "… it is essentially a gentlemen's agreement between all professional cyclists to present to the public the image of a drug-free sport." On the force of omerta (not judged a foreign term in the accepted cycling usage), Moynihan judges: "This omerta was so strong, unified and impenetrable, that it allowed an enormous and stunningly bold fraud to be committed, the biggest lie sport has ever seen" (ibid., 1).

5   Riders, managers, regulatory bodies, owners, sponsors, and journalists (that is, stakeholders generally) began showing changes of commitments and presuppositions about cheating and lying after what has been identified here as a "fulcrum" marking a separation of a previous set of assumptions underlying Tour de France business and a

The term "exigency" used by writers on the variability of hypocrisy across space and time denotes the import of context. Features of the context bear on the processes of lie-telling identified here as hypocrisy, where a wrongful deed is hidden or a claim is made dishonestly of an asset not possessed. The array of stories emerging at the end of the 2013 Tour de France alert us to how in practice components of this context are arranged, indeed organized into a system of factors that prompt the deceits, sustain them, and lead to resistance of revelations of truth.

The disqualification of the Lance Armstrong victories from 1999 through 2005 did not occur until 2012. The French Senate report, focusing on events judged wrong in 1998, and the time delay in resolving the Armstrong disqualifications complement the delays of reported discoveries at Penn State and the Roman Catholic Church noted in Chapter 2. Hypocritical acts occur within, and are supported by, organizational structures. And hypocritical acts enhanced by features of culture add to the durability of the persistence of hypocrisy and the seriousness of consequences of these deceits.[6]

---

current system of doing business in the Tour. This is represented analytically in the figure. Culture and behavior systematically change in observances of the "shift" with degrees of accommodation, resistance, and inertia. The UCI (*Union Cycliste Internationale*) in two recent procedural acts (2014 and 2015) illustrates how the shift to a new normal has occurred, but in the process illustrates variable rates of change across all stakeholders. Brian Cookson, with a priority of supporting change, was elected president of UCI in 2013. On January 8, 2014, the UCI commissioned an independent investigative group to review drug use, including questions about past UCI culpability. The committee submitted the report in February, 2015. The report, now officially a vehicle of UCI, criticizes the past "normal" system of the Tour including criticisms of past leaders of the UCI organization itself. The report record of the Tour, past, is consistent with the combined record from four major sources represented throughout this book. The report, in describing productive efforts by the UCI against drug use and deceits in the system, evinces productive steps that occurred within UCI since the "fulcrum" of 2012. The report judges that problems in both cheating and lying within the Tour do still exist.

6   In the USADA letter to six principals, including Armstrong, on June 12, 2012 Armstrong was singled out as being non-co-operative in the agency's investigations. In the January 2013 purported confessional interview on an Oprah Winfrey show, Armstrong technically admitted drug use, but with qualifications in his response. Following the publication of the French report on July 24, 2013, Armstrong's response continues to be one of claimed non-culpability. The events, in effect, are described by Armstrong as "outside himself." Armstrong appears to continue to see the dishonesty in the Tour and his own documented culpability as exclusive relative to general norms of sport (as those specified in this book). His comment to *Golf Digest* (2014) about rule-compliance in that sport suggest this compartmentalization: "Golf is different from the culture of cycling when I was competing, and that's putting it mildly. Cycling, it was the Wild West. Nobody considered doping cheating. It was an arms race where absolutely anything went, and it was every man for himself. You might consider me the last guy to have anything to say about cheating, but golf is different. I love adhering to a code of honor that we in cycling didn't have. If I moved my ball in the rough and got caught, I wouldn't just regret it, I'd be heartbroken forever" (*Golf Digest*, 2015: 5).

Figure 5.2   Timeline for cheating in Tour de France

Date	Event
1903	First Tour de France
11/1964	France passes first anti-doping law
7/13/1967	Tom Simpson dies on climb (alcohol and amphetamines) on Mont Ventoux
1998	Festina Affair
1999–2005	Lance Armstrong wins seven Tour titles
2004	*L.A. Confidentiel* appears, and Armstrong enacts successful libel suit
8/23/2005	Damien Ressiot in *L'Equipe* claims Armstrong drug use
2006	Operation Puerto opens
2006	Landis denied Tour victory
2/2008	Operation Puerto continues, after temporary closing
6/10/10	Landis files Whistle-Blower law suit claiming Armstrong and others defrauded Postal Service. Named in the suit are Armstrong, Thomas W. Weisel (Tailwind Sports), Johan Bruyneel, William Stapleton, and Barton Knaggs.
2012	Armstrong stripped of Titles (US Anti-doping agency strips titles; UCI follows)[7]
1/2013	Armstrong claims "defeasibility" in Oprah Winfrey interview
4/2013	Operation Puerto trial results: Eufmiano Fuentes found guilty
4/2013	US Department of Justice joins Landis lawsuit
7/2013	Brian Cookson (British Cycling President) promises to investigate UCI Culpability
7/2013	French Government drug report (918 pages), includes cycling (with Festina Affair)
7/2013	Stuart O'Grady (named in French report) admits drug use in 1998, Retires
8/2013	The Sunday Times agrees to settlement with Armstrong to repay proceeds originally given to Armstrong (in libel suit) plus costs; agreement is confidential, with *The Times* originally requesting 720,000 pounds in costs
1/2014	Union Cycliste International (UCI) establishes a Reform Commission

---

7   The notification to Armstrong and six others occurs on June 12, 2012. After allowing for response from Armstrong, which did not occur, the USADA published its full report supporting the Armstrong disqualifications on August 24, 2012. The UCI, allowed 21 days to contest the sanctions, did not do so and the final act of disqualification, now applicable to the UCI, occurred on October 10. 2012.

12/2014	Two Armstrong associates settle "Whistleblower" suit[8]
3/2015	Cycling Independent Reform Commission: Report to the President of the *Union Cycliste Internationale* (UCI)
6/2015	Anti Doping Denmark publishes report on Danish Cycling: *Rapport Om Doping I Dansk Cykelsport, 1998–2015*

On April 15, 1989, in a semi-final soccer match for the FA cup (The Football Association Challenge Cup; founded 1871) between Liverpool and Nottingham Forest, just as the match was getting underway, a crush of spectators into fences and with one another led to 96 deaths and 766 injuries. It was not until September 2012 that the Hillsborough Independent Panel reported that the tragedy was in large measure the result of a failure of police control. That is 23 years that contained charge and counter-charge occurring in a series of panels, and efforts of persons and professional bodies to hide and deflect culpability. Mistakes were made on the day, but the insidious character of the event grows as persons and acts that were blameworthy are neutralized and hidden from view by the series of investigative panels.

Figure 5.3   Timetable of Hillsborough "stampede," 1989

74 soccer fans died in a riot in Port Said, February 1, 2012. The game, between Port Said's Al-Masry club and Cairo's Al-Ahly club, eventually led to 21 ostensive rioters given death sentences and seven police officers attending the event acquitted. Later that year, in a retrospective in October of a riot preceding the European Cup match between Liverpool and Juventus, the tragedy of 39 deaths was recalled. These records remind fans and observers of the prospect for violence in highly-charged soccer matches. In Hillsborough, GB in 1989 crowding in the standing-room areas of the stadium as the semifinal match for the Football Association Challenge Cup, first held in 1871–1872, between Liverpool and Nottingham Forest escalated to the extent that 96 fans were killed just as the match was scheduled to begin. These events, while exceptional within the population of all soccer matches, allow the expectation of something similar to occur, albeit remote in probabilistic terms.

4/15/1989	The Match
	The Crush of Fans and the Deaths
	Official and Police Response
May 3, 1989	Liverpool–Everton (First Division). 300,000 pounds raised.
May 7, 1989	Liverpool and Nottingham Forest Replay; Liverpool wins, 3–1.
May 20, 1989	Liverpool–Everton in Final FA Cup match; Liverpool wins, 3–2.
8/1989	The Taylor Report (Preliminary)

---

8   Bill Stapleton and Bart Knaggs on 12/19/2014 agreed to pay $500,000 in response to the Landis Whistle Blower lawsuit. The US Federal Government had not joined this portion of Landis' suit; the settlement will depend on US Government approval.

1/1990	The Taylor Report (Final)
1990, 1991	The Coroner's Investigation. Reports findings, but does not allow questioning either at each of individual reports to victims' families or in generic report.
1998	The Stuart-Smith Report. Begins with the presumption of non-culpability of police and stadium caretakers. Looks for "new" evidence.
2012	Hillsborough Independent Panel

"The Report of the Hillsborough Independent Panel" (September 12, 2012) is a fulcrum or a marker of a new conception of normalcy analogous with the USADA letter of June 12, 2012. Prior to the report addressed to the House of Commons, the conception of principal officials, disclaimers in earlier reports, and in defenses against claims of culpability from the April 1989 events to January 2012 had been to persist in the initial framing of the events as: originating with unruly fans, who had been drinking to excess, and were trying to enter the event without tickets—with a particular onus embedded in the framing of events since 1989 on the unruly Liverpool fans. Within the introductory summary from the 2012 panel, the shift occurs: "The disclosed documents show that multiple factors were responsible for the deaths of the 96 victims of the Hillsborough tragedy and the fans were not the cause of the disaster. The disclosed documents show that the bereaved families met a series of obstacles in their search for justice" ("The Report of the Hillsborough Independent Panel," 2012: 1).[9]

Acts of deceit identified as hypocrisy here are not simply lies exacted by single persons and isolated institutions. More completely, they are omissions of disclosures of past wrongful deeds and claims of credentials that are not so, but which are induced by contexts of high expectations and the realities that past errors are not completely avoidable and desired exploits can never completely be accomplished. The cases of Penn State, the Roman Catholic Church pedophile priests, and the events in this chapter on the Tour de France and Hillsborough provide the elements of an organization that sustains the falsehoods and resists disclosure and censure. Central elements of organizations which comprise a kind of "organizational imperative" that sustains hypocrisies are the governing institutions of the sport or church, the media, and even entities charged with ensuring order and proper conduct, such as the police.

This book takes seriously the scholarship within moral philosophy and within political science that has attempted to isolate the essentials of "hypocrisy." In the publication history of four reasonably representative journals on the sociology of

---

9   Primary and secondary sources used in the commentary on the Hillsborough case include: the Taylor Interim Report (August 1989); the Taylor Final Report (January 1990); the Justice Stuart-Smith report (February 1998); "The Report of the Hillsborough Independent Panel" (September 12, 2012); Scraton et al. (1995); Scraton (1999); Scraton (2013); and the film, "Hillsborough" (1996).

sport and the sociology of religion, there are 67 references to "hypocrisy." These range from a single word to a few titles of articles; there is no sustained treatment across the population of articles of definition, social contexts, social consequences, or tie with any branch of sociological theory (excepting general allusions to power and hegemony of some institutions). This population is used to provide a basis of comparison for descriptions of a "pure" meaning of hypocrisy sought in this project and related uses of the term.

The meaning of hypocrisy driving the start of the investigation is of actions of an individual or institution which either hide a dark side or pretend a false credential. Chapter 1 provides a definition of hypocrisy used in the book's program. Contexts, as noted, may alter the core meaning of the term (Chapters 2 and 3). Chapter 4 and here in Chapter 5 hold illustrations of the contributions from organizational influences on occurrences, seriousness, and consequences of hypocrisy. Crucial *differentiae* in this definition which emphasizes both dissimulation and simulation are the components of deceit and the fact that the propagator of the deceit gains something from the lack of disclosure or the claim of an unfounded credential that the individual or institution possesses.

Hypocrisy is a lie, but it carries a special perversity because it exploits the consumers' trust in the institution being represented by the hypocrite. In sport and in religion, the presumed character of the institution is one of integrity. So members of the institution when dissimulating or simulating have not just acted falsely, they have violated—in the ideal-typical cases of sport and religion—especially strong levels of trust. As ties with these forms of hypocrisy with other potential deceits or deviations from norms of religion and sport occur, a more variegated treatment of hypocrisy and other kinds of deceits and their social consequences will occur in this and later chapters of the book. But the strategy now is to begin with a narrow and serious definition of "hypocrisy" rather than the use of the term to refer to any kind of objectionable inconsistency or contradiction. (Within the United States, such a loose use of the term illustrates the issue. President Barack Obama was called a hypocrite by the National Rifle Association in opposing some kinds of gun sales when he uses secret service personnel to attend his children when they travel to school.)

There is not a record of sociological research addressing an obvious question about hypocrisy: What are the social consequences? Illustratively, there are four research journals on sport and on religion whose longevity approaches the proposed time frame of temporal assessment in this project: 50 years. *Social Compass* began publication in 1953; *Journal for the Scientific Study of Religion* began publication in 1961; the *Sociology of Sport Journal* began publication in 1984; and the *International Review for the Sociology of Sport* began publication in 1966. A systematic inventory of all volumes within those journals' histories show these quantities of articles devoted specific attention to hypocrisy in the respective institutions. On the basis of the research record, this project is a needed systematic study of social consequences of hypocrisy in sports and religion, especially within sociology.

There are to be sure elements of contradiction in both the hidden condition (dissimulation) and the claimed visible condition (simulation) within hypocrisy. This aspect of contradiction, though, without the attendant deceit and profit, open "hypocrisy" to applications of the term to a wide variety of other conditions which can be easily and sometimes more accurately denoted by a range of different terms. These include: "inconsistency," "contradiction," "irony," "satire," "carnival," "dilemma," "ambiguity," "farce," and "there are good things and bad things" (in sport). With perhaps three or four exceptions among the population of the 67 journal articles consulted, one of the other lexical terms better captures the meaning intended rather than the more precise meaning of "hypocrisy" that is sustained in this project.

A major intention of the project is to outline the social consequences of "hypocrisy" for individuals and institutions. Some of these have been described within the cases covered in Chapters 1–3; to be consistent with the five goals of the book program, some consequences of hypocrisies within the Tour de France and the Hillsborough case receive attention here. A major consequence from all these cases bears on levels of trust in societies, which is the focus, as noted, of Chapter 6. These connect clearly with hypocrisy as contradiction as well as deceit and individual and institutional profit. As will be noted in Chapter 7, none of these articles systematically describe and document the social consequences of what is being referred to by their use of the term "hypocrisy." There may be an implied criticism of the contradiction or inconsistency or "farce" as one writer calls a sporting event. But potential social consequences do not approach—if they even were described—those that are described in this book.

What makes hypocrisy unique, as an instance of deceit in Shklar's (Shklar, 1984) refined position, is that a person or individual makes their claim for belief or commitment on the basis of the spokesperson's special integrity. An imagined invocation might sound like: "You can trust me, so believe me and commit to my position."

In the past few years there have been highly publicized scandals in both the sport area and religious area which represent violations of trust. But these violations can be seen as institutional failings without the factor of a clear embodiment of a person appealing for trust on the basis of his or her personal characteristics. Thousands of riders have competed in the Tour de France. The presumption about moral complexity of these athletes is not continually in view by the public and journalists. The event itself is the appeal and the story. Hundreds of soccer matches occur in England yearly and throughout the world; again, the event itself is the appeal to fans and to journalists. The moral machinations of players is not on the minds of these audiences. In the cases already noted, athletic coaches at major universities in the United States and coaches of highly vulnerable young athletes, like age group swimmers, the fidelity and blamelessness of the coaches is assumed and is tied up in a level of trust by those who consume the sports and the sport services. Priests and Protestant clergy are assumed to be blameless in their roles by lay persons; one engages them with the presumption of service and at worst benign inattention. One does not engage them as potential threats.

The general attribution of the administrators of college athletic events is not of a person identified for their irreproachable character, but it is certainly not an attribution of a highly compromised human being. The role Sandusky played at Pennsylvania State University and that college's administrators, and the roles of clergyman bring expectations of moral refinement. The roles of Tour de France athletes and administrators and administrators of major English soccer carry obligations to carry out the event for public viewing with accepted game guidelines—not continuously to invoke expectations of impeccable trust in their personal habits and honesty.

In this chapter in particular, the contributions of the surrounding organizational layers become more visible. "Mistakes are made" as recent designated culprits within the Tour de France report (Hamilton, 2012; Millar, 2012; Landis) and the 2012 report on Hillsborough concludes. What makes these and related situations similar to the Penn State case and the Roman Catholic Church pedophile pattern is the slowness of organization response. What makes the fallout especially disturbing, though, is not only the delays in organizational response; it is also the recognition in the cases of this chapter of how complex and potent the many parties to the institutionalized patterns are in creating and reinforcing a system where, as the chapter title states, the process: "lying becomes normal." In the Penn State case and the Roman Catholic Church case, flawed acts and persons have been identified, and though long in resolution, some efforts have occurred to exorcise the ostensive defective players. In the Tour de France case and in the Hillsborough case, the lessons and stakes for general social trust may be even more consequential. Through member presumption, acquiescence, and collaboration, two institutions of sport seem to have created systems where falsehoods were protected and corrections of the falsehoods resisted.

From what has developed in Chapters 1–4, there are several defining features of hypocrisy in the cases described thus far, and which exist in the ones in this chapter. The importance of success is elevated and depends on being superior to others; success and superiority carry moral currency. This is the meaning of Shklar's term of "exigency." The more intense the exigency and the more scarce the opportunities for success make the propensity to lie by denial (dissimulation) or fabrication (simulation) increase. Here the special importance of "organizational imperatives" receive more illumination.

Hypocrisy and Exigency: Four Conditions that Allow Intrusion of the Organization

First, there are variable expectations for performance (winning, money, or personal sanctity). Note that sanctity may include real or feigned claims for modesty, such as with Molière's Tartuffe. The expectations may come from culture or the institution. They may be variably internalized. Generally individuals and institutions susceptible to the dangers of hypocrisy are "true believers." The winning, the money, the personal sanctity or reputation hold high priority.

Secondly, there are variable chances for success. Examples include the evolution of competition within the Tour de France (Wieting, 2000), increasing stakes and diminishing chances to win in NCAA football, and problems of success in the Roman Catholic Church.

Thirdly, both of these factors themselves are conditioned by the ability to compartmentalize. Roles and evaluative dimensions within individuals may be isolable. Institutional public relations services may be able to separate spheres; or different departments may deal with different issues. The ruling of the Catholic Church to keep secret the discovery of pedophile priests was couched as being a greater need for the reputation of the Church, than was the need to protect vulnerable victims from the assaults of priests. An important part of this is the type of excuse and justification that the organizational culture prompts and will allow (Scott and Lyman, 1969).

Fourthly, with the elevation of the stakes organizations compete to conceal lies, against other organizations intent on detecting lies (Chapter 4).

Within these essential characteristics of hypocrisy, there exist highly visible cases where some, if not all, of the conditions exist. First, there has been a major distribution of decisions of oversight groups charging Lance Armstrong and his cycling team with cheating through at least the Tour de France races from 1999 through 2005; and then, the continuation of illegal activity when Floyd Landis was disqualified after an apparent win in 2006. The second case in view in this chapter is the Hillsborough soccer tragedy of 1989.

Two Key Cases in Overview

Lance Armstrong and Le Tour de France Violations

Among other penalties, on the basis of a lengthy investigation, the United States Anti-Doping Agency voided Lance Armstrong's titles in the successive Tour de France races from 1999 through 2005, and has disqualified him from participation in any event sanctioned by the Olympic Committee.[10] The primary source for this section will be: "Reasoned Decision of the United States Anti-Doping Agency on

---

10   The World Anti-Doping Agency (WADA) was established in 1999 with the specific responsibilities of monitoring for 600 sports organizations the World Anti-Doping Code. The United States Anti-Doping Agency (USADA), established first in 1999, and given recognition by the US Congress in 2001, governs drug use in US Olympic, Paralympic, and Pan American sport in the United States.

Disqualification and Ineligibility. Report on Proceedings under the World Anti-doping Code and the USADA Protocol of October 2012."[11]

The Tour de France, a venerable world sporting event contested first in 1903, entered United States sports consumption with the victories of Greg LeMond in 1986, 1989, and 1990. In 1998, coverage of the Tour as it approached its starting point in that summer grew due to a discovery of illegal drugs being transported to some teams. The event was contested, with riders suspended or dropping out as a form of protest. The intrusion by the police and, by acquiescence, the event organizers gave a sense of resolution of what was a possible drug problem in the event, and the 1999 event was a renovated Tour de France. The Tour that year was won by Lance Armstrong, who proved to be an extraordinarily popular winner in the United States, due to the fact that he had dealt with testicular cancer prior to his recuperation and victory.

Armstrong had ridden the Tour on occasion before 1998, having won Stage 8 in 1993 and winning Stage 18 in 1995, placing 36th overall. Following the win in 1999, he won six more times, with visibility of a positive kind growing yearly with his success. His victories, as a cancer survivor, prompted a philanthropic movement surrounding his and his teams' successes, which encouraged a kind of survivor activism by cancer peers and generating money for "Livestrong," the name given in 2003 to what had been known as the Lance Armstrong Foundation (elaborated later in the chapter). The continued success in the event, eventually exceeding with his seven victories the highest number achieved by any other competitors, was complemented by disqualifications of some riders from the event for using performance enhancing drugs, compromises which sustained negative press as well.

The Hillsborough Disaster in 1989

"In September 2012, the Hillsborough Independent Panel concluded that up to 41 of the 96 who had died [in 1989] might have been saved had some failings been addressed. The report revealed 'multiple failures' by other emergency services and public bodies which contributed to the death toll. In response to the panel's report, Attorney General for England and Wales, Dominic Grieve MP, confirmed he would consider all the new evidence to evaluate whether the original inquest verdicts of accidental death could be overturned."[12] The primary source here will be

---

11   The sequence of disqualification includes: a letter to Armstrong and five other principals in the alleged conspiracy on June 12, 2012, the judgment of lifetime disqualification of Armstrong on August 24, 2012; and the "Reasoned Decision ..." of October 12, 2012.

12   The summary comment comes from http://en.wikipedia.org/wiki/Hillsborough_ disaster. The reference to the inclination of the Attorney General to continue inquests refers to http:www.liverpoolecho.co.uk/2012/09/12/attorney-general-to-consider-overturning-hillsborough-inquest-verdicts-100252–31823481/. *Liverpool Echo.* 12 September 2012.

The Report of the Hillsborough Independent Panel, September 12, 2012, Ordered by the House of Commons.[13] This report shows the sequence of the definition of "normalcy" from the earliest characterizations from participants and subsequent official reports (in footnote 6) of what occurred in 1989 until 2012 and since that time. These cases extend the geographic reach of the book treatment, by looking at a major sporting event in France and an important stage in the resolution of a major championship in soccer in the United Kingdom.

These additional cases display the long period of time it may take before an individual or an entire institution may be brought to account for illegal activity. And as such they provide requisite records for the analysis. An important distinction between these two cases and the Penn State case and the expression of abuse by priests in the United States is that the initial acts of the bicycle racers, in the French case, and the police in the Hillsborough case were not judged as a compromise of prevailing norms of conduct in those events. At the times, presumptions surrounding the Tour allowed that some cheating in the past had been identified, but Armstrong escaped this association, and at first Landis escaped the association as well. The initial presumption following the Hillsborough events was a situation that had occurred at some similar soccer events, where unruly fans needed to be controlled by police. The police faced with the difficult situation were considered initially to have done their best to prevent the disorganization that led to the tragic deaths. Armstrong was at first in 1999 judged a hero, as was Landis in 2006. What unfolds over several years after the victories was a long period of negotiation among the riders, the press, the various judicatories that govern the sport of bicycle racing, and the public. So we are able to see how in claims and counter claims the moral rightness (or lack thereof) was given some kind of stable substance. With the Hillsborough situation, similarly, there was a long period between 1989 and the final report coming out (2012) where the various factions in the eventual definition of police cover-up and dishonesty can be viewed and evaluated.

Acts judged hypocritical by society and actors attributed with such valuations are considered deceitful. But the act and the actor display obsession with success, enviable intentions, and can betray understandable "attempts to do the right thing." Also, in the unfolding of the deception, actors and institutional entities show the ability to compartmentalize and separate disparate portions of their activities. This may initially be seen as concentration and focus. These social arrangements and styles of activity are why the duration of the concealment can be long; and these can account for the range and severity of negative consequences from hypocrisy.

The events and actors described in this chapter are prototypical of the long period of discovery and the unintended negative consequences of hypocrisy. The episodes—involving key figures in nearly 25 years of the Tour de France and the denials and labeled officials in the Hillsborough soccer tragedy where 96 fans died in 1989—differ somewhat from central sports figures and respected Church

---

13 "Hillsborough: the Report of the Hillsborough Independent Panel," September 2012.

leaders treated in Chapters 1–4. Hypocrisy violates expectations in institutions as illustrated with Penn State and the problems within the Roman Catholic Church. Beyond moral criticisms advanced by Bok and others (Bok, 1999), the focus has been on the social consequences of such deceits for those institutions charged with and assumed to be honest and faithful in meeting their official mandates. As Chapter 1 recounts, there are sizable consequences for individuals, relationships, and the organizations themselves. Chapters 2 and 3 alert us to the crucial sociological questions of variation by context. If there are deleterious consequences, then under what conditions—here time and geography—are they higher or lower?

Success in gaining from the deceits of hypocrisy (or through avoiding an unmasking) depends on the ability to control outside access to the accurate knowledge. Concomitantly, the success of uncovering the deceits would—so security services contend—come from the ability to detect the concealed information and challenge the suspect claims of public actors. This was the focus of Chapter 4.

In this chapter, consequences and context are joined somewhat differently. If there are consequences as described in Chapter 1, and they are variably concealed and detected depending on the relative success of the respective information technologies involved, are there prospects for a *general* attenuation of aspirations toward fidelity and a growing cynicism by consumers over whether to expect fidelity of sports and religious figures? The cases of the Tour de France charges and the Hillsborough revelations open up prospects of a general lack of constraints on acts of hypocrisy and perhaps a lessening of public surprise when the acts of deceit are discovered. Sadly, this reduction of surprise may align with a net reduction of trust in these and related institutions, as considered in Chapter 6.

The Cases in Detail

The Tour de France Since 1999

An overview article in *The New York Times* places the revelations from Floyd Landis and Lance Armstrong at the end of 2012 in some cultural context: "Since 1998, more than a third of the top finishers of the Tour de France have admitted to using performance enhancing drugs in their careers or have been officially linked to doping."[14] Depictions of the riders follows, with representations of those within

---

14   *The New York Times*, October 10, 2012. Updated, *The New York Times*, January 24, 2013. The United States Anti-Doping Agency published their "Reasoned Decision of the United States Anti-Doping Agency on Disqualification and Ineligibility" on October 10, 2012. The report confirmed the promised sanctions of Lance Armstrong, made in an August 24, 2012 letter stipulating a lifetime competitive ban against Armstrong. Travis T. Tygart's announcement of the report describes over 1000 pages of evidence used in the report, and testimony of 26 individuals, including 15 riders. Journalistic coverage was broad and immediate. Examples include articles by Jerè Longman (Longman, October 10,

the top ten of the 15 races provided (and those with sanctions dropped blacked out.). The collage offers an economical view of a culture of bending the event's rules. The following table illustrates the density of violators in the event from 1998 through 2012.

Table 5.1   Rule violators among top-ten placers, 1998–2012 Tours

Race Placement	Number over Period
1st Place	12
2nd	6
3rd	9
4th	4
5th	7
6th	6
7th	4
8th	6
9th	6
10th	2

Both the stories of Floyd Landis and Lance Armstrong have played out broadly in popular media since 2010, with Landis effectively re-writing his vigorous protestations of innocence with regard to his 2006 ban from the Tour in *Positively False: The Real Story of How I Won the Tour de France* (Landis, Mooney, 2007). Armstrong has admitted to reporters that he is not now defending his innocence of doping since 1999, but he continues to engage reporting and public opinion in efforts to alter the valence of rule breakage or reframe its meaning. Landis continues his enterprise, seemingly on two connected fronts. He, on one hand, claims he wants "to come clean" about his past sins in biking by revealing what he and others did. But he also is in trouble with the law on a contingency basis. He must pay back funds given to him for his essentially fraudulent defense, or he risks imprisonment. He has elected one medium to raise money (elaborated below) by claiming to reveal Armstrong's and other Tour officials' culpability,

---

2012) and Juliet Macur (October 10, 2012). Both articles refer to a multimedia display of rider disqualifications among the top ten place winners of the Tour from 1998–2012. An article and pictorial by Alan McLean, Archie Tse, and Lisa Waananen (on January 24, 2013) provide what they describe as an updated accounting of these disqualifications. The distribution occurs in the table. They cite their sources as: the United States Anti-Doping Agency, Court of Arbitration for Sport, International Cycling Union, French Agency for the Fight Against Doping, Amaury Sport Organization, news agencies and European news reports. In the 2013 and 2014 Tours no disqualifications have occurred within the top three general classifications riders as of the time of the 2015 event.

under a "whistleblower" law that can give him a percentage of money recovered from Armstrong in promised Federal prosecutions. In February 2013, the US Federal government joined Landis' whistleblower law suit.

Floyd Landis

The contribution of Floyd Landis' career to the account here begins with the attribution by the public and peers of athletic respect. On a late mountain stage of the 2004 Tour de France, Floyd Landis was supporting Lance Armstrong at the front of the peloton as they came over the Col de la Croix-Fry. Landis had driven the pace for a small group of competitors along with Armstrong. As a gesture of respect, Armstrong suggested that Landis push down the nine mile descent toward Le Grand Bornand (the end of the stage which began in Le Bourg-d'Oisans) to claim a victory for the stage. Despite Landis' efforts, he gave way to two competitors in the break and Armstrong won. With this finish for a *domestique* in the stage, and 23rd overall in that Tour, this represented a turning point for Landis as he moved into position to be named a leading rider on a team. As the leader of the Phonak Hearing Systems team in 2005, Landis finished 9th overall in the Tour, the last of Armstrong's seven victories in the event.

This respect hit a high point with his miraculous win in 2006—but the regard was followed by Landis' immediate suspension. Landis sustained a hip injury during a training ride in 2002, and this debility continued to be evident in races through 2006, with pain, a gradual shortening of the leg, and the need eventually for prescribed (and legal) cortisone shots. In September 2007, he received a new hip for the deterioration. He was leading the Tour de France of 2006 into the 16th Stage. In the last ten kilometers continuing through a series of mountain stages, he "cracked" and lost touch with the leaders. The stage up to the summit of La Tousiere in the Alps, was won by Michael Rasmusson, a Dane, and Landis dropped to 11th position, 8'08" from the lead. Potentially, and apparently, having lost the race, the next day he made a remarkable comeback—which put him into position to win the race, with a performance which became the basis of his disqualification from the 2006 event. From that point, he pursued a strategy of denying that he used prohibited drugs, wrote the book defending his activity, and remained true to his claim until May 20, 2010 when he admitted use of banned supplements during his career. His case had been arbitrated by a USADA panel and eventually by a committee of the Court of Arbitration for Sport. In succession they found him guilty, and he was banned from cycling until January 2009.

A consequence of first the success and then the ignominy of disqualification prompted a type of moral crusade by Landis beginning in 2007. Following the initial ruling that suspended Landis and the decision by the appeal board, Landis spent time appealing his case in the public domain. (as noted, steps that included *Positively False*, 2007). The caveat at the beginning of the book is instructive: "This book is a memoir. It reflects my present recollections of my experiences over a period of years, as well as information from interviews and other research performed by Loren Mooney. Conversations and events have been recounted to evoke one or more participants' recollections of what was said or what occurred, but are not intended to be a perfect representation" (Landis, 2007: i).

Consequences come from acts of deceit, and these are evident in the continuation of the Landis story. These include suicide, divorce, retraction, and recuperation. Once Landis admitted to drug use in 2010, a number of implications of deceit, at least from his marred 2006 victory in the Tour de France, emerged. A close friend, David Witt, had committed suicide in 2006 (acknowledged by Landis as possibly linked to his own dishonesty). Mr Witt had married the mother of the woman Landis married in 2001, Amber Basile. Landis' own marriage to Amber ended in divorce in 2009.

In 2009, Landis had been convicted of false appropriation of funds. The funds had been secured for his defense of his innocence. Once the suspensions were followed by the admission of guilt, then the reason for the request for legal funds became illegal. The court in its holding deferred to the priority of repayment as opposed to imprisonment. If Landis would repay the donors, then the jail time would be waived.

At least one strategy to recoup needed funds was to enter a whistleblower suit in 2010, accusing the Discovery Team of which he was a part of receiving illegal funds from the United States Postal Service. In this suit, invoking provisions of the False Claims Act, he could receive 10 percent of the recovered proceeds. The suit was sealed initially, but it became unsealed, and in March 2013 the Department of Justice joined the suit. Such suits can be focused on recovering three times the original contested amount, so the stakes rose from \$31 million to \$93 million. The record shows that the likelihood of success in such suits elevates to 80 percent if the government becomes involved. In this instance the claim is that the cycling team illegally asked for and received support from the US Postal Service for \$31 million during the years that they funded the team. Landis could receive as much as 10 percent of the amount recovered.

Lance Armstrong
The accounts of the early racing career of Lance Armstrong often start on Stage 15 of the 1995 Tour de France. During that portion of the event, Favio Casartelli shot across a turn on the descent of the Ponten d'Aspet, crashed, and died from head injuries. The following day of the Tour was neutralized when the competitors rode together and finished *en masse* in Pau (a stage subsequently officially cancelled). The competition began the following day with Eric Zabel winning Stage 17. In Stage 18, Lance Armstrong broke from the field in the stage running from Montpon-Ménestérol to Limoges, winning his second stage of his Tour de France career (his first in the 1993 event). His image of raised arms and fingers pointing toward the heavens to recognize his Motorola Team comrade, Fabio Casartelli, opened his world recognition as a dominant figure in the Tour.

In the 2013 "testimony" of Lance Armstrong within a highly public medium in the United States in an interview with Oprah Winfrey, Armstrong discusses two crises in his life: the life-time disqualification, which is the center of the

Oprah interview, and, earlier, his illness and recovery. Armstrong rose high in the international cycling world by 1996, being ranked the number one cyclist in the world. He was the first American to win the Fleche Wallone, was a member of the 1996 Olympic, and signed with a new team, Cofdis. He started the 1996 Tour de France as a moderate favorite but dropped out after the 5th Stage due to illness. He was diagnosed with testicular cancer in October, 1996. After what has been recognized as a series of remarkable surgeries and aggressive treatments and dangerous therapy, he was judged cancer-free by February, 1997. An important book, *It Is Not about the Bike* (Armstrong and Jenkins, 2000), described the harrowing and courageous displays of the patient and his doctors. At the height of a reputation for both being a superior athlete and remarkable cancer survivor, he started the Lance Armstrong Foundation in 1997 with the purpose of providing support for cancer survivors.

Philanthropy and conjectures about morality combine with the athletic trajectory of Armstrong. The "Livestrong" brand emerged in 2003, to give more generality to the original Lance Armstrong Foundation, with a mission "to inspire and empower" cancer survivors. Following the USADA actions against Armstrong, the Lance Armstrong Foundation title was changed to the Livestrong Foundation in November 2012. Armstrong resigned from being chair and then fully from the foundation. No immediate effect occurred on the giving to the Foundation, with $33.8 million given through September 30, 2012, which is an increase of 5.4 percent over 2011. Over the history of the foundation, $500 million has been raised.[15]

---

15   This question of a negative "fallout" in contributions from Armstrong's, Landis', and Hamilton's deceits is an important consequence. Regarding Armstrong, Livestrong Foundation (formerly Lance Armstrong Foundation) was founded in 1997 to provide support for persons affected by cancer. Following the series of censures of Armstrong, he resigned as chair of the foundation in October 2012 and from the board of directors the next month, and the organization made the name change at that time. "Figures provided by the foundation to the ESPN media organization, in October 2012, reveal that, despite the 2012 Armstrong doping controversy, revenues were up 2.1 percent to US $33.8 million, through September 30, 2012—according to ESPN, this total represents a 5.4 percent increase from 2011, with a 5.7 percent increase in the average dollar amount of those donations (from US $74.99 in 2011 to US $79.15 in 2012). Over the duration of its existence, the foundation has generated more than US$500 million worth of funds. The foundation, though, has revealed that its 2013 budget is 10.9 percent less than its 2012 budget" (in Wikipedia). Floyd Landis started a foundation, Floyd Landis Foundation, located in Lincolnshire, Il 60069 with the objective: "To support research for the treatment and prevention of degenerative arthritis, artificial joint replacement and the funding of treatment for individuals, including disadvantaged youths, suffering from the condition." According to GuideStar, which monitors non-profit organizations, the Foundation is not registered with the IRS. In the fiscal year starting on Jan 1, 2007 revenue was $16,598 and expenses were $17,208. In *The Secret Race* (2012) Hamilton mentions an organization he founded, Tyler Foundation, Inc.

Despite the component of philanthropy within Armstrong's career, a long legal war against him and his team occurred. The United States Anti-Doping Agency (Claimant) released their condemnation against Lance Armstrong (Respondent) in October 2012: *Reasoned Decision of the United States Anti-Doping Agency on Disqualification and Ineligibility.* The report disqualifies him from Olympic sports for life. The substance from an array of Armstrong's associates who were witnesses against him and a summary of investigative tests proceeds backward from the most recent evidence from 2012 through his competitions in 1999. Most expansive in the conclusions is taking away his seven Tour de France championships from the first in 1999 through 2005.

The Anti-Doping Agency "caught" Armstrong; not uncommonly for people in such circumstances he attempted, with his personal history of acute competitiveness, to escape the judgment. What do we do when caught in a lie or deviant acts when our response may be different depending upon the weight of evidence arrayed against us? Is it different depending upon our real or imagined sense of power and perhaps possession of moral currency? The response over the past year by Mr Armstrong lies on an imagined continuum, but not a predictable location.

First, affected parties acted immediately on the report. Nike, a longtime associate of Armstrong dropped him immediately. Armstrong did step down from his post as chairman of Livestrong, and on November 4, 2012 he resigned from the board of governors of the organization. In October, the International Cycling Union, which traditionally can struggle to retain the rights of governance in such matters, indicated it would not appeal the ruling by the USADA which would have been to the Court of Arbitration for Sport. The UCI, under its own auspices, stripped Armstrong of his seven Tour titles.

Mr Armstrong's response since October 2012 to the report and the confirmation of its rulings has been enigmatic. As Juliet Macur of *The New York Times* reported in a series of articles (subsequently compiled in *Cycle of Lies*, 2014) the progression of a kind of prolonged resistance ebbing into an acquiescence to the charges. Armstrong's legal team from June through the summer of 2012 sought to exclude Armstrong from the sanctions and also to try to discredit USADA. Armstrong in August dropped his formal fight against the USADA (expressed most fully by Macur, 2014). He did in a meeting with officials of the USADA (December 14, 2012; Macur, 2014: 382 ff.) make an effort to broker a deal of providing information on drug use and in return receive a reduction in the length of his disqualifications. (Subsequent meetings to proceed in the brokerage did not occur.) In news of an interview to be screened on the Oprah Winfrey show in January 2013, Armstrong admitted his doping. But his ambivalence (or machinations) have continued as Macur has described (2014: "Epilogue").

System of Hypocrisy in the Tour de France

The Organizational Imperative

Cycling is organized into teams, cycling unions, national and international judicatories, and event sponsors. In the case of Tour de France athletes, each contributes to appropriate conduct and may induce and sustain rule deviance. Lance Armstrong's first professional team was Motorola which he joined in 1992, with whom he competed in the 1992 Tour de France. He did not complete the event that year. After several successful performances in races, he joined the French team, Cofdis in 1996. In quick succession of his signing, he was diagnosed with testicular cancer, requiring surgery. Following the testicular surgery, brain tumors required removal. He was declared cancer free in 1997.

His salary at Cofdis had been $600,000, but they dropped him from the agreement after his cancer exposure; he signed with the United States Postal Service team for $200,000. The Discovery Channel Pro Cycling Team took over sponsorship of the US Postal team, which had been in existence since 1996, in 2004. They competed until 2007, when Tailwind Sports the license holder of the team ended sponsorship.

The competitors in professional cycling are organized within a professional union, Union Cyclist Internationale (UCI), founded in 1900. Each country with riders competing in international events sustains a cycling organization, such as USA Cycling in the US, in France (Fédération Française de Cyclisme), and in Italy (Federazione Ciclistica Italiana). The first national expression of a unified sport was the Amateur Bicycle League of America (1920, which changed its name to the United States Cycling Federation in 1995). A complementary entity, USA Cycling, developed in 1995, and the two streams of organizational development united as USA Cycling in 1995.

As evidence has emerged about rule infractions in the form of illegal use of drugs in high-profile races, monitoring bodies have emerged internationally such as the World-Anti Doping Agency (WADA) established in 1999 and nationally, as in the United States Anti-doping Agency (USADA) established in 2000.

The Tour de France event first occurred in 1903, as a medium to increase circulation of a news medium, *L'Auto*. Since that time, the continuous support of the event, excluding the years of the two world wars, has come from news agencies. Organizationally now, the Société de La Tour de France is part of the Amaury Sport Organization (ASO), which sponsors several large sport events including the Tour. The ASO lies within the larger communications organization, Editions Philippe Amaury, which publishes *Le Parisien* and *L'Equipe*.

A final layer of organization may be a Federal government. After the hiatus of the Tour between WWI and WWII, the French government considered itself the "franchise-holder" of the event and took steps to assign it to an elect entity. The United States Congress periodically has held hearings about illegal drug use in sports.

Once discovered, individual and institutional actors take steps to account for, explain, or neutralize their deceits. The form that these narratives take instruct us about prevailing norms within a context and within a particular time. Marvin Scott and Stanford Lyman's classic "Accounts" (1968) provides a vocabulary and analytical suggestions for linking the efforts of individuals and organizations to reconcile themselves to the expectations of the wider institutional order.[16] The statements of Lance Armstrong—over a period of many years—both in kind and in variability provide illustration within the Tour de France event. Similar efforts at reconciliation with social expectations when sanctioned for use of prohibited drugs in the Tour de France occur with Floyd Landis, an apparent winner of the 2006 event who, as described, was disqualified and Tyler Hamilton who was induced to admit to illegal drug use within several events, including the Olympic Games.

Armstrong, Landis, et al. Maintain the Normalcy of Lying

Armstrong
The fact of Armstrong's near-miraculous cancer, his strong cycling performances following his re-entry into elite events, and the positive attention paid his philanthropy, Livestrong, created a sympathetic atmosphere among the public and media. He was accused many times of PED use. For a long period of time, his posture was one of *denial* while invoking the negative findings of tests.

After being stripped of his seven Tour titles, in the fall of 2012 Armstrong admitted doping while cycling, a posture which might be one of *admission as charged*. Following his admission of using PEDs, three lawsuits surfaced based on the admission. One of these included claims for repayment of an award from an insurance company made to Armstrong on the basis of his false claim of not using drugs in the 1999, 2000, and 2001 Tours. A second sought damages for his falsely endorsing a nutritional supplement. The third, initiated by Floyd Landis, is a whistleblower suit now sustained by the US Federal government on the basis of defrauding the US Postal Service. Armstrong's legal defense against the whistleblower law suit is a combination of the justifications of denial of injury, denial of victim, and of condemning the condemner. He has said that the US Federal government received value from his performances (albeit subsequently

---

16 "An account is a linguistic device employed whenever an action is subjected to valuative inquiry" (Scott and Lyman, 1968: 46). "*Excuses* are socially approved vocabularies for mitigating or relieving responsibility when conduct is questioned" (ibid., 47, italics in original). These include: "… *appeal to accidents, appeal to defeasibility, appeal to biological drives, and scapegoating*" (ibid., italics in original). "… *justifications* are socially approved vocabularies that neutralize an act or its consequences when one or both are called into question" (ibid., 51, italics in original). However, "… to *justify* an act is to assert its positive value in the face of a claim to the contrary" (ibid., italics in original). "Relevant to [Scott and Lyman's] discussion of justification are the techniques of 'denial of injury,' 'denial of victim,' 'condemnation of condemners,' and 'appeal to loyalties'" (ibid.).

deemed illegal) because the US Postal Service received valuable publicity, which was what they wanted. Further, he has claimed that the US Postal Service is at fault for not detecting the fact that Armstrong was using prohibited drugs in the events.

A further line of justification is in the form of "everybody was doing it, therefore I had to do it." Here the neutralization efforts use both the condemnation of the condemners (referring now to other riders) and appeals to loyalty (the durability of omerta, again). The implications he has drawn, even though his victories in the Tour de France have been vacated, are that on the basis of the generality of use he remains the winner of those events, and the winner of the most Tour competitions.

Floyd Landis

Landis appeared to win the 2006 Tour de France. Urine samples provided by his team, Phonak, proved positive for an elevated rate of testosterone. He was disqualified from the race in August. The ultimate determination had to come from USA Cycling, and they asked USADA to determine the case. On a vote of 2 to 1 on September 2006, the disqualification was upheld, and he was banned from cycling for two years. Landis appealed to the Court of Arbitration of sport which upheld the USADA ruling. A subsequent effort by Landis in US Federal court to throw the CAS decision ended in both parties agreeing to dismiss the case. Landis pressed his case of his innocence with a book written with Loren Mooney, *Positively False: the Real Story of How I Won the Tour de France* (2007).

During the period of claiming his innocence, he sought to raise money from potential donors to his legal defense, termed the "Floyd Fairness Fund." Since he was disqualified from the sport on the basis of his involvement with doping, Federal prosecutors in the United States claimed his request for funds were made under false pretenses. Landis and the prosecutors on August 24, 2012 deferred prosecution depending on his paying restitution to donors who gave him money to defend himself—even though his claim to innocence was fraudulent.[17]

In May 2010, Landis altered his statements on drug use, admitting to both organizers of cycling and anti-doping groups that he had used drugs from June 2002 through the 2006 Tour de France. He has made allegations of drug use by Lance Armstrong and other cyclists, and accused the director of the US Postal Team of trying to cover up positive drug tests for Armstrong. Further marking his movement away from his claim of innocence of using drugs, Landis has included Armstrong in his whistle blower lawsuit stating that Armstrong's drug use during the sponsorship by US Postal Service cycling teams represented a defrauding of the US Federal government. US prosecutors have entered this law suit.

Tyler Hamilton as a further representation

Tyler Hamilton was on the US Postal Team in 1999, 2000, 2001, during the first three wins by Lance Armstrong. He had considerable reputational currency within

---

17 The amount demanded of Landis, as of August 2012, was $478,000 in restitution following his admission of fraud (*VeloNews*, 2012).

the sport for his substantial support of Armstrong in major races and for his own reluctance to accommodate to injuries (He raced with a fractured shoulder in the Giro D'Ialia in 2002, and he competed with a cracked collarbone in the 2003 Tour de France.). He was accused of blood doping or illegal drug use during his career. His win of a gold medal in the 2004 Olympics was questioned from a drug doping test. Because there was not a confirming test from another sample, he was permitted to keep the medal. Several suspensions followed, and in 2010 he admitted illegal use of blood doping and drug use over his career; he returned the Olympic medal to the USADA, and in August 10, 2012, the International Olympic Committee took the medal away.

Mr Hamilton through most of his career denied illegal supplement use, or through his lawyers argued for anomalies in the tests or procedures. As with Armstrong and Landis, he later changed his story and admitted the infractions. Is there an excuse? With Hamilton there is broadly a book-length "contextualization." He does provide a form of excuse in *The Secret Race* (Hamilton and Coyle, 2012). Basically he appeals to readers with the plaint: "If you had been in my position, wouldn't you have done the same thing?"[18]

------

18 Confederates who share a lie find their relationships corrode when one wants to divulge the deceit and another does not. Such has been the case for Armstrong and Hamilton, who once were teammates and close friends, and in the relationship between Armstrong and Landis, where the relationship was affable and now is bitter. Daniel Coyle notes the separation Hamilton felt, once he had described his drug use whilst Armstrong continued to deny his own: "Hamilton sometimes expressed fear that Armstrong and his powerful friends would act against him, but he never expressed any hatred for Armstrong. 'I can feel for Lance,' Hamilton said. 'I understand who he is, and where he is. He made the same choice we all made, to become a player. Then he started winning the Tour and it got out of control, and the lies got bigger and bigger. Now he has no choice. He has to keep lying to keep trying to convince people to move on. He can't go back. He can't tell the truth. He's trapped'" (Hamilton and Coyle, 12).

Hamilton records a bitter exchange at an Aspen restaurant following Hamilton's interview on 60 minutes which aired on May 22, 2011, where Hamilton spoke of the team's drug use. In this account, Armstrong was alerted to come to a restaurant where Hamilton was eating with friends, and there confronted, provoked, and threatened Hamilton (pp. 254–61 in Hamilton and Coyle). The storied break between Armstrong and Becky Andreu in a hospital room in 1996 occurred over Andreu's remembrance of doctors discussing EPO use with Armstrong, and he from that point denying the admission and indeed the conversation ever having taken place at all. Hamilton's own retrospective can be seen in contrast with a different time. His, the retrospective after revelations of drug use in 2011; but here is a considerably different remembrance as the Postal Service was set to start its run of Tour victories starting in 1999. "It may not look like it, but bike racing is the quintessential team sport. The leader stands on the shoulders of his teammates—called *domestiques*, servants—who use their strength to shelter him from the headwind, set the pace, chase down attacks, and deliver water and food. Then, just out of sight, there is a second level of *domestiques*: the team director, the *soigneurs*, the mechanics, the drivers, the interconnected grid of people who are essentially doing the same thing. Every race is an

The Consequences of Hypocrisy: Inside and Outside the System

Those who become aware of deceptions and inconsistencies such as those of Armstrong, Landis, and Hamilton as well as others in the sport can themselves neutralize them with disinterest or by attaching some form of recompense from the athlete, or their own, to the act. So, the crucial question within the commitments of this book: what are the social consequences?

At a personal, social psychological level the marriages of all three ended in divorce during the deliberations with cycling and legal authorities. This may, of course, be purely coincidental. Floyd Landis' father in law and close personal friend, David Witt, committed suicide in August 2006. Landis in later years surmised that the death was partially caused by his own implication in the use of illegal drugs.[19]

The legacy of Armstrong and Landis included incorporation of philanthropic organizations, Livestrong in the case of Armstrong and the Floyd Landis Foundation in the case of Landis. Livestrong asked Armstrong to end association with the charity, and it appears to have been unaffected by the notoriety of Armstrong's censures. The Landis foundation never did have a durable record of gifts. Armstrong's continuing legal cases are potentially costly for his personal fortune. The government case to retrieve funds fraudulently given to the US Postal Service includes as defendants Johan Bruyneel and the team owing the cycling team as well as Armstrong, and could go as high as $90 million, with Armstrong being the most damaged. Estimates place Landis' legal bills to defend himself at $2 million, with $1 million raised for which he is liable in his Federal case. So, as noted, he must repay these contributions.

Broad public news coverage about drug use in the event occurred with the raid on drug providers at the start of the 1998 Tour. Commonly for publically supported sporting events, claims of cheating or mis-management bring efforts from new agencies and governmental entities to detect, deter, and to penalize such rule violations. WADA, USADA, efforts by the French national government, and occasional efforts by the US legislature represent such consequences.

Two remaining recipients of deceit of athletes include the result for the public reception of the event, and reactions of constituencies that have benefitted from the successes of the athletes such as philanthropic organizations. Armstrong, Landis, and Hamilton all started organizations intended to provide philanthropic services. In the cases of Penn State and the Roman Catholic Church, charges of lying by organizationally important persons had a negative effect on income generation,

---

exercise in cooperation—which means that when it goes well, it creates a kind of high like I've never felt anywhere else a feeling of connectedness and brotherhood. All for one, one for all" (Hamilton and Coyle, 2012: 78).

19 Armstrong divorce in 2003 (Wikipedia, 2015); Hamilton divorce in 2008 (Hamilton and Coyle, 2012); Landis divorce in 2009 (*Gather*, 2015); Witt suicide from self-inflicted handgun on August 15, 2006 (Wikipedia, 2015).

and may have had an effect in consumption of the sports product or support of the institution in the form of attendance at sponsored events. GuideStar reports this foundation filed an IRS Form 990 2004. The organization, with a physical address of Boulder, Colorado 80304, lists no recent revenues or expenses, and has not filed pertinent IRS forms recently. In October 26, 2004 the Foundation announced the believetyler.org, with the goals of Hamilton of: reach the podium, to win a Gold Medal, to cure MS, and to change the face of US Cycling. The new foundation was affected by the drug finding following the 2004 Olympic victory. Internet news still records some activity for the Foundation, continuing to be located in Boulder, Colorado. In a footnote on p. 227, Hamilton says his Foundation closed in 2008 (Hamilton and Coyle, 2012).

The popularity of the Tour as measured by US TV viewership seems to depend less on taint from the drug scandals than on the specific presence of Lance Armstrong during his participation in the event. However, recent general popularity continues high as indicated by viewership figures in 2013. Eurosport (owned by France's TF1 Group and Discovery Communications) claimed 17.1 million viewers for the early stages of the 2013 Tour, a 50 percent jump from the same period the previous year, and the highest figure since 2007. NBC Sports Network recorded 560,000 viewers for the last stage of the 2013 event, in their rendering an increase of 67 percent for that stage from the previous year.

Lying and the personal efforts of concealment and deflection may lead to decrease of loyalty to friends. In *The Secret Race*, Hamilton recounts a conversation with Armstrong during a 2004 Tour stage, after Landis has told Hamilton about Armstrong's divulging to the UCI Hamilton's use of drugs (Hamilton and Coyle, 211, 212). Is it the case that liars are inclined to label other people as deceitful, following accusations made about themselves? Also, if one is lying then the worry about being caught can be an extremely heavy burden (Hamilton and Coyle, 214). Additionally, there appears to be a certain social psychology when caught: they do not confess because they do not consider themselves to have cheated. Also, there is worry about how others will be adversely affected, and this is a deterrent against being truthful (Hamilton and Coyle, 223; further enumeration of deterrents to telling the truth). In Hamilton and Coyle's summarization: "You realize you have been sacrificed to keep the circus going; you're the reason they can pretend they're clean. You're alone and the only way back is to spend years and hundreds of thousands of dollars on lawyers so that you can, if you're lucky, grovel your way back to rejoining that same messed-up world that chucked you out in the first place" (Hamilton and Coyle, 226). In Hamilton's recounting, Pantini, Jakshe, Landis, Ullrich, and other storied riders, had a bad reaction to being "popped." Hamilton said his legal bills reached 1 million dollars in the 2004 cases (Hamilton and Coyle, 228). Once somebody on the Tour has been caught, other riders make them outcasts (Hamilton and Coyle, 236, 237). Hypocrites may believe they are right for so long that they may appear never quite to understand that they have lied and are culpable. This can yield to a kind of permanent barrier of ever being able to be honest and see the world as it is. The consequences for trust for alternative theories about the viable prospects for integrity and trust in human societies receive attention, as noted before, in the final two chapters of the book.

The normative system within which riders, coaches, and oversight groups in the Tour live within and contribute to has been one of lies. As the beginning of this chapter describes for this event, this normative system (to use standard sociological terminology) is a cycle of lies (Macur), conspiracy (Albergotti and O'Connell), or machine (Hamilton and Coyle), to use more evocative terminology, which constrains behaviors of members and requires collective participation of members in sustaining the system. Lies of concealment are told and lived and then concealed (dissimulation); lies of fabrication are told and lived (simulation). The essentials of hypocrisy exist. What the journalistic accounts, along with the legal depositions, show, and what has effect on biographies is that maintaining a lie requires some special contrivances in comparison to the management of hypocrisy within the Penn State case and some of the Roman Catholic Church cases described.

In hypocrisy, one may or may not recognize the contradictions evident in one's behavior. The variable of exigency, though, elevates not only the predisposition to lie but also the salience of lies we are calling hypocritical. The use of the term to condemn a competitor is a technique available as well as the array of excuses and justifications that Scott and Lyman list as available to human actors (Scott and Lyman, 1968). The very strength of exigency from Shklar, though, may lead to the grim acknowledgement of personal accountability from hypocrisy that requires self-destructive acts. The self-awareness and possibly the associated self-destructiveness may come from a variety of sources such as an alternative loyalty, publication, or the demand for disclosure from an instituted authority.

Riders in the Tour are socialized into the system through education, and with enumeration of member obligations to maintain the system (cycle, conspiracy, machine). The substance being maintained itself is dishonest, so this is why the demands for maintaining the system eventually turn out not to be sustainable. Comparing the before period and the after period of the June 2012 fulcrum clearly attributes culpability to Armstrong (Figure 5.1). The difficulties in continuing the deceitful system appear.

The Hillsborough Tragedy: Good/Bad Cops, Bad/Good Fans

Strange things happen at sporting events. The average attendance at one of the larger football stadia in the US, the University of Michigan, is over 100,000 fans. Just in the small range of time in focus in the report reviewed here (considerable background of course, but principally coverage for the most part between 2011 and 2015), a fan has fallen from an upper deck ("Fan Falls …," 2013), fans have been married in a parking lot ("A Wedding Fit for Ducks …," 2015), and a couple has been observed in sexual congress by thousands of fans in Yankee stadium ("Quite a Show …," 2012). The University of Iowa, the University of Michigan, and Bever Stadium of Penn State University compare with small cities. Over the course of a contest which may last three hours, a wide range of humorous, conflict-ridden, annoying, and sometimes tragic events occur. The average attendance at a major league baseball game such as with the Chicago Cubs at Wrigley Field (32,589 in 2013) or Yankee Field (40,489 in 2013), would comprise smaller sized towns. But this group of people at these athletic events come together in an emotionally charged setting. This is to say emphatically, that within the elation, aesthetic wonder, surprise, and sadness associated with watching a sporting event, life can display distributions of occurrences not unlike non-sporting life. The whole range of experiences, good and bad, occur. This would be expected in any demographic concentration of the respective sizes mentioned here as illustrations.

Along with this emphatic acknowledgement, however, the vast record year by year, sport by sport, and, if one is candid, the whole sequence of one's own experience with sport is that sport provides a singular experience of joy, relaxation, excitement, and unalloyed fun. This is, as the terminology of the previous chapters and here convey, the "normal state of affairs" for sporting events. Anticipation is high, emotion is high, customary worries about eating and drinking and appropriate decorum may be relaxed. But—with the definition of sport as intrinsic, physical, rule governed, and consummative—we as players or fans want to be there with a vengeance and do not want to be anywhere else. This normative frame of anticipation and levity and, importantly, a "time out" from all outside the frame is so crucial in order fully to understand the Hillsborough soccer tragedy. An important record of this frame comes to us now about many groups of people attending the soccer game in April 1989.

On May 11, 1985, 56 soccer fans attending a league match between Bradford City FC and Lincoln City FC died due to a fire that started five minutes before half time. The fire most likely started from a match or cigarette dropped beneath the stands which ignited rubbish long-accumulated under the seating area. On May 29, 1985, at Heysel Stadium just before the European Cup final between Juventus and Liverpool, a rush of spectators grew into an uncontrolled stampede which led to the death of 39 fans (32 from Italy, four from Belgium, two from France, and one from Northern Ireland). On April 15, 1989 just before an FA Cup semifinal match started between Liverpool and Nottingham Forest at the neutral Hillsborough Stadium in Sheffield, England, a crush of fans developed as groups moved erratically into viewing sites and 96 people died.

Such events had occurred before in the UK, such as the Bolton Disaster where 33 people died at an FA Cup match and the 1971 Ibrox Disaster when 66 people died at the end of a Rangers-Celtic game. Contemporary soccer fans may view such events as somewhat ordinary, when hearing of violent episodes at the end of a February 2013 soccer match in Port Said between the home Al-Masry and Cairo's Al-Ahlya, where 74 spectators died. Short of participating in such events, and similar ones, or being drawn in by accident of location, it is not easy to contemplate with one's mind and emotional stocks what takes place. Some war experiences are similar, as are public protest incidents or purposive marches where marchers are attacked viciously by police or military authorities.

The Hillsborough incident, news of which re-surfaced on September 12, 2012—23 years after the deaths in 1989—with the publication of a report of the Hillsborough Independent Panel carries special import in this project. The length of time that elapsed before some extraordinary effort was made to clarify the event coincides with the perplexing delays associated with the controversy surrounding abuse by clerics in the Catholic Church, the Tour de France controversies, and the Penn State scandal. And the events now arranged in something approaching a complete overview in the panel's report display, again, how parties to an initial malfeasance, or breach of law, or dishonorable act may continue to exhaustion, to make reputational appeals to "the court of public opinion."

A central theme of assessments of the acts of hypocrisy is to describe consequences, as has been stressed in the program of the book. The consequences for many levels of society in the cases of Chapters 1 and 2, with focus on priest abuses and illegal conduct by Sandusky at Penn State University (and at least tacit acquiescence on the part of administrators), are fairly clear-cut. The cases of Floyd Landis, Lance Armstrong, and the prototypes that follow, such as Hamilton, and the apparent police cover-up in Hillsborough are less immediately evident in their social consequences. Enumerating these when they exist is important. But as important is the issue of working through long periods in which principals changed their minds about their culpability (partially as a result not of personal moral compunctions but external discoveries and potential penalties). If figures lie, often hypocritically in their failure to disclose or their claim of moral purity, if there are no ready victims how do we assess the consequences? Does not the possibility exist that the actors are presuming on a kind of moral thinness in the structure of society such that ultimately in their "appeal to the public" they will be absolved by public opinion? Here, the assumption of such actors is that trust for veracity of sports and religious figures is so tenuous anyway that violations of such low levels of trust really are not too serious.

An analysis of the social organization components of deceit, acquiescence, detection, and consequences—that is to say, the sociology of hypocrisy—here becomes complex. But at the same time the stakes for understanding how personal and institutional deceits can influence public trust become correspondingly dear. Who are the "public," and what can and should components of the public do to contribute proportionally to more honesty in sport and religion rather than diminishing amounts? The following are some players in the institutional arrangement, with a range of options available to them: media and, specifically, reporters on persons and events; insurers, and the most direct constituencies such as beneficiaries of philanthropic yields of sport figures, fans, and donors to philanthropic organizations associated with athletes' performances. The media, for example, are powerful contributors to the contexts surrounding deceits and the consequences of deceits. A continuous question about them tries to decide whether they are reporters of truth or confederates in deceit.

Phil Legitt and Paul Sherwin have long been associated with the world-wide television coverage of the Tour de France, and the subsequent production of video recordings of successive Tours through the summer of 2013. There are few reporters of any sport more knowledgeable, informed, and refined in their presentation of the event. In the 17th Stage of the 2005 Tour de France, they witnessed and duly reported on the singular breakaway of Floyd Landis. As reporters of an event they were variously attempting to be accurate to what they witnessed, brought to bear context to the effort, and sought to place the event within a long history of outstanding competitive performances. As the history of the event unfolded, they were reporting a large fraud as Landis was within a few days stripped of his victory, and after a long period of contestation, he was found in several judicatories not only to have used illegal drugs, but also to have defrauded supporters who had donated to his legal defense fund. In formal terms, what are consequences of a well-intended report by the most accomplished of sport reporters which in retrospect the truth of what they have reported has become compromised?

The debatable elements become more visible when sport spokespersons make their case to a "court of public opinion" through memorials and biographies. Such are the cases, for example, in the instances of Sally Jenkins assisting Lance Armstrong in the production of his first two books on his defeat of cancer and early success in the Tour, or Loren Mooney who co-wrote with Floyd Landis, *Positively False*, and Daniel Coyle, who co-wrote with Tyler Hamilton, *The Secret Race*. What is the analogy for the cooperation of journalists here? Is it the lawyer representing a client with no interest in the trustworthiness of the client? Is it as the centuries-old amanuensis? Or is the claim of identification with the sport figure, from exposure on dust jacket and inside title page as co-author, grounds for scrutiny when the story reported becomes challenged? If the credit as a traditional research document carries this journalist's work as co-equal, then is the culpability from the later admission of deceit shared? As opposed to the position that co-authors took with Lance Armstrong and Floyd Landis, other authors have assumed different identities with the Tour controversies since Armstrong's first victory in 1999.

Within an ostensive court of public opinion, if searching for criteria for documenting consequences or even negative consequences within sporting events one might look for audience response. Has attendance or television viewing been affected by the recent scandals of Armstrong, Landis, and others? With respect to physical viewership on the road during the 20 or 21 days of on-road competition during the 2013 Tour, no claim for a decrease has been made. Television viewership in the United States and in France appears to depend on the centrality of native contenders rather than challenges to the fairness of the race. Revenue production for causes from the activities of these sports figures receive impetus from the athletes' successes, and in the "court of public opinion" compromises of the athlete's moral coin may be in turn bolstered in varying degrees from the reputation of the particular foundations. As mentioned above, no immediate effect occurred on the giving to the Livestrong Foundation.

Two additional points of discussion that interested persons will debate concern consequences for how the event is contested, with the disqualifications and fines so visible recently for the Tour de France; and controversy over public protections that need to be exacted by institutions to guard against violators of event rules. On the first question, the effect on the racers' performances from a drug free event, calculations are precarious since each year the route alters so there is no standard -measured distance nor constant terrain from year to year. But, again, this is a domain for discussion for interested persons and journalists. The average speed for the race winner in 1903 was 25.7 km/hour. The top average speed occurred during Lance Armstrong's seventh victory in 2005, at 41.4 km/hour. The wining average speeds since, have been 40.8 km/hour (2006), 39.2 (2007), 40.5 (2008), 40.3 (2009), 39.6 (2010), 39.8 (2011), and 36.8 (2012). On the second question, before a "court of public opinion," can violations become so common as to be items of risk control by institutions and sponsoring organizations? On the manifest instance of a criminal act, such as with Sandusky at Penn State, the word of the insurance industry in the United States is that there is no insurance liability for illegal acts. Whether promoters such as Amaury are able to purchase insurance to cover breaches of event rules is an uncertain matter.

At the end of his third book covering Lance Armstrong and the Tour de France, the Scottish writer, David Walsh, announced with some finality that October 22, 2012 was the date USADA judged Armstrong complicit in a web of illegal drug use in cycling. In the report, Armstrong is stripped of his Tour titles and banned from participation for life in any sport overseen by the International Olympic Committee. Mr Walsh does not gloat in the evaluation, but journalist peers conveyed to him that the substance of the evidence from the 164-page (exclusive of appendices) report coincides closely with claims by Mr Walsh and his co-author in the first book, *LA Confidentiel* (with Pierre Ballester, 2004) and the often unpopular judgments Walsh was recording through Armstrong's seventh victory in 2005.

By the explicit definitions of hypocrisy emphasized in this project, Armstrong's continued pattern of hiding illegal behaviors and denying them fits. Trying to advance discussion of a larger effort of the book, to document consequences of hypocrisy, becomes difficult, though, despite justifying Armstrong's inclusion as an appropriate case for discussion. There are direct penalties affecting Armstrong, most directly the loss of approximately $500,000 for each of the seven Tour victories. Nike, among other major contributors to his career have cut him from their system of sponsorship. The United States Postal Service supported one of the teams he competed for during the years 1998–2004, and the US government now seeks return of some thirteen million dollars from him, Stapleton, and Johan Bruyneel the coach. The *Sunday Times of London* paid 300,000 pounds to Armstrong when his group sued for liability over a published summary of some of the offending claims from *LA Confidentiel*. The newspaper sought to recover this amount plus additional funds (estimated to be $1.6 million) for costs from Armstrong once the USADA confirmed much of Walsh's evaluation. The newspaper reported a confidential settlement on August 2013.

These are sizable monetary consequences for the individual. But, of course, if the seriousness of the cheating is evaluated in permanent, social terms one should expect broader institutional outcomes. Moving slowly beyond Armstrong himself, Walsh does mention principals in cycling and directly associated with Armstrong's team who earlier renounced the cycle of systematic drug use. Some, such as Emily O' Reilly, a trainer who had earlier quit and testified against the program might see some vindication in the October 22 end-point. Some cyclists from the Tour wrote books about their drug experiences, with degrees of reticence expressed over their personal usages of drugs. While these might be considered as evidence that the growing strength of investigations by judicatories into the deceits of the sport yielded the disclosures and some repentance, the books and recounting came after the authorities discovered the athletes' drug use and exacted penalties.

The point of the context of a sport or religious organization creating a frame of presupposition about practices, which may or not be wide of norms of honesty or fairness, cannot easily be assessed here when evaluating the consequences of actions against Armstrong. The event in its three-week continuation supports the largest group of fans of any sporting event in the world. Viewership on television and in person have continued at their high levels; newspaper coverage—which as noted has at times itself been a sponsor of the event—continues. Does the formal judgment that Armstrong and his team cheated over seven years and denied, falsely, doing so bring cynicism and departure from fans of the sport? The news coverage, world-wide daily viewership, and masses of people lining the roads around the course into Paris do not show this.

The frame of presupposition about rule compliance had always included the prospects of cheating since the event started in 1903 (Wieting, 2000). The large police raid on team trainers and on cyclists in 1998 could give fans reason for caution if enthusiasm depended on honesty and fidelity in the sport. But the rule infractions historically and the penalties and the 1998 discoveries seem either to be anticipated by fan presumptions or to be inconsequential in their loyalty to the event.

Chapter 7 considers three competing prospects for collective organizations. The stakes are high, because they in each case make claims about species characteristics and possibilities for trust among communities, at least within those whose essential character such as sport and religion presume trust. A few summary points can be made here in anticipation of the discussion later. In a Goffman-inspired approach, the norms of activity exist in a web of managed performances that maintain each other and in net create a semblance of order. The deviations within the Tour de France were not surprising since the rules to begin with are artifice; the only surprise is that a pattern of rule deviation did not last longer before detection and attempted resolution (which did, as noted, still take 13 years). Again, as anticipated in Chapter 1 and as will be discussed in Chapter 7, with Goffman, so long as artifice keeps the system running, there is not an immediate reason to alter the system.

In a conflict perspective where information is the capital of value, competition continues over the technology of concealment and the technology of detection and disclosure. In the Armstrong case, the battle was long and hugely costly for both the Armstrong groups and the USADA. But for the moment, at least, the detectors are ahead. There are symbolic gestures among athletes, team managers, and team owners that advocate the necessity, for the sport, of cooperative acquiescence to norms of fairness and honesty. For now, on those teams, they show heavy uses of external controls in the forms of tests to assure the desired end of a "clean" sport. But there are sports and varied cultural contexts that show realistic prospect for a third theoretical alternative, a contractual approach.

Institutional Imperatives, Deceitful Actions, and the Concept of Normalcy

In the cases of Penn State and the Roman Catholic Church, there is a personal departure from societal norms which is then deflected by the actor. The departure falls within consensual definitions of lying (Bok) and the condemnations of hypocrisy that exist in the sacred texts of the Bible and the Koran. Coupled with the initial acts, the records described here of institutional hiding and deflection of the information extend the wrong and may indeed contribute to the lists of negative consequences for the original actor, the organization itself in losses of monetary support, penalties, and even criminal sanctions.

The Normal within English Soccer: Alternatives Contend

Two intense descriptions of the Hillsborough events provide a clear juxtaposition of conclusions that can be dependent upon presuppositions of a normal state of affairs observed by different reporters. One lies in this statement by Bill Buford in his study of English supporters of football published in 1990. He writes: "Hillsborough: the most famous stadium in the world. What happened there confirmed something in me. There was something inevitable about the ninety-five dead, relentlessly overdue" (Buford, 1990).

A contrasting view comes from a recent article from a long-working commentator of the Hillsborough events, Phil Scraton:

> In April 1989, ninety-six men, women and children, supporters of Liverpool Football Club died in a severe crush at an FA Cup semi-final at Hillsborough Stadium, Sheffield. Hundreds were injured and thousands traumatized. Within hours, the causes and circumstances of the disaster were contested. While a judicial inquiry found serious institutional failures in the policing and management of the capacity crowd, no criminal prosecutions resulted, and the inquests returned 'accidental death' verdicts. Immediately, the authorities claimed that drunken, violent fans had caused the fatal crush. Denied legitimacy, survivors' accounts revealed a different story criticising the parlous state of the

stadium, inadequate stewarding, negligent policing, failures in the emergency response and flawed processes of inquiry and investigation (Scraton, 2013).

As the first description of soccer played in England shows, one can conclude a propensity to violence. In his widely distributed book published in 1990, *Among the Thugs*, Bill Buford the author makes the case that there is a unique sensibility of English fans, supporters euphemistically, which contains a propensity to violence. The violence, which occurs with a crowd consumed by some nationalistic loyalty to a city's or nation's team, driven by various narcotics and alcohol, ultimately thrives on the "rush" of danger even though factually one may be injured in the crowd events. Buford relies heavily on interviews of spectators, and depends on his own lived experience in participation in these violent events. He watches the tapes of the crowding that was allowed by the police and led to the deaths and injuries; his conclusion follows presumptions of his life within the supporters through many matches.

In daily, lay observances, and also in forms of regularized research, what one expects to find will often be found. The violence in the history of English football contrasts with the activity of "supporters" of American college football. As the following table shows, despite the dramatic framing of these events, large attendance, and high levels of emotion, evidence of social disorder is very slight.

Table 5.2   Delinquency records at the University of Iowa football games (means)*

	2011 (N=7)	2012 (N=7)	2013 (N=7)
Underage 21 Possession	7.7	4.7	4.7
Assaults	.14	.14	0
Public Urination	1.14	.43	.57
Interference with Official Acts	.57	1	1.29
Operation of Vehicle under Influence	.43	.57	0
Open Container, Person	44	43	9
Drugs	.29	.71	.29
Trespass	.71	.29	0
Consume Hard Liquor	0	.57	0
Public Intox	11.4	16.6	10.3
Disorderly	.14	.14	0
Open Container in Vehicle	.14	.14	.14
Providing False ID	N/A	.57	.14

* The average home football attendance for the University of Michigan (Ann Arbor, Michigan) in the 2012 season was 112,252. The University of Iowa (Iowa City, Iowa) was ranked 21st among 169 major programs listed, with an average attendance of 70,747. Information provided by The University of Iowa Department of Public Safety.

There are instances with English soccer supporters that stand out in contrast with the prospect in similar instances with hugely popular sport events on college campuses in the United States. The supporter of events within this American context considers normal, an unusually small amount of disturbances. If the expectation of normalcy is of fans primed for violence, then the tragic circumstances in Hillsborough by default may yield to a conclusion of inevitability. Relatedly, if this inevitability and its associated blame of liabilities of supporters exists, then an account of the Hillsborough events follows one line towards a conclusion. However, if the expectation is selective, then the construction by police and literally years of attachment of accountability show a systematic perversion of truth by police and other oversight bodies. This is the conclusion of three careful research bodies, which begin with very different preconceptions of the "normal" condition of English soccer matches: a group associated with the sociologist, Phil Scraton; a group who interviewed survivors who lost friends and family in the crush at Hillsborough (Taylor et al., 1995); and a governmental panel which published its report in 2012.

The cases of Armstrong and Landis, and to a certain extent others who lied about taking drugs within the Tour de France, and the various layers of deflection and hiding information that occurred in successive reviews of the Hillsborough incident do not begin with a visible, obvious, mal-intentioned person who is lying. The initial actors are trying to work within existing expectations of their teams, their sport or church, and in terms of what consuming publics expect. In these cases—and others—the weight of the deception lies with a set of institutions that surround the initial set of acts such as those of Armstrong and Landis and the police who made serious mistakes in the handling of Liverpool fans at the soccer match. The situations in these cases contain a set of what might be called organizational imperatives that sustain the original deviance or deceits of the athletes or the caretakers of crowds at the soccer matches. The fact that the very offensive steps in denying a mistake or deviance without the clear original act, as with priests and Sandusky, provides two shadings of an understanding of hypocrisy that add to the overall treatment of the sociological study of this phenomenon. The cases fill in dimensions of how hypocrisy operates. One contribution is that even without an initial deviant act by what somebody labels as a hypocritical individual, a set of organizational imperatives can jump into action with similar and even exact processes and consequences. The second point is that the strong demonstration of the role of surrounding institutions that may act independently of an original hypocritical act, gives leverage in interpreting why so many news story labels of "hypocrisy" seem to die or end with the original discovery and the journalistic finger-pointing (Tables 2.1 and 2.2 in Chapter 2).

A participating actor in a sporting event (or religious event, also) could act in ways that various layers of institutional awareness and oversight would condemn, but they don't because the discovery and public condemnation of the individual and act could compromise their own interests. There is, in short, a set of institutions who respond to the transgression with secrecy and with manipulation of information because there are imperatives that they do so to protect themselves. These institutions include teams, the judicatories that govern (and promote often at the same time) a sport, journalists, and the spectators themselves.

The use of the word "hypocrisy" is common (see Tables 2.1 and 2.2). The negative meaning is virtually universal, in the US, Iceland, and France, across the population of 50 years of appearances in representative, major journalistic media. Other countries attach negativity to the term. Invocations of the term in the journal population do not draw consequences; the history of sociological coverage does not either. The records of cases covered to this point, though, clearly show such negative consequences. Affecting and exacerbating the harm are organizational constraints that delay action when deceits occur and may become implicated directly. Given these imponderable condition of hypocrisy, the explanatory lacunae cry for guidelines for some resolution.

The definition of sport used in the project stipulates rule governance, along with physicality, intrinsic value, and a level of intensity in the participation. The preoccupation with rules at the elite levels easily displays this. But, importantly, analyses of sport activity at other levels enhances this concept, too. One can note, again for an example, writing on "street" basketball such as that provided by Pete Axthelm in *The City Game* (1970). The definition of religion above from Geertz itemizes general dimensions of this institution. Each dimension and the whole imply permanence and dire consequences upon deviations. Formally and in practice, sport and religion carry strong expectations from participants and onlookers of normalcy. The two primary cases in this chapter, lying within the Tour de France and within layers of officialdom in the Hillsborough tragedy, show the effects of presumptions about normalcy in sport, which create a context for both organizational complicity in hypocrisy and the slowness of observers in acknowledgement of this hypocrisy.

The Normal within the Tour de France

Economic ends existed in the early Tours de France, so sponsors, participants, and spectators attended to rule definition—and infractions. Twelve of the 27 riders in the second edition of the race in 1904 were disqualified for various infractions. An important indication of interest in violations from consumption of illegal substances begins with France's anti-doping law of 1964, and the first death in the race of Tom Simpson (partially from alcohol and amphetamines) in 1967. Inventories of disqualifications for all pro-cycling races include a 33-page listing from 1886 through 2013 (Wikipedia). Notable recent instances in the Tour de France include the Festina Affair in 1998 and the Spanish investigation, Operation Puerto, in May 2006.

The conduct of the event, however, which incorporates participation of riders, support teams, administrators, spectators, and journalists, has harbored presumptions of the integrity of the event (parties and actions being honest being considered is normal). Despite the fallout from the Festina Affair in 1998, where only 96 riders finished after the rider expulsions from Festina and TVM, a pattern of general reorganization of administration and serious punishment of riders did not occur until 2012. Some adjudications at the team support level were still continuing into the beginning of the year 2013. All this (that is, long-delayed corrective actions and still remnants of rule violations), despite the fact that information on Lance Armstrong's use of illegal drugs existed in 1999.

The Normal within International Football: the Hillsborough Case

Sport is physical, intrinsic, rule governed, and consummative. These characteristics make it species-specific, and account for its contribution as a highly serviceable vehicle of cultural memory, as well as the obvious outcomes of being entertaining and just plain fun. The strength of the characteristics means, with slight turns of excess, problems can occur. The physicality of sport, such as in boxing, football (soccer and American football), and rugby creates a context of freer expression of physical contact among fans in the form of hugging, high-fives, passing bodies through fan populations, and on rare occasions exchanges of physical violence. The time-out character of an intrinsic sport may lead to a binge analog where licenses of consumption and behavior may occur. The centrality of rule governance, makes rules explicit and salient, and may lead to unnecessary conflict over rule compliance. The personal and group satisfaction of sport participation and success from early childhood to the Olympics may spill over to meanings well beyond the import of the contest itself. There are indeed excesses at every level of sport. At the most preliminary level of youth sport, Little League, recently an observer at a game in Washington State pulled a gun on another spectator over an argument. In Columbus Ohio, in 2012, parents engaged in a brawl at a Little League game. These extend the reach of what sport-import can bring, in ways that have occurred more internationally and visibly such as at international soccer matches.

But importantly—and, indeed, critically so—these are outliers, exceptions, marks on a plot far off the grid of important sport and compliant behavior. In the case of the Hillsborough tragedy that occurred in April 1989, where 96 people died, the conclusions of Scraton, the group studying survivors of Hillsborough, and the 2012 government panel, an understanding of the event should not conclude just the role of thugs, and fan conflict, and fans lacking tickets. The consensus of these analysts is fully to acknowledge the malfeasance of responsible authorities, and also to acknowledge years of deceptions and cover-ups by these authorities.

Representative of sport enthusiasm in the United States are attendance figures at football games in the Big Ten Conference. These are noted in Table 5.1. It is the case that security issues do occur, as the figures show. But what is essential for understanding deviances like the Hillsborough disaster is to appreciate the overwhelming sense of normalcy that governs such sporting events. The contest in 1989 was important, as a semi-final match between Liverpool and Nottingham Forest, but the presumption, the state of mind of spectators is one of normalcy (which includes safety, entertainment, and comfortable diversion). Jenni Hicks (a Liverpool supporter commuting to the match in Sheffield) recounts: "We arrived in Sheffield at about 12:30 or 12:45. We found suitable parking. We were actually parked in a mixed car-park with Forest and Liverpool supporters. It was predominantly Forest supporters, but there was a very jovial atmosphere amongst the Forest and Liverpool supporters who were there—'We are going to win today' sort of thing—and no animosity. It was a glorious day, we had taken a packed lunch, and the atmosphere was tremendous in the car-park. We were all out of our cars having our picnics. No problem" (Taylor et al., 1995: 17).

Jenni Hicks' perspective on the sporting event, and that of her husband, Trevor, changed. Within a few hours their two teenage daughters who had accompanied them to Sheffield were dead.

> Sarah and Vicki were just on these very low trolleys in body bags. I didn't realize what they were. I had never seen a body bag in my life. They were just there and the relief, it seemed to me, that I had found them. The first sensation was that I had found Sarah and Vicki. I could take them home. I remember getting down on my knees, and Vicki was this side and Sarah was the other side. I picked Vicki up and lifted her up and really cuddled her and hugged her. And I can remember how cold she was. She had a little hospital gown on because obviously with dying in the hospital, the hospital had laid her out. She had their little white gown on. And then I went to give Sarah a hug and I remember the contrast in body temperature because Sarah was warm. Vicki was how I imagined. It was like taking something out of the fridge. Sarah felt as if I had pulled her duvet back in bed and given her a cuddle. When I picked Sarah up, I looked up and said 'Are you sure she is dead, because she is warm?' These two CID officers went in with us, two typical officers, quite young, in their leather jackets and jeans, and they had tears running down their faces. These big husky, bulky guys. We were allowed what seemed like a couple of seconds (Trevor et al., 1995: 159).

The searing, yet researchable (remember, sociology both should and can add illumination, Chapter 1), implications here for social trust concern the patterns, continuities, and changes in what are considered normal patterns of conduct in these two sport cases. Through the investigative work, and the use of a decisively critical lens over a ten-year period, the presumption of the "normal" in the Tour as being honest, fair, and non-hypocritical (as sport should be) has been challenged. The challenge has presented a different picture of a system which was a "conspiracy" of deceit, a "cycle of lies," and a machine run be collusions. The argued for actual normality of the tour is one of a continuity of non-truthfulness. The provocation for a change to a system of participation, governance, and understanding that reflects more idealistic features of sport—fairness, honesty, and transparency—has been slow in coming, but evidence exists that it may be underway (Figure 5.1). Many within and outside the sport hope the conception of normalcy within the event and the sport of cycling will now more closely approximate honesty in action rather than as a fiction.

Different conceptions of normalcy existed from the setting and the unfolding of events of the Hillsborough tragedy. One led to attributions of blame of the spectators and even of the victims at the beginning of the football match. Another, from several sources over the years from 1989, considered the activities of the fans to have been excited—per spectators at major sporting events—but not inordinately unruly. The first conception exculpated officials who dealt with the crowds and who responded to the injured and dying. In 2012, a turning point, as has been described, occurred at the highest levels of government in the United Kingdom and exacted judgment on both of these long-running, competing conceptions. The fans and their behavior were judged consistent with engaged observers, but not exceptional for regular human conduct in public settings: The authorities' claims of unruliness (stressed as what one usually would expect from football crowds, as an excuse) was discredited. Culpability was placed on layers of authorities responsible for maintaining order and for not adequately attending to the needs of victims in the situation

Lessons about the influence of organizations in maintaining lies whose substance serves them, adds sobering information to the book's consideration of the organizational imperatives in hypocrisy. In the history of the Tour de France, a system of deceit developed and in practical terms became for many contributing parties the normal way of doing business; that pattern of operable deceit was masked by public pronouncements of an idealistic and honest sport institution. In the case of Hillsborough, the system of dishonesty among layers of officials who shared considerable blame for the tragedy sought for many years to remove themselves from accountability by claiming the source of the behavior that escalated into unruly behavior and then injuries and death had roots in traditional bad behavior of fans. The placement of blame on the fans, and claiming it was the customary pattern of activity, for many years was used as a shield for the concealment of the errors and falsifications of authorities. Lying, and here hypocrisy, can be systematic, durable, and in these instances very consequential as the lies are maintained by organizational entities.

Continuing the Program

The selection of the strategic cases of sport and religion are the limiting cases where honesty should prevail. Sport is physical, intrinsic, rule governed, and consummative. Religion is "what concerns us ultimately" (Tillich), or, in Geertz' articulation, a system of symbols that stresses "powerful, pervasive, and long-lasting moods and motivations in men [and women]" (Geertz, 1973: 94).

If any institutionalized activity warrants our trust, sport and religion should. Cases in Chapters 1, 2, 3, and 5 show compromises. There are consequences, as noted in these chapters (Goal 4 of the program of research). The question engaged in Chapter 6 is whether compromises in the institutions of sport and religion connect with the diminution generally of trust institutions described within several current research sources.

The sociological program makes use of the disciplinary priorities and resources of context, ideal-typical cases, and attention to organizational influences. But it carries an obligation—central from the beginning of the book coverage—to make a contribution to an unrecognized topic of consequences and, always an obligation, theory expansion. This occurs in Chapters 6 and 7.

Chapter 6
Hypocrisy and Levels of Trust within Cultures

Introduction: Meaning and Variability of Trust

Adam Smith wrote, in 1759 in *The Theory of Moral Sentiments*, about deceit and the consequences for deceiver and deceived in this uncompromising and unadorned way:

> It is always mortifying not to be believed, and it is doubly so when we suspect that it is because we are supposed to be unworthy of belief and capable of seriously and willfully deceiving. To tell a man that he lies, is of all affronts the most mortal. But whoever seriously and willfully deceives is necessarily conscious to himself that he merits this affront, that he does not deserve to be believed, and that he forfeits all title to that sort of credit from which alone he can derive any sort of ease, comfort, or satisfaction in the society of his equals (Smith, 1817: II, 208).

Hypocrisy represents a lie, but with special ingredients of deceit. With the denial of a past wrong (dissimulation), compromised actions in terms of prevailing standards are denied or hidden in order to create an advantage that could be lost if the real situation was disclosed. In simulation, a condition of the present is claimed, even though the reality is not true. Again, in terms of prevailing conditions in the context of the claims, an advantage is asserted without true warrant. In all the cases described in this volume, such as in Chapters 2, 3, and 5 and similar ones in this chapter, the mechanisms of the dissimulation or simulation may be complex. In illustrations within Chapter 5, Tyler Hamilton the cyclist was caught, punished by the cycling community, and lost his 2004 Olympic Gold Medal. In his account in *The Secret Race*, his final "fall-back position" to exonerate himself or to neutralize his acts, was to argue that "anybody would have done the same thing if they were in my place." After many years of suspicion about the use of illegal drugs, Lance Armstrong formally admitted some years after he retired from competition in the Tour de France that he used drugs.

The moral reference, or the context of explanation or justification that he made in 2013, was similar to that of Hamilton. Armstrong described in a *Le Monde* interview that the reason he used drugs was that this was the only way to win the Tour. The intimation was that drug use was common, if not universal. He implied—as did Hamilton—that the context was culpable. He was not personally to blame; he was doing what was normative. He even goes so far as to suggest that he should be respected because he did it (that is to say, cheated and got away with it through various artifices) more effectively than his competitors. What are the general issues here? Is Armstrong correct that everybody cheated? If so, is this a principle of honesty that can be sustained generally? With regard to Hamilton, is it the case that given the chance at advantage in a sporting event, anybody would take the unfair advantage?

Over the last 20 years, sociology has given notably high attention to trust issues. One reason has been the evidence of decreasing trust in institutions, an ingredient long felt important for the quality and stability of social life. A related reason has been the recognition that some societies show higher rates of trust than do other societies, and these relative rates persist (e.g., Olivera, 2013; Traynor, 2013; Marozzi, 2014; Mackie, 2001) A third reason comes from the evidence of breakdown of societies considered authoritarian, with the changes in 1989 in the Soviet Union, Germany, and Romania being illustrative. The sociological premise is that if there is a prospect for democratic institutions as alternatives in these countries, the democracy will depend on a store of civic trust, a resource of social capital as it has been named by Putnam and others (Putnam, 1993).

This book intends a program of work in the sociology of hypocrisy with attention to social contexts of meaning, methodological attention to ideal-typical cases, recognition of organizational influences on lying, consequences of hypocrisy, and development and application of relevant theories. Several specific consequences of hypocrisy at the personal, interactional, and institutional levels have been described thus far. The conceptualization of hypocrisy as concealment of untoward acts or fabrication of valued acts falsely, that is, dissimulation or simulation, provides instances where social acts violate social norms that are necessary for trust. When the acts are compounded by protection and concealment at the organizational level, threats to generalized trust in institutions within societies exist. The goals of the sociological program require joining this developing attention to trust issues, as an obligation from the book's attention to hypocrisy. The addition of attention to trust as a consequence further establishes the bases of consequences of hypocrisy as a valuable domain for development and application of theory (Chapter 7).

The sociological work on trust itself is in a state of development. Statements advocating attention are inventories of conceptual definitions, aggregations of disparate research efforts, and admonitions for continued work (e.g., Fukuyama, 1995; Cook, 2001; Cook et al., 2009). The material of the chapter here is a modest effort to contribute to the trust research by explaining the relevance to the general efforts of sociological attention to trust (our sociological obligation, again), by noting further why hypocrisy can be deathly serious (rather than trivial from its redundancy). Hence, using information from the specific cases in the book, attention can suggestively turn to how the sociology of hypocrisy can link with particular views of trust—which stress the general import of fidelity to the quality of social organization.

Sport and religion in their ideal-typical forms could be excluded from incorporation into trust analyses, given distinctions existing between faith, confidence, and trust conditions (Heimer, 2001; Farrell, 2009). Violations of expectations should not occur, by definition, with faith conditions and confidence conditions (the writers on trust note as contrasting with trust). Trust as these and other authors in the chapter write, want to include some element of risk which is overcome when one trusts. A ball made of safe materials in a contest or a child free from untoward advances by a priest may veer into faith and confidence, rather than the trust components articulated in efforts at refinement of the term. The record of the cases in this book, even as ideal-typical, do show risks, though. The level of risk depends on special features of variation of salience and are contingent on the investment on the part of the organization to preserve control of the valued commodity (winning, success, for example) and hence can move sport and religion into the domain of interest for trust study. Also, organizational investments may hold propensities to conceal actions that my compromise chances for success, further posing concerns about trustworthiness of institutions.

Sport and religion, then, even though they could be circuited and placed in the categories for faith and confidence can show compromises that pose risks. And, as such, they become institutions open to study about trust. Again, as the stakes increase, risk may increase, and with these conditions sport and religion can remain as limiting cases on the basis of their ideal-typical definitions (Chapter 1). Sport and religion still serve well as limiting cases for the examination of implications for general trust in societies, in ways consistent with already noted implications of rule violations for the respective institutions themselves. The inventories of trust meanings, trust research, and trust implications allow several openings for the sociology of hypocrisy within sport and religion to make contributions.

Beginning in the 1990s, at least partially as a response to broad-based evidence of diminishing trust in institutions, expansive, inventive, and provocative research within the social sciences has stretched the reach of coverage of issues of trust and provided some tentative clues about factors enhancing or diminishing trust, sustaining high levels of trust, and showing how levels of trust at various levels of society aid or inhibit success and order of human groups. From the unqualified statement of Smith (above: Smith, 1817: II, 208) to the present, the inventory of relevant factors and processes inherent in trust levels grows—bringing satisfaction as threads of knowledge contribute to a durable theoretical and empirical fabric, but frustrating as the possibilities for contributing factors to the whole decline of trust continue to increase.

"Trust is the expectation that arises within a community of regular, honest, and cooperative behavior, based on commonly shared norms, on the part of other members of that community" (Fukuyama, 1995: 26). Francis Fukuyama is talking about the bases of trust within economic systems. Central to his analysis, though, is attention to cultural differences that may define standards and conduct of trustworthiness in societies, which are viewed in this book across time and in three societies. Also, the values and habits that make up displays and expectations of trust are carried through a society's relatively informal institutions such as families, neighborhoods, churches, and presumably sport organizations. The judgment here is that religion and sport are not the only two organizations through which trust in a society is sustained, but their very character makes them limiting cases where trust and trustworthiness, that is the fidelity of the reference institutions, should be high.

Quoting Foddy and Yamagishi: "In this chapter, trust is defined as an expectation of beneficent reciprocity from others in uncertain or risky situations (Brann and Foddy, 1987). Trust reflects a belief that others will act in a way to benefit or at least not harm us, before we know the outcome of their behaviors (Dasgupta, 1988). Trust is not required when others' interests are totally allied with our own; these are the domains of assurance, faith, and confidence (for example, Hardin, 2001; Buskens and Raub, 2002). Rather, trust is needed when another person has the potential for gain at our expense, but can choose not to do so (Yamagishi and Yamagishi, 1994; see also Knight, 2001). Trust is most important in uncertain, not certain relationships (Cook et al., 2005)" (Foddy and Yamagishi in Cook et al., 2009: 17; references included in original).

The situation with sport and religion is that the very nature of the institutions renders them on the low end of the continuum of risk. They should fall into assured expectations or confidence (Farrell, 2009), or what Heimer (2001) calls faith. Relying on the leadership of a church, a priest or pastor, should not be a matter of risk. Similarly, one participates in sport and watches sport under the assumption that the rules and levels of compliance of participants are not matters of variability. One can bet on a sporting event, and that involves risk, but when one does bet on an event, the gambler assumes the event itself is not "rigged" and the system of betting itself is an honest one. Therefore when lying and cheating occur as described in the earlier chapters, the magnitude of disaffection is proportionally greater from investing in what was assumed to be an honest process (assurance). This disaffection yields potentially, too, a disproportionate level of disillusionment and negative consequences. Even when the non-risky prospects of fidelity in sport and religion veer into activities with some risk—more realistic and certainly common within the cases of the book—sport and religion in principle self-define themselves as high in levels of trustworthiness.

Hypocrisy and Trust

William Shakespeare in *The Merchant of Venice* and *Twelfth Night* inserts a provocative thrust into a culture about inconsistencies in behavior of important people. Molière turns a light on an apparent friend who in a room of the host's house attempts to seduce his friend's wife. The Bible and the Koran note several instances where contradictions of character are held up for scrutiny and censure. The depth of historical appearances and the generality prompt a question about how important for the integrity of institutions, indeed life, acts of hypocrisy are. While suggesting commonalities of censure through time and space, are these only comments on personal failings that readers and followers of social commentators and hallowed teachers that we should attend to if we are self-critical? The juxtaposition of two periods of time (1940 vs. 1990) in Chapter 1, where episodes of ambiguous endings to college football contexts, suggests two styles for resolving similar contested events. In the first, a coach and a college president see the reference for resolving the ambiguity to be rules of the game, a greater good than the specific game itself. In the second case, the principals who are beneficiaries of a ruling conclude that the momentary gain from a referee's error is a gift of fate undeserving of a second thought over any larger meaning.

In illustrative material covered to this point, hypocrisy is condemned, and the negative valuation is durable in time and across different cultures, even where the meanings of the concept may differ somewhat by context (Chapter 1), but does its appearance matter for broad questions of social order? Hypocrisy is lying, manipulation of the truth, one of the examples of "moral choice" soberly identified by Sissela Bok (Bok, 1999). But does it matter for institutions, or is there, as her delineation allows, moral choice in private life but not necessarily in public life? In this chapter, advances on this question occur. If the issues really are private, then, like all manner of personal errors and vagaries of habit, we can use them to castigate others and use them as standards for self-refinement if we seek personal improvement. If so, analyses of current and past instances lie in the realm of ethical philosophy and the history of manners.

But if acts of hypocrisy—dissimulation or simulation—illustrate fissures in assumptions about fidelity of persons who occupy positions in institutions who have misled us in dealing with consequential facts, then the events, processes, and outcomes are topics of social order, and therefore sociological questions. Hypocrisy is lying. If the lies betray personal foibles and are a source of annoyance about intimates, or dark spots on personal tallies of behavior, then hypocrisy as many other objectionable habits we or others show are just one more annoyance of life. But if hypocrisy of people within influential positions, or hypocrisy as part of an institutional way of doing business, affects the ways influential people are received and institutions evaluated, then the issues of such deceits are larger. Is trust in societies, then, affected by cultural predispositions toward hypocrisy and by specific instances where influential people or institutions hid information or pretended information was true when it was not?

Francis Fukuyama wrote on trust at a time in American society and within social analyses when patterns of trust in institutions among publics were falling (Table 6.1). The decline continues, so here the prospect of the larger implications of hypocrisy in sport and religion are viewed—since Fukuyama (1995) and others (examples in Cook et al., 2009) identify lack of fidelity as one source of the diminution of trust, and thus hypocrisy as a form of deceit should be included. For Bok, trust fundamentally depends on the fidelity of information. "Imagine a society, no matter how ideal in other respects, where word and gesture could never be counted upon. Questions asked, answers given, information exchanged—all would be worthless. Were all statements randomly truthful or deceptive, action and choice would be undermined from the outset. There must be a minimal degree of trust in communication for language and action to be more than stabs in the dark" (Bok, 1978: 18). Hypocrisy, by definition deceitful, should be considered within these general sociological discussions of trust.

The dynamics of hypocrisy are complex (an acknowledgment made throughout the chapters thus far), and, fairly, the idea that personal ethical failings (which appear in all of us) should be given the weight of social consequence dictates caution in the treatment in this chapter. First, data on the general trust problem are displayed. Two sets of examples of the potential relevance of hypocrisy to these general issues of trust lie before us. One of these sets comes from issues of meanings of hypocrisy which exist in literature mentioned in Chapters 1–3. Then some examples of possible connections of hypocrisy to general issues of trust come from Chapter 5 and material in this chapter on how individual and group acts of hypocrisy may be made consequential for trust levels through organizational influences. The sequence of treatment here, then, will be presentation of trends of trust. Following, discussion of the combined prospects for how hypocrisy within the cases in Chapters 2, 3, and 5 (and here) can affect trust proceeds within the chapter. If hypocrisy does affect general levels of trust, then the consequences for individuals, group interactions, and institutions are not minor: they can be severe. The non-incidental, again, severe, prospects of hypocrisy for diminution of trust counsel pause for reflection on how individuals should act and how institutions preferably will operate: issues of morality. Some of these implications add to a basis for attention to connections between hypocrisy and sociological theory, anticipated in Chapter 1 but treated more fully in the last chapter, and fifth stage, of the book's program.

The Diminution of Trust

The Gallup Opinion Poll has asked this question 35 times since 1973: "Now I am going to read you a list of institutions in American Society. Please tell me how much confidence you, yourself, have in each one—a great deal, quite a lot, some or very little." The following set of evaluated institutions over 40 years illustrates the point made commonly by analysts that trust in all institutions with the exception of the military, has dropped. The figures come from combining the two positive alternatives, "a great deal" and "quite a lot."[1]

---

1   Preoccupation with public trust of governments and institutions among politicians and the priorities of journalists is high in countries outside the United States. Particular interest focuses on variations of trust in different institutions and prospects for changes in trust when fundamental forms of national governments change. For example, "Strengthening Trust in Government," ORCD, 2005; Yu, de Haan, and Beugelsdijk, 2001. The World Values Survey (started in 1981) includes the topic, and allows cross-time and cross-country comparisons. These data come from "Confidence in Institutions: Gallup Historical Trends," June 7–10, 2012. http://www.gallup.com/poll/1597/confidence in institutions.aspx.

Table 6.1   Degrees of trust in select American institutions (percentages)

	2012	2002	1991	1981	1973
Military	75	79	69	50	58 (1975)
Church or Organized religion	44	45	56	64	65
Public Schools	29	38	35	42	58
Newspapers	25	35	32	35	39
Banks	21	47	29	47	60 (1979)
US Congress	13	29	18	29	42

Hypocrisy, Organizations, and Trust

Descriptions of consequences of hypocrisy to individuals, relationships, and organizations recognize the importance of context. In conditions of exigency, as Shklar describes them, the contexts hold high chances for hypocrisy and in turn negative consequences. Exigency exists when there are high expectations for success (here within the institutions of sport and religion) paired with strong constraints limiting success for all. Despite the limitations the demand for success is so high, even with moral components that delineate one's status vertically, there is a push toward either to dissimulate or to simulate information about performances—the elements of hypocrisy. The process as described in Chapter 4 reflects levels of success in making available information for personal use (for concealment or fabrication) and, alternatively, capabilities of information control that allow access and detection to concealment and fabrication. These resources show a second set of contextual factors bearing on the accuracy of information that may affect levels of trust and levels of trustworthiness.

Trust, in the literature reviewed in this chapter to this point, depends on these contextual factors. The exigency elevates prospects for dishonesty, which raises fears about the truthfulness needed from actors to ensure trust in them and to demonstrate their trustworthiness. The ease of creating information that is suspect (and consequential for trust and trustworthiness) and the availability of means to evaluate this information increases the chances trust will occur and individuals and institutions will be considered trustworthy. To illustrate more fully the import of these contextual elements of exigency and information control, examples using some of the lines of trust literature and the case material from the book serve productively.

The emphases of Russell Hardin about trust (2001) and two fundamental factors in determining consequences of trust by Carol A. Heimer (2001) aid the second example on how hypocrisy bears on levels of trust—as consequence. For Hardin, "In modal trust relationships, the trusted party has an incentive to be trustworthy, and incentive grounded in the value of maintaining the relationship into the future. That is, *my trust of you is encapsulated in your interest in fulfilling the trust*" (Hardin, 2001: 3; his emphases). He also stresses that issues of trust need more fully by social scientists to emphasize trustworthiness (that is, of people, institutions, organizations) (e.g., Hardin, 2001: 22). Trust is necessary when there is doubt about the action of other persons or institutions. Carol Heimer (Heimer, 2001) isolates levels of uncertainty as a central variable, that is, "... the inability of an actor to predict the outcome of an event because he or she lacks information about the intention and competence of another actor who directly controls the outcome" (Heimer, 2001: 43). Pivotal too, in her conceptualization, are levels of vulnerability. "Vulnerability has to do with the amount of risk an actor incurs by engaging in a particular interaction and is a function (nonlinear and increasing) of the proportion of the actor's total assets that are at stake in the interaction" (Heimer, 2001: 43, 44).

As institutions, both sport and religion sustain expectations of low uncertainty and the dominant pattern of participation in either does not carry high levels of vulnerability. Critical, too, from Hardin is that by the definitions followed through analyses of this book, sport and religion claim moral mandates for trustworthiness. What this means for the cases described is that the magnitude of the violation of trust that has occurred, and the potential consequences for layers of victims grows proportionally with these facts of high standards of integrity and relatively low levels of uncertainty and, initially, low levels of vulnerability. As described in the first chapter, these conditions make sport and religion a pair of limiting cases for implications of the deceit occurring within the two institutions. A condition of sport organization and hypocrisy within the national organization of swimming in the United States, gives illustrative substance to these four factors from Hardin and Heimer and point to prospects for trust that come from hypocritical acts.

On May 23, 2012, Montgomery County Circuit Judge Marielsa A. Bernard sentenced Rick Curl to seven years in jail, with five years of probation, for sexually abusing one of his swim team members during her activity in his club from 13 to 18 years of age. Mr Burke founded the Curl-Burke Swim Club in Washington, DC which was known as an incubator of high level swimmers for college teams and as Olympic Games prospects.[2] "I have in my mind this picture of a little girl," Bernard said. "She trusts you. She respects you. She's madly in love with you. There is [so much] psychological damage your actions have done to her." The victim in July 2012: "I trusted him, and my parents trusted him, everybody trusted him, and that trust was broken."

---

2   News accounts of the Curl sentencing distinguish Curl's club as both large and successful as a conduit for swimmers intent on elite success. *The Washington Post*: "She [Kelley Currin] swam for the Curl-Burke Swim Club, one of the nation's largest such organizations, through which Curl, now 63, had guided athletes to Olympic gold medals" (Brittain and Trevino, 2012). *The New York Times*: "She [Currin] was one of the top swimmers in the world in 1987 and a finalist at the 1988 United States Olympic trials. Curl oversaw one of the largest, most successful clubs in the United States, and his top swimmers included Tom Dolan, a two-time Olympic gold medalist" (Crouse, 2013).

The period of abuse, recreated in the courts over the spring of 2013, embodies a clear definition of hypocrisy. A person of enviable reputation, occupying positions of considerable power and influence over young children (and their families) conceals a long period of inappropriate—and eventually designated criminal—behavior. Mr Curl's behavior was hypocritical. The court and the victim state without hesitance that trust was broken. This case, which is not exceptional, illustrates two special ingredients about hypocrisy in this situation of compromised trust. Drawing on the analytical priorities of Carol Heimer noted above, uncertainty and vulnerability are both low in principle and low based on assumed practices within the respective institutions.

The athlete began training with Mr Curl's club when she was nine years old. The sexual relationship continued from the time she was 13 years old until she was 17. A young athlete, of junior high age, can assume considerable certainty about the authoritative person and hold reasonable expectations for athletic success. As a person's body changes in adolescence and other priorities enter for this age of person there may be a degree of ambivalence about the work-investment in the sport and likely future success. In this instance, the parents themselves strongly reduced some of this potential ambivalence by agreeing to a settlement ($150,000 paid by Curl to the family in exchange for non-disclosure) in the late 1980s, to assure Ms Currin would not forfeit a chance of an athletic scholarship to the University of Texas.

Hypocrisy creates a relationship between the enactor (either hiding an untoward secret or claiming false credentials) and the receiver (or target) of the act because the coin or credit the hypocrite claims is so valuable to those who are potentially deceived. The elevated belief by the student in the teacher's honesty, or the athlete's faith in the coach, or the person's confidence in the caretaker gradually create great vulnerability for the persons who do question the authenticity of the acts of the service provider or superordinate. The potential losses for the student, athlete, or person cared for, on discovery of the deceit are commensurately high.

Similarly, when a child is abused by a Catholic priest, this is deeply offensive to those who discover the act for its abuse of status and power, and the discovery may give warrant for the claims for criminalization. The hypocritical characteristics embedded in this particular kind of relationship make the offensiveness of the act and the potential damage to the victim extreme. The adult has the physical strength to assault the child. But added to this is the institutionally based and perhaps family based reputation that the priest holds for the child. The intensity of the child's regard for the priest in the relationship elevates the vulnerability of the child to the assaults of the clergyman. As the recognition by the victim emerges about the dishonesty of the priest, the negative consequences again are commensurately heightened for the child. The coin of the clergyman was dear to the child, so its loss when the hypocrisy becomes evident is proportionally as great as the value of the coin. The relationship has begun with certainty over the integrity of the priest, coach, or caretaker; and, as such, initially there is assumed safety carried in the assurances of integrity.

The weight of the value in the respected person adds to the costs for the one who is deceived, be it a young athlete or a young church goer. The force of the role toward perfection, be it honored coach or clergyman, creates an "exigency," as Shklar says, which should guide our analysis. "Sham faith is a haunting shadow for a genuinely religious mind. The striving for religious perfection is interminable, and the demand for greater fidelity is ever more exigent. The stricter these requirements of faith are, however, the more likely real or imputable pretense becomes. But the only weapon against it is to insist on even greater efforts, which in turn encourages the very vice that is to be extirpated" (Shklar, 48). Mr Curl was a highly respected coach of a very successful age-group swimming program. He betrayed his remorse at his sentencing, where his lawyers cited his repentance and morally upstanding behavior since the assault on the young swimmer. The defense team submitted 70 letters supporting Mr Curl's moral virtues; an estimated 50 people appeared in the court room, ostensibly to support the former coach. This was a person committed to success and who valued morality. But he assaulted the athlete not just once but over a period of several years, followed the events with a career as a leader of the sport while knowing of his deceit, and only at the beginning of 2013 did he publically admit (following the formal criminal charge) the dishonesty of the past.

By combining the conditions from Hardin and from Heimer, an inventory of stakes of trust for participants in the relationships created in the cases in view in the book exists. The judgments of conditions do not rest—nor can they—on iron-clad attributions of psychological states and individual actions. But the set of expectations people can be reasonably thought to bring to situations in which they engage in relationships with caretakers, or coaches, or priests is high. The very nature of religious organizations and sport institutions allows a set of expectations of young persons, students and athletes that are trusting and it is the violation of such conditions of trust on the part of clergy, coaches, or administrators that makes the outcomes in view in the cases so reprehensible.

Table 6.2   Trust conditions in select institutional environments

	Shared Interest	Presumed Trustworthiness	Uncertainty	Vulnerability
Priests	Yes	Yes	No	No/Yes
Sandusky/Penn State	Yes	Yes	No	No/Yes
Hillsborough	Yes	Yes	No	No/Yes
USA Swimming	Yes	Yes	No	No/Yes
Tour de France	Yes	No	Yes	Not Assumed

The history of the development of a standard of dishonesty in the Tour de France poses the prospect that the situation with its components of hypocrisy, organizational influences, and eventual consequences for trust was unique. The record now from the other illustrative cases does show considerable commonality with the Tour case. One might conclude that there may be quantitative differences among the cases, with the similarities dominating, particularly when organizational influences are considered. With such a judgment from the comparison, the implications for general conceptions about trust from the Tour may blend with estimated implications from the other cases. One could, as some commentators have, draw from the history of deceit in the Tour de France a conclusion of inevitability brought on by a culture of deceit nurtured by lucrative rewards for successes that evade challenge. Allowing for the similarities of the cases, the uniqueness of the Tour, from its history through the series of demonstrations of cheating, and then lying (particularly from 1998 through the present) encourage a conclusion of unique features of the Tour. And the special features of the Tour prompt consideration of some qualitatively different consequences for levels of social trust, and subsequently for evaluation of applicable theories to the cases in view in the book.

The Tour de France began in 1903 with commercial motives driving its organizers. The 1904 event provided early examples of rule violations by both riders and spectators. The victories of Greg LeMond in 1986, 1989, and 1990 began to open up interest in the event in the United States. Hence, when the broadly publicized "bust" of riders at the start of the 1998 race in the Festina Affair occurred, the exposure was far beyond Europe. The drugs, the layer of dispenser-drug experts, and questions about riders and teams created a large network of journalistic commentators dealing with the event and its provocative stories of cheating. A competing pair of management and riders, intended to create competitive teams on one hand, and layers of judicatories on the other hand to control illegal activities started their dynamic of concealment and detection. The Wikipedia entry for "List of Doping Cases in Cycling" lists 45 pages of entries from 1886 through 2013. So, contrary to the bases of expectations about trust in the other cases used as illustrations in the book, these appear not to exist in the history of the Tour de France. To counter illegal drug use in sporting events, The World Anti-doping Agency was founded on November 10, 1999. The United States Anti-Doping Agency started on October 1, 2000.

Along with comment over the last two years about drug use in the Tour de France growing, there have been suspicions about winners and suspicions about the whole group of competitors since Festina. David Walsh had been claiming drug violations by Lance Armstrong early in the 2000s. But the weight of journalistic judgment and claims of the administration of the sport continued to conclude violations were an exception. The judgment of "honesty is normal" that has ended by current reporting (e.g., Macur, 2014; Albergotti and O'Connell, 2013) starts to change with the disqualification of Landis following the 2006 Tour de France. Landis, himself supported by enough of the honesty presupposition, wrote his book (Landis, *Positively False*) countering the disqualification in 2007. The USADA took Armstrong's Tour titles away in 2012, followed by the international cycling union's actions disqualifying him (UCI). Aside from accused riders continuing to claim honesty, various management entities such as team leaders, and sport judicatories denying complicity, the weight of evidence supporting conclusions about the Tour de France having a history of drug use and deceitful denials for nearly a decade now predominates. (As Chapter 5 describes and Figure 5.1 summarizes.)

Landis's own effort to gain return for his Whistleblower lawsuit against cheating by Armstrong's teams received legitimacy when the US Federal government joined his suit. David Walsh, who had settled with Armstrong's supporters who had sued him earlier in the decade, had a sort of last word in his *Seven Deadly Sins*, and his paper has successfully sought reprisal payments from Armstrong (who had originally been successful in suing Walsh and his paper). The "Normal" state as being cheating, collusion in covering up the cheating, and lying about cheating (up until the turning point discussed in Chapter 5) was the current state within two major recent books by writers from the *Wall Street Journal* (Albergotti and O'Connell, 2012) and *The New York Times* (Macur, 2014). Their picture is complemented by the United States Anti-Doping Agency Report of 2012, "Report on Proceedings under the World Anti-doping Code and the USADA Protocol: Reasoned Decision of the United States Anti-doping Agency on Disqualification and Ineligibility." A fourth medium of information, a film by Alex Gibney, "The Armstrong Lie" added additional redundancy to the picture.

The presumptive condition of deceit within the event contrasts with the presumptive conditions of the cases of pedophilia among Catholic Priests, the Penn State situation, Hillsborough, and some other cases such as United States swimming. Trust as Smith's excursus says at the opening of the chapter is a highly valuable condition. Trust was lost in the Church, a major United States university, and layers of civil judicatories in the Hillsborough case. The strong line of commentary now about the Tour is that trust never should have existed. In the latest, Macur and Gibney organize their statements on the existence of lies within each overlapping layer of Armstrong and his team, and often most aspects of the event itself. The net of the other two documents, even without the conclusion in their titles, is consistent as well. Lies do not provide a basis of trust. All should know, during the period of 1999–2012, the Tour was untrustworthy.

Circumstances where expectations of safety and fair play were violated and where vulnerability was exploited create an outcome that is harmful to potential victims and diminishes continued trust in the institutions. The violation of trust and the consequences of the violation are termed "bad," "harmful," "destructive." These are moral terms and when considering the various social costs of hypocrisy, the criteria of moral and not-moral enter here. The assessment becomes complex when the issues of moral implications become attached to the Tour case. Here, the system has tried to proffer a legitimate image. But the paper record of incidents, unsuccessful efforts to change drug use from at least 1998 onward, and then the current failure of efforts at detection, exclusion, and penalties which followed the drug charges yield an alternative picture. Now as the system shows, organizers claim, journalists allow, and almost all riders argue the deceit was embedded in the system. So, who is harmed, and what is the moral cost of the rule violations? There was not trust in one another's fidelity to begin with, so when rule breakage occurs, the costs of violations of trust are hard to demonstrate, and the moral implications do not come easily to view.

With the meaning and consequences of hypocrisy in the cases, and now with the extension of these cases to considerations of trust in view, similarities and differences can be identified.

1. Tour de France, at least partially from the historical circumstances of an event not clearly premised on honesty, isolates that event as partially unique.
2. But reading back now, through the other cases, similarities do exist from material in Chapter 5 and material in this chapter about the existence of fulcrums at key points in time where the presuppositions about what is normal and what is deviant may change. This pattern does occur in the priest case, at least partially with the appearance of the Boston newspaper stories (2002); and with the Parliamentary review in the UK about Hillsborough (2012). Since the event occurred at Hillsborough in 1989, the presumptions of persons and groups to blame and persons and groups to keep from blame led to a persistent and consistent account based on presuppositions of disobedient fans, excellent work by monitors on the scene of the event, and caretakers of the injured after the riot who struggled honorably with difficult conditions. But with the report, which acts again as a fulcrum, ideas about normalcy and departures from normalcy have changed. Just before and just following Curl's conviction, the long-standing presumptions of altruistic and responsible coach behavior have changed.[3]
3. Thirdly, consequences for the organizations involved with hypocritical acts of members and potential for conclusions about hypocrisy and trust are refined by the comparison of the Penn State and the Roman Catholic Church responses to information about violations by personnel. As noted in Chapter 2, the comparative speed of organizational response by Penn State compared to a slower and less complete response by the Roman Catholic Church has led to different organizational costs. Penalties dictated by the NCAA toward Penn State regarding bowl appearances were reduced; and the record of the former head coach, Joe Paterno, has been re-stored at least

3 USA Swimming was established in 1960. A sequence of formal regulation of coach and athlete behavior stats with USA Swimming Safe Sport in 1987. In 2010, the program aims directly at the conditions of possible victimization of athletes that occurred with Curl. E.g., "Implemented comprehensive Safe Sport Program—update Code of Conduct; recommended best practice guidelines; expanded model policies" (usaswimming.org/protect, 2015).

so far as wins of games are concerned. The monetary costs for the Church, the continuation of legal cases, and the evolution of watch-dog groups bent on both identifying faults of the clergy and exacting penalties continue, due in part to the perception of a slow response of the Church in admitting errors and through establishing internal corrective measures.

Morality Enters: Is it Wrong to Violate Trust When Violations are the Norm?

In Smith's evaluation, trust was violated in all cases used in the book as illustrations. The conduct and the implications for self and others hold moral weight. But the Tour situation and now similarities between the Tour and some of the other cases raises the haunting prospect of a system where a system where dishonesty is the norm becomes self-perpetuating. The *difference* in consequences in practical terms and certainly implications for theory, when norms of deceit become normal, as they did in some of the cases presented are sizable. The question of the durability of a system which by estimations of all involved is deceitful provides a very sturdy test for the theoretical alternatives in view earlier in the book and further in the last chapter. As reviewed in Chapter 5, the "normal" system of a consistent pattern of dishonesty has proved unworkable and has to a degree been supplanted within the Tour. The change schematized in Figure 5.1 challenges the workability of the system of "deceit as normal." Similar sequences of shifts of ideas about normalcy occurred in the Hillsborough case, the situation in the Roman Catholic Church in the United States, and the situation with US Swimming. Now by extension of implications, the question rises about the workability of such a social system generally—a system, as it were, where trust focuses on the continuity of others being dishonest.

Beginning with four largely consistent documents about the Tour de France that have appeared in the last two years affords grist for the most consistent cynics and misanthropes among us. The material, indeed, represents a huge test for those with optimism about effective and fair social institutions, especially with institutions which organize sport activities. The titles alone should deter choices to consume the material in conditions of repose or in anticipation of slumber: *Reasoned Decision of the United States Anti-doping Agency on Disqualification and Ineligibility* (USADA, 2012); *Wheelmen: Lance Armstrong, the Tour de France, and the Greatest Sports Conspiracy Ever* (Albergotti and O'Connell, 2013); "The Armstrong Lie" (Gibney, 2013); and *Cycle of Lies: the Fall of Lance Armstrong* (Macur, 2014).

The value for the cynic grows and the aggravation for the optimist heightens because of the quality of the documents, which are thorough, creative, courageous, and each prepared with an obvious sense of obligation. Further, the running definition of sport before the project here of an activity that is physical, intrinsic, rule governed, and consummative is presented with an exceedingly stern potential exception. The sociological storehouse of terms, explanatory strategies, and of course general theoretical options is severely tested in the process of consuming and somehow accounting for the social system described by the four documents.

There are formulaic definitions of sociology—the enterprise here—available in historical accounts and dictionary definitions. One of the strongest representations of assumptions of social order as the focus of sociology is Émile Durkheim: "It has been pointed out that the word 'institution' will express this special mode of reality, provided that the ordinary significance of it be slightly extended. One can, indeed, without distorting the meaning of this expression, designate as 'institutions' all the beliefs and all the modes of conduct instituted by the collectivity. Sociology can then be defined as the science of institutions of heir genesis and of their functioning" (Durkheim, 1983). The current distribution of practices occurs in any inventory of presentations to a professional meeting or a running tally of new specialty journals within sociology. In addition to the evidence of variability and elaboration of the field, there are patterns of practice and consensual assumptions close to what Kuhn calls "normal science."

"Normal science," within a discipline often refers to the constellation of substance in the most widely distributed textbooks within a field of study. The course "Introduction to Sociology" is taught in almost every college in the world and in an increasing number of secondary schools. There is textbook literature that conveys the normal features of a *discipline*. One by Robert J. Brym and John Lie, *Sociology: Your Compass for a New World* (3rd edition) devotes one chapter of 22 to "Deviancy and Crime" (30 of 659 pages). Another, *Sociology* (12th edition) by John J. Macionis, devotes one of 24 chapters to "Deviance" (31 of 655 pages).

Within the range of work and central to commonalities there are assurances of social reproduction, possibilities of concerted social actions, valuations of some social stability, and support mechanisms to reduce threats to these social fixtures and maintain collective efforts of communal life. The record in the overlapping accounts of the team lead by Tygart at the United States Drug Agency, USDA (2012), Juliet Macur (2014), Albergotti and O'Connell (2013), and Alex Gibney's film, "The Armstrong Lie" (2014) tests many of these canons of the discipline upon which researchers depend, and certainly gives a picture of a type of social organization that is outside of what many need in the course of mundane human existence. At every level—participation, group organization, management, commercial support, oversight, and consumption—they document an institutional structure premised on regularized patterns of deceit.

Because the effectiveness of the deceits commonly depends on concealment of information (dissimulation) or claims for actions which are dubious or false, central processes of this institutional structure are rife with hypocrisy. This activity is "out there" and it is subject to and the responsibility of sociology work to address it. What can sociological wisdom provide? And what contribution is made to theory in the process, and what can or cannot be exploited from existing theoretical tools in the discipline? These topics define the priority of attention in Chapter 7.

By way of transition from the accounting of sites nurturing hypocrisy in earlier chapters *en route* to theoretical growth in the last chapter, several provisional answers to these questions will be offered:

1. The situation of the Tour de France contains different meanings about trust within the context of origin of the event compared to some of the other cases. But following the processes of the other cases shows similarities in how fundamental presuppositions of the normal way of doing business may change.
2. The Tour de France case gives useful illustration of the organizational imperatives in the sustenance of hypocrisy. But again, importantly, each of the other cases show how the surrounding organizations may have influenced conceptions of honesty, by aiding concealment of deceits or maintaining support of individuals who later proved to be dishonest.
3. We see a range of consequences of an organization premised on deceit. These include commercial implications; changes in the status of potential beneficiaries from the existing dishonesty; and personal consequences. In the case of the Tour de France, the lack of alteration in the standpoint toward and consumption of this sport production for many years is worthy of note also, as one might say, there was initially a lack of consequences from the patterned dishonesty. But with the changes at the point of the "fulcrum" in 2012, negative consequences became more visible. Similar patterns exist in the other cases as well.
4. One of the ingredients in all of the cases of organizational neglect toward detection an even protection of deceivers gives the persistent and resulting question of where correction can come from. In the record of the four focal documents, some suggestion of the import of outside entities such as journalism, entertainment, and independent control agents enters the process under view. Enabling conditions for all, though, include some level of legitimacy, and sufficient material resources to conduct their work.
5. On review, two of the four differentiae of sport seem compromised in the Tour case, the institution of professional bike racing being compromised and strongly influenced by money, means the centrality of an intrinsic and rule-governed activity is questionable. But the very extreme character of the intrusion of commercialism and winning at any costs (the outer edge of being consummative) does authenticate these two criteria of sport.
6. The cases prompt the question for sociology of the extent to which this system is different or the same as the other cases in view in the book, and relatedly, how the institution of the Tour de France is similar or different from institutions whose public face is represented as being truthful and transparent. In the documents cited, the words "moral" and "morality" enter, though infrequently. Attention is suggested to questions of goodness and badness within institutions of sport.

7. The etymology of "morality" suggests its importance for the questions with which sociologist deal. Christopher Powell (2010) provides a useful reminiscence of work by early theorists in the discipline. He arrays Max Weber, George Simmel, Karl Marx, and Émile Durkheim across a methodological individuals-to-holism dimension; also in this overview, a potential, and underdeveloped fifth prototype, "heterarchical theory," reflecting post-modern influences. The discipline displays contemporary energy, and conceptual options, for a new "sociology of morality" (Hitlin and Vaisey, 2010).

Proceeding, there are two important distinctions in past and current treatments of morality that bear on the discussion here. One concerns the emphasis on some kind of objective standard against which acts and individuals can be judged. This includes the contrast between normative vs. descriptive views of morality, realism vs. anti-realism, and approaches that stress absolute standards against those who advocate the salience of context. The other, related distinction lies between what amounts to a morality *of* action as opposed to a morality *in* action (one alternative implies an objective reference or standard for conduct, the other emphasizes the maintenance of the existing order as routine).

Regarding the first distinction, the visibility of strictures against lying within the texts and teachings of major religions is a major example of an absolutist or realist alternative. The instances of proscription of hypocrisy specifically in religious texts were noted earlier. Teachings against falsehood occur within the Judaic-Christian tradition in Exodus and Deuteronomy, for example ("You shall not bear false witness against your neighbor"); and are Number 4 within the "Precepts of Buddha" which states "A disciple of Buddha does not lie but rather cultivates and encourages truthful communication." The Koran says, "Truly Allah guides not one who transgresses and lies" (Surah 40:28). (Note, though, qualifications in both the Talmud and Koran.)

Within the classic tradition of sociology, Émile Durkheim's conception of social order as premised by a collective consensus over norms of conduct leans toward the realist pole as well as religious ideas and proscriptive philosophical ones such as those of Immanuel Kant.

Chapter 1 described the work of Erving Goffman which stresses the fundamental importance of self-presentation to others and mutual response of the intended audience as the core of social life. With this constructionist view at the level of interaction, I expressed the expectation that patterns of deceit, including hypocrisy, would be a substantive topic of interest to Goffman. Importantly, it is not. The connotation of falseness embedded in the related forms of hypocrisy as dissimulation and simulation does not occur. The essence of the interaction order is the mutual accomplishment of two or more people acting in concert where the senses of self—who they are—supported by each other. Façade, deceit, self-promotion (or self-derogation) are not a problem if the other acts in concert with the expression of self of the first person.

This analytical priority introduced in the tradition of Goffman's books receives current expression in the work of interpreters of Goffman such as Anne Warfield Rawls (1987; 2010), and to a certain extent with the traditions of ethnomethodology and conversation analysis (e.g., Turowitz and Maynard, 2010). In her earlier statement, Rawls seeks to redress any hesitancy readers have about Goffman's preoccupation with the "interaction order." In Rawls' interest in emphasizing Goffman's uniqueness (and in her effort to refine the position) the closeness of actions and responses by one and then another in their expressions of their selves and recognition of the others' self-hood an "interaction order" is defined and maintained. If one wants to introduce an idea of morality the criterion is the accuracy of the congruence in the behaviors of parties to the interaction order underway. The priority exists:

> If however, one treats at least some essential social facts as constituted in and through order properties of interaction (that are not themselves properties of institutions). Based on a mutual commitment among participants to do so (which also has nothing to do with social institutions), then the crucial patterns of behavior in question and the social facts they generate are not constituted by social institutions or by an individual orientation toward goals and values. They are constituted, rather by their relationship to mutual commitment of participants to the practice, which includes a commitment to reciprocate with one another to protect both self and interaction from damage should problems develop (Rawls, 2010: 96).

If the mutual understanding of self and other includes acts that acknowledge the relationship of mother and child, continued maintenance of selves to this interaction is moral because it is consistent and consensual. If the mutual understanding of a bike-racing self and a resourceful coach includes the elements of denying publically the use of testosterone or blood doping, the interaction order is moral so long as each is consistent in the deceitful fabrication. The sin in this interactional order is not the violation of statutes; nor is it a violation of the public's expectation of drug-free sport. The sin, the moral violation, is publicizing the illegal acts and divulging the deceits.

The elevation of the "interaction order" to central analytical and practical importance in the work of Goffman and Rawls serves the task of interpreting and analyzing the seemingly inchoate—and to the optimist citizen—depressing social system describe by the USDA, Gibney, Macur, Albergotti and O'Connell. An apparently endless population of micro-arrangements are negotiated among cyclists, coaches, cyclists and coaches, and all with sponsors that seem *ad hoc*, but they are of enormous import for the parties. This makes sense in terms of Goffman and Rawls, because one's very self is defined and protected to the extent that the small interaction order is maintained.

Participants at many levels of the Tour de France and commentators speak of a prevailing norm underlying many variations of expression in the hiding of deceits and conveying false information. The code, Omertà: "is a cultural expression and code of honor that places legitimate importance on a deep-rooted family sense of a 'code of silence,' non-aggravation with authorities, and non-interference in the legal actions of others" ("Omertà," 2014). The citation to this code and allusion to its properties occurs often within the culture of the Tour de France. The allusion to Omertà as a possible explanation for the seemingly non-traditional patterns of interaction among members of the bike culture adds a conceptual layer to the normative system in view that is located somewhere between the more encompassing set of laws and religious norms which Durkheim would assume to constitute society, and the micro, variegated exchanges among pairs of people termed interaction orders. The descriptive record of the four documents in view, however, continually illustrates how the ostensive external constraint of Omertà is broken.[4]

The Consequences of Hypocrisy for General Levels of Trust: and Continuation of the Program

Because of high standards which drive individuals—and sometimes organizations—to great lengths to achieve them, even though they may ultimately be unobtainable, hypocrisy occurs. Consequences for hypocrites, institutions, and persons deceived do not necessarily occur. But they can occur, as noted in the examples developed in earlier chapters. The likelihood and severity of negative consequences grow as the hypocritical conceits remain undiscovered or unacknowledged. A major factor in the delay of discovery or acknowledgement is the reluctance of superiors or confederates to aid the discovery, and the subsequent disqualification or penalization of the deceiver.

The Assignment Record Project, available within BishopAccountability.org, attempts to list every US Catholic priest who has been accused of sexual abuse since 1940. The dominant news about the priest scandals over the past two years has included information that layers of the Church administration have for decades covered up or ignored priest malfeasance.

It was not until the Hillsborough Independent Panel installed by the British government provided their final report in September 2012 that some official sense of national closure over the 1989 events occurred. Following the report, the Prime Minister registered national and general sentiment expressing his sympathy and regret.

Now, United States Swimming claims and displays in a recoverable listing, athletes and parents are protected by an inventory of coaches proscribed from being allowed to deal with athletes. The listing, "Individuals Permanently Suspended

---

4   As footnote no. 4 in Chapter 5 explains, the term is borrowed, resists definition within the culture of the Tour, but is commonly understood as a code of silence about secrets within the cycling culture.

or Ineligible" contains this caveat: "The following is a list of individuals who have received a lifetime ban, permanently resigned their membership, or been declared permanently ineligible for membership in USA Swimming. The fact that an individual's name does not appear on this list does not necessarily mean that he or she is eligible for membership in, or in good standing with, USA Swimming."

Chapter 7

Ethical and Theoretical Implications of Patterns of Hypocrisy: Artifice as a Species Constant or a Variable

Introduction: Looking Forward

John Milton sold *Paradise Lost* to Samuel Simmons on April 27, 1667 for five pounds, with the provision of an additional five pounds when successive editions of 1,300 items were sold. Milton's widow received payment, following sales of a third edition, on December 21, 1680, which was six years after Milton's death. The initial release from Simmons for five pounds was the equivalent of an amount today for 714 pounds or $1194, for the most famous of Milton's books, and by consent one of the most important books ever of English literature.

Milton was blind by the time he began *Paradise Lost*, depending on scribes to record his dictation. His life from 1608 where he protested, at cost, against presumption and constraints from both political and religious institutions lies at the center of the historical period Runciman identified as a defining period for hypocrisy and hypocrites (2008).

Milton's words in Book III of *Paradise Lost* alert us to the importance of hypocrisy within human societies; his intimation of the opaque character of hypocrisy represents the difficulties attached to understanding patterns of hypocrisy. He gives this respectful view of hypocrisy, along with a sober view of the task of illumination that defines the central intention of this project: "Neither man nor angel can discern hypocrisy, the only evil that walks invisible except to God alone" (Milton, [1667] 1940).

The mystery in Milton's characterization contains an awareness of hypocrisy as common and also perplexing. Both features can deter sociological attention. It is all around us, that is to say, so what can be added that is new? Paradoxes and inconsistencies do not strengthen researcher confidence in devoting resources to a topic. The features in Milton's cryptic comment, though, can remind us of our disciplinary obligations which have prompted the present endeavor. The foci of this project are traditional within sociology, even routinely so: a descriptive record of occurrences with a sensitivity to cultural contexts; strategic selection of ideal-typical cases; organizational aspects which affect occurrences; consequences for society; and investment in exploiting and developing theoretical resources. This chapter attempts to frame a foundation for continued work on the sociology of hypocrisy: by summarizing the components of the program from the preceding chapters, and pushing the potential of available theoretical options for penetrating the resistant features of hypocrisy, as John Milton characterizes them.

Hypocrisy and Sociology: Five Components of a Program

Hypocrisy: The Meanings in Contexts

Reprising some of the etymological notes introduced in Chapter 1, the words "hypocrite" and "hypocrisy" have roots in fourth century BC Greek use within the theater, where an actor is providing a fiction of an ostensive reality in the drama, and an actor's interpretation, one of alternative meanings; and also within the combination of the words "hypo," signifying under and "krinein" meaning to decide: hence a deficiency in judgment. Again, foregrounding definitional material included in the beginning of the project, the meanings from scholarship on the seventeenth- and eighteenth-century use, and preoccupation by Runciman (2006; 2008) and Shklar (1984), combine the practice of dissimulation, where an unfavorable characteristic is hidden, or simulation where a favorable characteristic is claimed falsely. Initial features of interest of the topic for sociological theory are the generality of the term, and the nearly completely consistent negative valance attached to "hypocrite" and "hypocrisy."

The empirical store from the beginning chapters provides illustrations of how culture, perused through time and national comparisons, suggests variability of frequency, saliency, and patterns of hypocrisy of individuals and institutions. "Hypocrisy," when used as a term, consistently carries a negative meaning, that suggests appearances are bad for society, and also implies that alternatives to hypocritical acts would support society. Despite the potential of the topic for traditional sociological priorities, the field has, as the material throughout the project illustrates, avoided systematic attention. The potential importance coupled with the marginality within the discipline has introduced a contradiction to which attention has been given as successive cases where hypocrisy appears have been treated. As examples of Max Weber's ideal-typical cases, religion and sport—the strategic limiting cases—offer prospects for the analysis of import for society and for sociological theory.

Paired with the universality of a negative cast when the term is employed, the volume of usage varies when religion and sport are discussed in public media in different settings. The term as reference and the term used pragmatically as an intended invective occur more prominently in the popular media of the United States than either in France or Iceland (Tables 2.1, 2.2). The explanation incorporated from scholarship by the political historians Runciman and Shklar suggests that the saliency of hypocrisy in the United States and earlier in Anglo settings is a consequence of cultural preoccupation with the standards of self and others for successful personal endeavors. The preoccupation, coupled with the realities of inevitably not reaching perfection, creates the *exigency* surrounding promises not fully realized that can lead to the deceits called hypocritical.

The histories of religion in each country show interest and significance of religion for political and social institutions. But there are differences. Attendance, importance, and continuous patterns of support for conservative strands of religion in the United States differ clearly with comparable patterns in both France and Iceland. Religiosity in its generality and potency within the United States potentially creates the striving for perfection that makes the United States stand out. The saliency and visibility of religious expectations potentially create a context of exigency, which is the context of anticipation of prevarications that can become hypocritical.

Fictional literature by virtue of its attention to biography in detail, representation of the most durable norms of a culture, and existence as a vehicle for an elaborate simulate of a social order provides additional grounds for the prospect of cultural differences of exigency as sketched in Chapter 3. American novelists across many decades of writing history, Hawthorne and Sinclair Lewis, for example, provide a social simulate of religious standards and consequences when standards are not reached which is noticeably different from the treatment of religion and an apparent clergy transgression in Iceland. For Hawthorne and Lewis, the claims by religious spokespersons were extraordinarily demanding. Connected with the high standards In Hawthorne and Lewis, in both scenarios the prospects of compromise became matters of life and death. Potential malfeasance of clergy in Laxness' novel (the Icelandic literary representative) pique the Bishop's curiosity and require administrative action but the facts of the case, when an observer reports it, show quite minor deviation from serious religious doctrine. The acts investigated by the Bishop and his emissary are matters of social decorum. Exigency for absolute purity is low; commensurately prospects for deception creep downward, and the costs and benefits—the implications of the malfeasance—should be considered partially humorous and ironical rather than disastrous as with the principals in *The Scarlet Letter* and *Elmer Gantry*.

As noted previously, Protestant Christianity enters frequently into the fiction of John Updike; and also in his recounting of biographical details (*Self-Consciousness*, 1989). Mr Updike's home-bases of Pennsylvania and New England explain his particular evocation of New England Congregationalism (Puritans) and the Presbyterianism of Pennsylvania. Three novels in particular serve to illustrate continuation of religious hypocrisy themes within the American writing history from Hawthorne and Lewis.[1] Updike, as a recent United States writer, allows present visibility as a continuation of cultural themes in Hawthorne

---

1   Hawthorne (1804–1864), Lewis (1885–1951), and Updike (1932–2009, and Laxness (1902–1998), and Molière (1622–1673) hold religion salient in their personal biographies and in their priorities for aptly representing their respective cultural themes. Autobiographical and biographical sources illustrate this: Hawthorne's birth in Salem, Massachusetts sets the stage for his interest in Puritan "exigency." Lewis' biography and impressively systematic style of work receive illustration in Hutchisson, 1996; for Updike,

and Lewis. As a contemporary of Halldór Laxness (1902–1998), the Icelandic representative in the cultural comparison between the United States and Iceland, considering Updike (1932–2009) assures both are current as well as both clearly representing their own cultural histories.

The dynamic of religious expectations by culture and its religious leaders, and the inevitable failures to realize the expectations—again, the exigency—appear within the roles of the clergy figures and those around them. Some assign the classification of "The Hawthorne Trilogy" to this group of Updike's work.

The Scarlet Letter appeared in the United States in 1850. The book was a best seller. The period of writing occurred toward the end of the Second Great Awakening and before the growth of the Third Great Awakening continuing from the late 1850s into the twentieth-century. Both movements were post-millennial describing the second coming of Christ within Christianity to follow periods of social development by believers. In practical terms, progressive reform movements, with religious association, flourished from these admonitions. The saliency of religion in associations, beliefs, and in investment in practical policies shows special features of religion in the United States. The period in focus in *The Scarlet Letter* is the mid-seventeenth-century in Salem, an earlier example and foregrounding of this penchant for religious belief and practice, and the associated standards of individual religious purity.

The period of the Third Great Awakening of the early twentieth-century was closing by the time of the publication of *Elmer Gantry*. Perceived decline in church membership and diminution of religious orthodoxy among US citizens prompted denominational preachers or sometimes independent preachers to engage in extra-church revivals. Billy Sunday (1862–1935) was a popular evangelical preacher in the first quarter of the twentieth-century. Aimee Semple McPherson (1890–1944) followed Sunday, increasing her broad appeal through use of radio. Elements of Sunday, a former major league baseball player who had played for the Chicago White Stockings of the National League, with the Pittsburgh Alleghenys in 1888, ending his career with the Philadelphia Phillies as he began his religious carrier as an evangelist, enter the image of Elmer Gantry. McPherson's life and work anticipate the popular evangelist in the novel, Ellen Falconer, whom Gantry meets, works for, and continues for a time as a lover.

A Month of Sundays appeared in 1974. Updike, as noted, reflects his personal religious and ideological history and the religious settings in Philadelphia and New England. The God is Dead Movement noted above was temporally associated with

---

again, 1989; for Molière, Scott, 2000; and for Laxness, Chapter 3, and in Guðmundsson, 2014; Hallberg, 1971a and 1971b; and Sigurjónsson, 1986.

Sometimes the three novels in which Updike gives particular attention to religion in the United States, *A Month of Sundays* (1974), *Roger's Version* (1986), and *S* (1988), combine as a key way-station on the cultural lineage from Hawthorne through Sinclair Lewis to the beginning of the twenty-first century. Clergy figure prominently in these pieces, as in *The Scarlet Letter* and *Elmer Gantry*.

highly publicized criticism of US society, with changes in sexual morality, civil rights activity oriented to improvements of Blacks and women in the country, and protests against the United States' involvement militarily in Southeast Asia. The middle-class religious culture of Updike's *Sundays* takes into account the widely attributed changes of the late 1960s and early 1970s. But, critically, by intent in characterizations, plot, and preeminence of central themes, *A Month of Sundays* continues the preoccupation with religion of the earlier ancestors, and retains remnants of the complex dynamics of the exigencies in culture that make ancestors of Puritan culture vulnerable to hypocrisy.

The Reverend Thomas Marshfield is a Lutheran clergyman (with decided Puritan and Reformed proclivities) who has been sent to a make-shift resort area for a certain kind of rehabilitation due to violations he showed in his role as a pastor. There are other temporary residents of this rehabilitation site, a reasonably expensive motel with access to a golf course. Three, Woody, a Roman Catholic Priest, Jamie Ray, a visitor from a Southern evangelical denomination, and Amos ("the pastor of a happy little outer-inner-city church," Updike, 1975: 183) feature in the account. Residents of this rehabilitation site must provide a journal of their religious life and presumably give some accounting of errors they have made as members of the clergy. The substance of the narrative is Reverend Marshall's record of his life in his church and its culmination in mistakes, discovery, consequences, and movement out of his job with the rehabilitation assignment a point on his devolution.

It is not in Updike's orientation as a writer to be just provocative, or just satirical, or just a writer of parody. He shows this clearly in the large corpus of novels (which appeared at approximately two year intervals until the end of his life) and in his own non-fictional criticism. However, his attention to common factual details and the oddities of human behavior (as opposed to searching for the deep motivational forces in his actors' minds) means that he responds with care to what are the reported contexts of his heroes and heroines. Hawthorne writing in 1850 makes the mid-seventeenth century his object, but his sense of religion in New England is unavoidably framed by his experiences in the mid-nineteenth century. Lewis systematically sought out biographical details of contemporary members of the clergy in the 1920s and carefully immersed himself into the religious life of the period of writing. This attention to detail illuminates his own characterization of the common themes of religion within the US, and aptly adds his way-station along the trajectory of Hester Prynne and Dimmsdale, Gantry and his love, Ellen Falconer, and Thomas Marshfield.

The deeds of Reverend Marshfield may seem to be caricatures of a member of the clergy too soundly and easily corrupted by the norms of the surrounding culture—sufficiently strong even to mar the professionalism and purity of a pastor. Thomas Marshfield, though, is a leader of a mainline Protestant church, with expectations for prudent staffing, accomplished and orthodox sermons, professional counseling of parishioners, and displaying a faultless family life. Marshfield, though, has had an affair with his organist, slept on occasion with women whom he counsels, and as the ultimate violation of his expectations attempted a sexual life with the wife of the head of the Deacons, or the governing body of his church. Reverend Marshall is a hypocrite.

Within the notable attributes of Updike as a writer, which include productivity, good citizenship as a public intellectual, and assiduous care to detail, he is true to unrelenting and often mutually contradictory features of American religion. The religious, and certainly religious leaders, are to be good, aspirants to improvement if not perfection. Their training, predispositions, and surrounding evaluators demand these credentials. This is so for Marshfield. As with the objects of interest for Hawthorne and Lewis, Updike's hero can never meet the expectations. The American religious hero or heroine in this American trajectory is always prompted to deceptions, from the intensity of the exigencies of the culture. Marshall is a student of Karl Barth (popular among seminarians in the late 1960s) and not Paul Tillich. Barth lies clearly in the lineage of Jean Calvin. "To sum up, and to bring my day's trial to an end, I had no choice but to follow my father into the ministry; the furniture forced me to do it. I became a Barthian, in reaction against his liberalism" (Updike, 1974: 25).

A person strongly within the contradictory currents of Puritan religion must energetically pursue the ethical mandates; but inevitably one errors, and because of the broad expectations for conduct the hypocrisy can occur. In the narrative Marshfield is writing, "I love myself and loathe myself more than other men" (Updike, 1974: 9). His most intense personal and romantic attraction among his examples of adultery is a refined, attractive, older woman who is the wife of the head of the Deacons. Her name is Frankie Harlow, and she is a believer of unusual strength and unmitigated consistency. In attempted sexual relationships with Ms Harlow, Reverend Marshall is impotent.

With the three sport-emphases described for the United States in Chapter 2 (collegiate expense in providing sport, the centrality of gender civil rights issues in the history of sport, and the role of professional leagues), sport displays a generality, a tie to social traditions of success and invidious distinctions, and a centrality in overall trends in social priorities that differ from culture patterns in France and Iceland. If the formal definition of sport is applied, being physical, intrinsic, rule governed, and consummative, all dimensions and certainly the last have an enhanced pattern in the United States. Here with sport there is again the elevated condition of exigency for deceits: high standards, competition which leaves all unfulfilled at some point, and then the possibility of compensating constructions termed hypocritical.

There are variable expectations for performance (winning, money, or personal sanctity). The expectations may come from culture or the institution. They may be variably internalized. There are variable chances for success (Wieting, 2000). This characterizes the increasing stakes and diminishing chances to win in NCAA football, and the combination of demands for success in the Roman Catholic Church along with the possible diminished realities of success. Suzy Favor's account included the strong internalized expectation to be "perfect." As she aged, prospects for "perfection" seemed more remote, leading to her depression and need for new demonstration of "perfection." She received accolades (ranked third best) within an evaluation scheme oriented to prostitutes.

These factors themselves are conditioned by the ability to compartmentalize. Roles and evaluative dimensions within individuals may be isolable. Suzy Favor had post-partum depression following the birth of her child, and her husband had opposed her being a prostitute. These were framed as ways to reduce culpability. Her agreeing to be an "escort" was really only for a year; she was good at it, as was her "constitutional" predisposition for perfection—even though she now admits that the choice was a mistake. Institutional public relations may be able to separate spheres; or different departments may deal with different issues. The ruling of the Catholic Church to keep secret the discovery of pedophile priests was couched as being a greater need for the reputation of the Church, than was the need to protect vulnerable victims from the assaults of priests. An important part of this is the type of excuse and justification that the culture prompts and will allow (Lyman and Scott, 1968).

I have elected to use the term "tacit theory" to denote the features of a society that are assumed by natives for sufficient practical conduct. Mention of novels from the United States, France, and Iceland provide efficient illustration of these assumptions, and discriminate the cultures. Other terms comparable are "expectancy states" (rational choice theorists); "common sense reality" (phenomenologists); and the "generalized other" (social behaviorists). The unexpressed theory guide decisions about what to do, what to anticipate in the response of others, bases of planning when dealing with institutions, and beliefs about consequences when successes and failures occur. Tacit theories become more explicit when they prove unsuccessful, activities are blocked or sanctioned, or when one is asked to articulate the assumptions.[2]

---

2   1. Using novels as a source of comparative information relative to traditional sociological research meets a central principle of validation, which is to find similarities and differences between products using different methods. 2. The writing in novels provides a description of both behavior and motivation. These are usually not available together in a piece of systematic research. 3. The narrative of a novel provides a simulation of a social situation that has a temporal element. We can see what happens in groups over time in ways that we never or rarely can in systematic research. 4. The narrative of novels offers the chance to see different viewpoints from separate members of a group. 5. Non-public or non-obvious social relations in groups can be depicted in the novel's narrative in ways that rarely are visible in traditional sociological research. Examples include secrets, lies, instances of ambivalence (love vs. hate in a relationship), complex communication, conflicts, the predisposition to save or hoard, and how groups deal with unexpected events such as accidents, windfalls, or loss of a life or a job. 6. The criterion for use of the novels here is not just that they are representational. Rather, the records of the hypocritical acts are each intelligible from the standpoint of its respective context and less intelligible from the standpoint of an alternative context. Rather than just representing the culture, they each discriminate their culture.

Sociological theory, in its more explicit forms, does not differ widely from tacit theories. Drawing from the content of the book, hypocrisy, tacit theories include: (a) ideas about what is salient or significant (in Weber); valances of reward and punishment attached to significant domains of activity; markers of evaluation; and consequences of failure and consequences of success from varieties of human action. Each of these—still not fully articulated assumptions about behavior—draw close to the coverages of Weber, the Chicago school of Pierce, Mead, and Goffman, and Durkheim mentioned throughout the book.

Table 7.1   Tacit theories of religious experience*

	France	Iceland	US
Salience, significance	Medium	Low	High
Ways to success, accomplishment	Regular, infrequent ritual conformity	Politeness; ritual respect	Ethical purity; adult confirmation; belief in scripture
Markers of evaluation	Attendance; confession	Secular sociability	Renunciations; baptism; resistance to scriptural alternatives; relative superiority
Consequences of failure or success	Deferred[3]	Breach of cultural bond	Self-inflections; public remorse; predisposition toward fabrication

* Tacit theories are non-expressed beliefs about self, others, and institutions enabling natives to proceed daily in their lives. The substance is not appreciably distinct from **prevailing** sociological theories. Tacit theories have relatively non-explicit assumptions; they use stories as a primary means of memory and communication. Tacit theories may become explicit when they prove unsuccessful, their directives are blocked by institutions, or when others ask actors for an explanation of behaviors.

Religion and Sport as Test Cases

Even with the denotative meaning of hypocrisy, of course, it can occur in a wide variety of institutions. Runciman and Shklar have addressed their work to politics. Machiavelli, if read literally, advocates hypocrisy or any other useful prevarication as appropriate for the Prince. The idea of the corporation as a central organizational principle of business in the United States does not eschew hypocrisy but may sustain it so long as corporate obligations are met to generate profits. I note the

---

3   For a useful recent journalistic example of public neutrality to private morality in France, see Dan Bilefsky, "France Crosses a Threshold in Examining Strauss-Kahn's Personal Life," *The New York Times*, February 19, 2015.

corporate business of cigarette sales and the common identification of hypocrisy in the document store for that business.

The reason I have elected to focus on hypocrisy in religion and sport is that these two institutions represent in their proclaimed purposes and generally attributed social obligations levels of honesty and opposition to deceit that make them unique. If hypocrisy has consequences in institutions—as is described in the project—then a defensible first step is to consider these institutions as "limiting cases." If hypocrisy exists in these two institutions where such hiding of information and manufacture of information is essentially considered anathema, then this gives a starting point to assessing degrees of hypocrisy and consequences of hypocrisy where such formal denunciation of hypocrisy does not exist. Conversely, if hypocrisy does exist in these institutions, then warnings persist about hypocrisy and its implications within other institutions, and for society as a whole.

I have used Clifford Geertz's definition of religion (Chapter 1). I believe this has broad use by researchers who want to identify common components of religion in doing comparative research. One might add Paul Tillich's definition of religion as "that which concerns us ultimately." While cryptic, this certainly is discriminating in identifying beliefs, rituals, and teachings which official religions maintain and which cannot be casually applied to the institutional purposes of other institutions.

As expressed earlier, for a definition to be useful it must refer to something and exclude something else. I believe my definition of sport as: physical, intrinsic, rule governed, and consummative does capture how sport was known from early records of the Olympics in the eighth century BC, and how it usefully can be used at present with the "boundaries in use" criterion along the lines of Durkheim's definition of moral systems. The boundaries of elite athletics (Olympic Games or Tour de France) are illuminated when violations are cited. These same essential components of sport appear in gymnasia all over the world on Saturday mornings where "pick-up" games of hand-ball, soccer, or basketball occur without formal referees. (Note discussion and citations on informal sport in Chapter 1.)

The Organizational Imperatives of Hypocrisy

Two of the somewhat surprising characteristics of the cases described in the earlier chapters included the complexity of actors and meanings within episodes of hypocrisy, and simultaneously the length of time a series of acts which are dishonest build on one another and become complicit in erecting an increasingly complex organizational structure. Timelines of representative cases given particular attention here exist as figures in respective chapters (Figures 1.1, 1.2, 5.2, 5.3). Contrary to, or at least strongly expansive of, the original meanings of the terms of "hypocrisy" and "hypocrite," both of which denote discrete actors and events, the record of a *system* of dishonesty in an individual's or an institution's biography of lies suggests a complex and durable character that becomes increasingly difficult to detect and to end.

Hypocrisy and Consequences

The presumption of hypocrisy as being a discrete act by an individual and institution which is dominant in the hundreds of uses of the word and attributions over 50 years within three countries completely circuits the record of personal and social consequences of hypocrisy (enumerated in Tables 2.1 and 2.2). Consequences from the case descriptions are anomalous at times, generally understudied, and largely under-theorized: hence, the perceived obligations of treatment of consequences in Chapter 6 and attending to theoretical prospects in this final chapter.

This book takes seriously the scholarship within moral philosophy, sociology, and within political science that has attempted to isolate the essentials of "hypocrisy." In the publication history of four reasonably representative journals on the sociology of sport and the sociology of religion, there are 67 references to "hypocrisy." These range from a single word to a few titles of articles; there is no sustained treatment across the population of articles of definition, social contexts, social consequences, or tie with any branch of sociological theory (excepting general allusions to power and hegemony of some institutions).

Evidence of interest in hypocrisy in the institutions of sport and religion does exist. Hypocrisy is eschewed by the texts of many religions. Journalistic coverage of instances of hypocrisy consistently condemns the occurrences. Instances of hypocrisy in sport and religion appear in journalistic coverages across a wide swath of cultures—always with a negative valence. Even though patterns of hypocrisy by individuals and institutions may persist over decades without publicity, when they are discovered and publicized the administrators concerned with consequences of hypocrisy may act severely and swiftly to reduce public censure.[4]

The meaning of hypocrisy driving the start of the investigation is of actions of an individual or institution which either hide a dark side or pretend a false credential. Crucial *differentiae* in this definition are the components of deceit and the fact that the propagator of the deceit gains something from the lack of disclosure or the claim of an unfounded credential that the individual or institution possesses. As ties with these forms of hypocrisy with other potential deceits or deviations from norms of religion and sport occur, a more variegated treatment of hypocrisy and other kinds of deceits and their social consequences has occurred in the later chapters of the book. But the strategy here has been to begin with a narrow and serious definition of "hypocrisy" rather than the use of the term to refer to any kind of objectionable inconsistency or contradiction.

---

4   Careful treatment of institutionalized sport where apparent deceit exists and is organizationally supported occurs in work on soccer by John Sugden and Alan Tomlinson (1998; 2003). References to hypocrisy can come within sociological books principally broadly focused on other topics. In Otis Dudley Duncan's masterful treatment of the history of measurement he takes note of the existence of material reward given victors in the ancient Olympics. "Actually, there was considerable hypocrisy in the pretense that the only reward for athletic victory was honor" (Duncan, 1984: 84).

A Formidable Consequence: Levels of Trust in Societies

It is, as noted, the case that hypocrisy may occur in a variety of institutions. Social consequences of hypocrisy come from perceptions of betrayal, lack of authenticity, and lack of integrity. These, among other factors, have been discussed as associated with national reductions in trust in all institutions (the US, for example). Evidence of diminution of trust in institutions has been documented for other countries as well, though with country variations. One continuous record of patterns of confidence in institutions comes from the Gallup Poll since 1973. With respect to organized religion in the US, "Quite a lot" of confidence has moved from a high of 68 percent in 1975 to 44 percent of the public in 2012. Confidence in television peaked in 1996 at 46 percent and now is 21 percent. Some of the lowest levels of confidence are with health maintenance organizations (19 percent), big business (19 percent), and the US Congress (12 percent).

While deceit and the particular form of deceit described here as hypocrisy may be part of this general loss of confidence, sport and religion alone as defined here represent institutions where the very character of the message or product or service is based on fidelity. There are large practical problems in dealing with hypocrisy across all institutions in the US let alone cross-nationally. And doing so broadens beyond manageability the persistence of the fidelity claim. Again, the lessons of the consequences of hypocrisy for social institutions can be drawn from these limiting cases of religion and sport.

Theoretical Options and Theoretical Stakes within Sociology

Hypocrisy as common, frequent, serious—and circuited by sociological theory

In the interest of identifying an accessible and common pool of research in sport and religion, I use the population of items attending to hypocrisy in the histories of four journals, described earlier (*Social Compass, Journal for the Scientific Study of Religion, Sociology of Sport Journal, and International Review for the Sociology of Sport*). In this population, conceptions of theory range from one word and an ostensive body of work of one author (e.g., Gramsci or Veblen or Marx or Weber), to some terms for moderately general lines of research such as on cognitive consistency, and to very general allusion such as "post-modern." Of relevance for describing the project in view here: (1) there is little attention to contexts; (2) there is almost no attention to how hypocrisy (however defined) fits into social systems cross-time and cross-culturally where trust is an issue; (3) there is no systematic attention to social consequences of hypocrisy; and (4) there are no items that compare pairs of theories, let alone compare three theories.

Minimal theory obligations

I express these points here regarding my theoretical intentions as priorities that I have. I well understand readership and scholarship display variability of definitions, priorities, and uses of sociological theory.

First, there should be description of social outcomes that have some temporal permanence, generality, and cultural range. Very few of the population of research articles address generality in terms of temporal permanence. There are three brief mentions of Roman Catholicism's influence on State structures that define sport policy and there is one article that deals with the Christianity of athletes. But of the 67 there is no effort to expand ideas of generality by comparing religion and sport (despite as stipulated here their inherent similarities). There is virtually no strategic effort to expand generality of theory across culture: 62 articles address one country, two address two countries, and three address three or more. The project here on hypocrisy illustrates the relative preoccupation with hypocrisy in major news sources in three countries over a half century, and describes representative cultural and organizational uniqueness of sport and religion in the three countries (United States, Iceland, and France).

Secondly, there should be lines of congruence identified among parts of the system, such as in this case relevance for concealment and simulation (types of hypocrisy) of new technologies. These new technologies affect likelihoods of concealment, access, and detection and relationships of hypocrisy (as defined here) with general trends of suspected compromises of candor and disclosure and concealment.

Thirdly, there should be attention to the assumptions of sociological theories that are in play. Assumptions distinguish theories but they also can make it difficult to evaluate theories. None of the articles in the reference population compare and contrast two theories, let alone three theories. The project here discusses the relevance of three theories in the examination of the two institutions, across a half century, in three countries.

Fourthly, theories should be able to add some clarity to "outlying cases" or non-obvious outcomes. This is a part of what Thomas Kuhn deals with in *The Structure of Scientific Revolutions* (2012) as anomalous cases. Can the cases be incorporated into a theory, or does the gradual enumeration of the anomalous cases eventually require an expansion of the theory or a shift in theoretical paradigm? This manifestly is not a project on idiosyncratic or sensational cases; but the project includes a collection of cases that have recently appeared in sport and religion literature and which occupy this anomalous status and hence represent potential for extensions of theory. These include the recent publication of Tyler Hamilton and Daniel Coyle: *The Secret Race: Inside the Hidden World of the Tour de France: Doping, Cover-ups, and Winning at All Costs*; the news coverage of Suzy Favor Hamilton's career as a high priced prostitute (e.g., Jeré Longman in *The New York Times*, December 20, 2012). Anomalous too is a broadly distributed account of an amateur runner in the United States who has persistently tried to cheat while running distance events (while at the same time going through related activities to mask and diffuse his cheating with claims to altruism [Mark Singer, "Is Kip Litton a Marathon Fraud?" *The New Yorker*, August 6, 2012]).

Given the potential seriousness of hypocrisy for institutions, it is a non-obvious outcome that many cases discussed in this project took decades to be uncovered. Social consequences of hypocrisy are not general. Shklar makes this point. William Ian Miller, an author consulted at several points here, makes this point (e.g., in Miller, 2003). The very idea that an act or pattern of actions may persist for years, and then when made public yield counter actions from putative victims, the criminal justice system, and administrations vividly illustrates the import of context. The cases of charged pedophilia within the Roman Catholic Church made visible in the last few years now are known to have existed for at least half a century. Current major economic, public, and legal responses to Floyd Landis and Lance Armstrong, respectively address occurrences that began in 1999 and 2005. Penn State University in the US in the past several months did act quickly to deal with prospects of hypocrisy within its athletic system through firings, removal of vestiges of honor to the designated culprits, enlistment of unhampered legal investigators, and firing of its own major administrators. All this closely following public disclosure; but the events occurred and were concealed since 1998. (Similarly, extensive records of Boy Scout groups in the United States are now being made public due to journalistic efforts to use legal gambits to obtain information on these kinds of cases.)

The volume of uses of the term: from common usage, from intricacies under a careful analysis, and from the potential of seeing the power of metaphor (e.g., Lakoff) point to some efforts to deal with these often costly delays in dealing with the deceits termed hypocritical. One is some recognition of the import of contexts and how globalization and associated homogenization smooth the meanings and implications of hypocrisy. Another, given the prospects of organizational imperatives in nurturing and sustaining hypocrisy, is to inquire whether there are realistic organizational implications for reducing these deceits (and then, potentially, enhancing trust). Further, if the record is as indicated here, with the breadth and durability of occurrences of hypocrisy, what can sociology do in suggesting ameliorative prospects for reducing these deceits within sport and religion and the associated costs?

Three theory contenders
Erving Goffman and his followers If Goffman's posture toward lying has informed or reflects the traditions of sociology then the absence of sociological treatment of hypocrisy is not an anomaly at all. Goffman's approach from the beginning of his rich production of insights and terminology considers all social life as artifice. In his whole scheme, the meanings of hypocrisy as probed here are ordinary and predictable. When we find in *Presentation of Self* the terms for disruption (inconsistencies or contradictions) in "face," for example, these are not problematic for society in terms of lost trust and cynicism.

Rather, the valence of treatment is that these are flaws in the maintenance of a social conspiracy erecting a social order. Goffman assumes the performance of all actors is not problematical with deceitful acts. By contrast, critics of hypocrisy see these as the fissures that can doom society. What is problematical for Goffman in the deceits is the discovery. This can only be resolved or repaired by a recovery individually created or aided by allies. The valuation of this deception is somewhat altered in *Stigma*. Here one's identity personally and socially can potentially become at risk. So one must work to "fit" into society. One learns to "pass" or to "cover" questionable acts and appearances.

Goffman's work, of course, comes from the social philosophical position of pragmatism developed in the United States by William James, Charles Peirce, and John Dewey. Here, criteria of reason and empirical demonstration are subsumed under practical consequence. Broadly, meaning exists in the consequence of the act. Truth lies not lie in the purity of the rational sequence or the hope for an empirical record. Truth lies in the material consequence that results from an act.

Émile Durkheim writing about pragmatism at the beginning of the twentieth century (Durkheim, 1983) sees this philosophical epistemological position untenable; and essentially at odds with his intention to establish a sociology based on empirical facts (social realities that lie outside ourselves and which yield sanctions when violated). For Goffman, as noted, lies—when they become visible from lack of social associations that conceal them and therefore don't "keep the social order moving"—are the only problem for the smooth texture of society. In the "Thirteenth Lecture" in *Pragmatism and Sociology* (Durkheim, 1983: 67, 68), Durkheim releases his antagonism toward the moral and epistemological faults of pragmatism:

> How could reason, in particular, have arisen in the course of the experiences undergone by a single individual? Sociology provides us with broader explanations. For it, truth, reasons and morality are the results of a becoming that includes the entire unfolding of human history.
>
> Thus we see the advantage of the sociological over the pragmatist point of view. For the pragmatist philosophers, we have already said several times, experience can take place on one level only. Reason is placed on the same plane as sensitivity; truth, on the same planes as sensations and instincts. But men have always recognized in truth something that in certain respects imposes itself on us, something that is independent of the facts of sensitivity and individual impulse. Such a universally held conception of truth must correspond to something real. It is one thing to cast doubt on the correspondence between symbols and reality; but it is quite another to reject the thing symbolized along with the symbol. [Here, a footnote to *Elementary Forms* is added by the editor of this English edition, John B. Allcock.] This pressure that truth is seen as exercising on minds is itself a symbol that must be interpreted, even if we refuse to make of truth something absolute and extra-human.
>
> Pragmatism, which levels everything, deprives itself of the means of making this interpretation by failing to recognize the duality that exists between the mentality which results from individual experiences and that which results from collective experiences. Sociology, however, reminds us that what is social always possesses a higher dignity than what is individual. It can be assumed that truth, like reason and morality, will always retain this character of being a higher

value. This in no way prevents us from trying to explain it. The sociological point of view has the advantage of enabling us to analyze even that august thing, truth.

Bruce Schneier: bounds and bounded rationality   For Schneier (2012), defection from norms of fidelity is a rational choice resulting from insufficient constraints provided by security resources in a community. "Our exploration of trust is going to start and end with security, because security is what you need when you don't have any trust, and—as we'll see—security is ultimately how we induce trust in society. It's what brings risk down to tolerable levels, allowing trust to fill in the remaining gaps" (17). For Schneier, liars are adaptive. If they lie so much that eventually nobody trusts them, then there is a limit. But does the aggregate limit ever destroy the trust basis in society? Schneier's point is that opponents reciprocally adapt. Is this evolutionary or strategic in one generation (ontogeny)?

Schneier either assumes rationality with perfect knowledge of alternative outcomes and associated positive and negative weights; or he cannot account for stable lines of action. Trust *ipso facto* cannot occur—only infinite security enhancements.

Hypocrisy itself—false display followed by detection—cannot conform to his action-reaction hypothesis because the exigencies of hypocrisy are culturally variable.

Specifically, hypocrisy depends on several conditions which may be different within different times and places.

1. An emphasis on and belief in purity and self-improvement.
2. Self-evaluation based on invidious distinctions. That is "my worth is determined relatively," and by criteria established outside of ourselves.
3. Signs or markers of performance become widely available (Thorstein Veblen, *The Theory of the Leisure Class*, 1967; Quentin Bell, *On Human Finery*, 1976).
4. Because of limited resources, inequality for everybody is unavoidable (see Jonathan Cobb and Richard Sennett, *The Hidden Injuries of Class*, 1993).
5. Social constraints on people who deviate: morals, reputation, institutional constraints, security measures.
6. Reasons why people deviate (Schneier, 2012: 145, 6): selfish self-interest, self-preservation interest, ego-preservation interest, other psychological motivation, relational interest, group interest of another group, competing moral interest.
7. Reasons why organizations defect (156): selfish interest, self-preservation interest, ego-preserving interest, other psychological motivations.

Considerable weight from the recent histories of religion and sport support the conflict view and Schneier's cases. By the expectations of sport and religious institutions, integrity of actors, either individual, group, or corporate, by definition must be assumed. The presence, and as evident in the chapters, the persistence of hypocrisy where lies occur and are sustained threatens sport and religious institutions. Sizable investments within the NCAA, national sport organizations such as USA Swimming, and the Tour de France are being made to detect lies, to publicize them, and to make lying costly with fines and suspensions. Lawful and accommodating actions of athletes, coaches, and team organizations represent coin of value—indeed essential value—for the integrity of sport. Non-hurtful, honest postures of church employees lie consistently with claims and expectations of religious organizations. When employees compromise the claims and thwart the expectations constituencies hold for church employees, again the coin of religious offerings can drop drastically in value.

So, the quick, public description of sport and religious organizations is to try to combat the threat to the lost value of commodities. This can come from detection, publication, and where possible, penalization.

On a general level, a refined, new technological tool exists as *Transparency International*. Specific to the sports covered, the installation of team monitors, USADA, WADA, and now Federal initiatives all illustrate efforts to control false information within cycling. First, Penn State, then the Big-Ten, then encompassing organization for that university, and then perhaps the NCAA took ameliorative steps during and following the Penn State problems. USA Swimming now publishes a list of banned officials. With respect to the Roman Catholic Church, any priest named as an offender appears on a list. The initial response to a recent scandal over judging in rhythmic gymnastics was to sanction judges.

In summary, these are theoretical ideas that essentially are aligned with conflict theory, but come from sources that include variables of differences in relative access to technologies that allow hiding information, but also can allow detection and publication of hidden information, and can allow consumption of the information. The idea that conflict over control of information as capital will continue (as progenitors of fictions are discovered and constrained by security), the pace, complexity, and relative success both of infractions (liars and outliers) and those responsible for security can be assessed both across time and culture. (Note: For hypocrisy to have social consequences, relevant consumers must have access to the description of hypocrisy. The sequence includes variable access of hypocrites to mechanisms of concealment, and then variable access of publicists such as journalists to the information, and then variable access of consumers through levels of literacy and physical access to media carrying the information—issues considered in Chapter 4.)

A social contract where pretense is modulated and evaluation of shortcomings attends to context   The weight of social and institutional response to lying in sport and religion supports impressively a conflict view of this kind of deviance and the attendant institutional reaction. Further, to expand general attention to conflict issues as opposed to alternative issues, the Human Relations Area Files (covering 285 cultures) finds 4,020 paragraphs in 1,261 documents in 254 cultures for "conflict." In contrast within the HRAF archives, there are 1,033 paragraphs in

422 documents in 160 cultures. This is between a two to one and four to one ratio of saliency of conflict to cooperation. Cases remain in general social organization and in sport, though, where the norm is cooperation and in the focus here this means truth-telling. The presence of the cases, particularly in light of the fact that in both sport and religion fidelity to rules and truth contribute to the essence of both institutions, demands that these additional theoretical possibilities be explored. They may be minority instances, but they define the essence of both institutions. Six possibilities can be considered.

These are theoretical ideas that I am terming here "contractual." As anticipated in Chapter 1, these theoretical ideas do not assume the basis of social order is artifice, as with Goffman. They do not assume the inevitable and unstrained predisposition for people, who can, to control information (yielding in turn continuing efforts to detect and publicize from opposing groups who want to control information as a form of capital). The examples in this third grouping allow variations in levels of honesty and levels of deceit as forms of capital in interactions. Cross-culturally and through time (and two institutions), variations in degrees of hypocrisy can be assessed. In this theoretical grouping, contracts to assure and maintain transparency and honesty when dealing with the coin or capital of information are established. This alterative is not "pie in the sky," since the examples address multiple scales of social organizations, such as dyads through nation-states, and they stipulate identifiable variables where more or less of contractual exchanges occur where honesty prevails. Illustrative examples include the following: Robert Axelrod, *The Evolution of Cooperation*; Tony Ashworth, *Trench Warfare: 1914–1918*; John Rawls, *A Theory of Justice*; Roger Fisher, William Ury, and Bruce Patton, *Getting to Yes: Negotiating Agreement without Giving In* (2003). Combining with these four are two groups of ideas that are useful to make up the six possibilities: contractual principles of honor societies, such as in Iceland, traced from the Early Commonwealth (William Ian Miller, *Bloodtaking and Peacemaking: Feud, Law, and Society in Saga*) to the present effort of Iceland to revise their National Constitution in the interest of re-establishing principles of contract that protect mutual obligations of integrity; and instances of sport where referees are absent or barely evident.

With respect to this last source of contractual ideas, within the array of highly visible world sports, curling and golf exist as exceptions where referees are not present. In golf, there are at larger events officials that can interpret rules to competitors. The contests in these two sports represent the epitome of rule governed sport where the players themselves maintain the integrity of the practices. If there are some features of the character, history, participant populations, or spectator expectations which can be identified supporting these athlete-run sports, then the possibility of transporting any of these to other sports (which apparently need increasingly elaborate policing systems) in principle does exist.

Curling has roots in Scotland and came later to Canada. The World Curling Federation lists 50 national member organizations, showing its international distribution. Curling has been an Olympic sport since 1996, and World

Championships occur yearly for men, women. World curling championships for wheelchair athletes started in 2002, and curling has appeared in the Paralympic Winter Games since 2006 in Turin. Because of separate national sport priorities and sport cultures, national memberships. Approximately one person out of 30 in Canada curls (1.3 million membership). In the United States, approximately 15,000 curl; but also interest within the United States exists in the number of colleges and universities that support teams. College Curling USA exists as an umbrella organization. Approximately 200 participants competed in sanctioned events in 2012–2013, representing 36 colleges and universities.

The norm of self-governance within curling exists in every piece of available information in print, in behavior, and in historical lore. The movie, "Men with Brooms," (2002) revolves around a rule violation by a local member of a curling team (known as the *Rink*). He touched a stone during its movement on the ice: a forbidden act. The severe violation was magnified when he (Paul Gross, a star in the film and the director) did not immediately admit to the violation. His mortification at his lapse led to his breaking up with his girlfriend, throwing the four stones used by the team into a lake, and leaving his home for an arduous (and out-of-the-way) job in the Middle East.

Curling historically is associated with sociability, with families traveling between towns for a match (bonspiel) and spending time drinking and eating following the event. This civility surrounds the sport today. As sport is rule-governed, sport is also consummative. Observers of curling players and events should never underestimate the intensity of the sport and the huge import of winning. In *The Black Bonspiel of Willie MacCrimmon* (Mitchell, 1993) a representative medium of the meaning of the sport to participants, a curler makes a Faustian deal with the devil to gain assistance in winning the Canadian national championship. (The civil and democratic character of curling in sport drive the unusual sequence where local teams [*Rinks*] always have the chance of moving through a series of competitions with the possibility of competing for the national championship). In the deal, if Willie and his rink win in a match with the Devil (a rink which includes Judas, Macbeth, and Guy Fawkes), the Devil will help Willie win the Brier (the name for many years of the Canadian National Championship). If Willie loses to the Devil, he must go upon his death to curl with the Devil's rink in hell.[5]

---

5 Golf is another sport that is noted for its reliance on self-policing by competitors, even to the highly visible efforts of elite golfers on summer weekly television who proffer to be replacing pieces of grass they have dug up in a stroke (that is, to keep the conditions fair to all other competitors). Lance Armstrong has said he would not cheat at golf; because there is an honor code in the sport that deters rule-breakage. Contingent on the demands of marketing and international expansion of player and spectators the two traditionally self-policed sports of golf and curling have elaborated and formalized the places for referees and express rules, divergences from the original norms of self-policing. The United States Golf Association publishes the 210-page rules of golf. The R & A, based in St Andrews,

Formally related to these sports where the visible presence of "third party" of referees is at a minimum or absent are the sport contests which are engaged in by amateur athletes, on a fairly regular basis, but at times, with personnel, and in settings that are highly irregular. For example, at every major university in the United States in an enclosed recreation space, on a Saturday morning from opening time at 8:00 a.m. into mid-afternoon a sequence of basketball games occurs on anywhere from two to two dozen basketball courts. Teams may be made up of two to five players, a "hold" on a court may be time-specified or result-specified. One or more teams, for example, may schedule a court for one hour. Or teams may be able to complete a contest with an identified end (number of points, e.g.), with the winner retaining the court until that team loses. There is no referee. Rules—which are vigorously enforced—are understood or briefly negotiated. The contests proceed with great seriousness, but all without a formal referee structure, because there is a reciprocal understanding of the rules. There may be minor variations at the many venues, possession may alternate or possession may continue with a basket scored, but critically the reciprocally understood norms for the game are iron-clad. What happens when referees are interjected, such as in an intramural game or in a formal intercollegiate game? The potential exists for some rule violators "to manipulate" and to gain advantage from the external referees.

There are doubtless infractions in golf. There are doubtless infractions in competitive events which hundreds of thousands compete in each year in small towns and cities throughout the United States. Thousands of runners compete in races like the Chicago Marathon, Bix 7 (Davenport, Iowa), the New York Marathon, and the Boston Marathon (36,000 expected in the spring of 2014.) But the crucial point is that the exception, and that is the extreme exception, is the rule violator who contains and does not divulge his or her violation.

Rosie Ruiz presented herself as the winner of the Boston Marathon on April 21, 1980, but assessments of her background and her own lapses in describing the

---

complements the jurisdiction of the USGA with "Rules of Amateur Status," "Equipment Standards." The United States Curling Association publishes its 56-page "Officiating Manual;" and the World Curling Federation provides a "Chief Umpire Reference Manual" (170 pages). The current rule book for the Canadian competitor published by the Canadian Curling Association was published in September 2014, and is 21 pages in length. The sheet of ice for participation is 44.501 meters to 45.720 meters in length. The width is between 4.318 m to 4.750 m. Each member of two four-person teams throws two stones (19.96 kg–17.46 kg) over ten trials, called ends. The point of release of the throw, the hack, is 1.89 m behind the outer edge of the 12-foot circle (the English foot being used colloquially to designate the series of circles) that defines the scoring area at each end of the sheet of ice; the opposite series of circles being the respective target of each rink, or team. Team members throw in an alternative sequence, with scoring occurring when in each end one team has one or more stones closer to the 4-foot circle than the other rink does. The aggregate score across the ten ends yields the winner. The location of a stone can be affected by hitting from the stone of an opponent, but not by touching that (or one's own) stone with the broom or with a body part ("Rules of Curling for General Play," 2014).

race led to the discovery that she had lied about completing the whole 26.2 miles. What is so representative of the event, though, is the extreme minority occurrence of this misrepresentation. To the hundreds of thousands of competitive runners who race each summer, this kind of violation is on the edge of belief.[6]

The Tour de France as a Test: Cooperation with Minimal or No External Control

Three recent major crises of integrity within the Tour de France are the Festina Affair, the Puerto Affair, and the decisive action against Lance Armstrong and his Team in 2011 that led to disqualification in the races from 1999–2005. The response in each case displayed the character of a conflict organizational perspective. The "lies" of athletes, trainers, coaches, and at length attributions toward ownership potentially compromise the "coin" of the event. Public good will, donations, news coverage, spectatorship all could be affected. The responses of the various jurisdictions (again, coaches, teams, ownership, police, states, UCI, the Tour de France organizers, such as ASO, national organizations such as France, and USADA, and WADA) could, upon the claims about drug use and cheating, lead to increases of administrative steps against such infractions.

The common system emerging from the accounts discussed for cycling and the "Armstrong Affair" in Chapters 5 and 6 allows a focal point for discussing the applicability and, in turn, the partial features of three theoretical alternatives: Goffman and the idea of an interaction order; a conflict-oriented tradition which stresses the necessity of external, powerful agencies with refined technology and

---

6   The application of the three theories to the highly visible—and still continuing case—of the Tour de France will show explanatory and predictive prospects of each, from the start of the book's program. Further, the theories hold alternatives for *design* as well. Actors may not make a theory prescriptive, but they can. This is particularly true of the contract tradition. The cases with their negative consequences can provide information from a Goffman approach; or from a conflict approach they may show how to deter such negative outcomes. The positive options driven from a contract approach may be less common from the cases, certainly given their overall negative tone in the chapter coverages. Thomas Hobbes (1558–1689), John Locke (1632–1704), Jean-Jacques Rousseau (1712–1778), and Immanuel Kant (1724–1804) provide foundations for social contract theory. John Rawls (1921–2002) has given us a powerful contemporary version, particularly with his *A Theory of Justice*, 2003 (1971). Rawls expresses an essential principle of the alternative: "Each person possesses an inviolability founded on justice that even the welfare of society as a whole cannot override. For this reason justice denies that the loss of freedom for some is made right be a greater good shared by others" (2003: 3). Some illustration of social contracts that could be made in sport and within religion come from Fisher, Ury, and Patton, *Getting to Yes* (2011). They express four principles for resolving disputes among contesting parties: "Separate the People from the Problem; Focus on Interests, Not Positions; Invent Options for Mutual Gain; Insist on Using Objective Criteria" (2011: 11). The force of hypocrisy, either as simulation or dissimulaton, creates bad consequences for sport and religion because it thwarts one or more of these principles.

money; and—true to essential features of sport and religion—types of theories that emphasize the relevance of social contracts among participants within these two institutions.

Inside the front cover of Reed Albergotti and Vanessa O'Connell's book, *Wheelmen: Lance Armstrong, the Tour de France, and the Greatest Sports Conspiracy Ever* (2013) they provide a web of connections among 30 principals that contribute to the "conspiracy," the system they describe. There are individuals, groups of individuals, organizational units from teams, event oversight entities, sources of money, and governmental bodies. The inventory is both very helpful for its economy in providing a map and ponderous for the job implied to explain their system with any completeness from sociological tools.

Within the narrative of their book and that of Juliet Macur's *Cycle of Lies: the Fall of Lance Armstrong* (2014) and usefully largely echoed in the USDA report (2012) and Alex Gibney's movie the population of team-member riders whom Armstrong interacted with provides an array of "interaction orders" that Goffman and Lewis might tell us is a theoretically appropriate place to begin. Both Albergotti and O'Connell and Macur regard Armstrong interacting with ten riders who at one time were members of his teams: Frankie Andreu, Tom Danielson, Tyler Hamilton, George Hincapie, Floyd Landis, Levi Leipheimer, Kevin Livingston, Christian Vande Velde, Jonathan Vaughters, and David Zabriske. Counting just pairs that makes 55 potential "interaction orders," of a minimum size of two.

Just considering Armstrong's relationship with each, the respective histories have included team membership, sharing of drug information, living together, and with all but George Hincapie moments of trust violation and very mean-spirited acts from Armstrong to the others. Hincapie is the only person from this set who seems still to be in a reasonably amicable relationship with Armstrong (note, particularly, Hincapie's recent biography, *The Loyal Lieutenant*, 2014).

From just the narrative segments in the two journalistic treatments (complemented from the USADA report and the film), the durability of these interactional orders is very modest and does not take analysis very far toward the large groups of people and the institutions that Albergotti and O'Connell show. A second level might include, as Scott and Lyman articulate, speech acts (accounts and justifications) which invoke in the interest of preserving interaction some consensual norms to which appeals can be made (Scott and Lyman, 1968). Turowitz and Maynard (2010) emphasize the momentary behavioral exchanges that Anne Rawls is interested in, but they do allow as Scott and Lyman do a kind of second-order body of information shared by the parties to the interaction order.

Rawls in her deference to the importance of her idea of "interaction order" excludes macro-references to accounts and justifications. Specifically: "There is no referee to which participants can appeal, and consequently, constitutive orders do not generate accounts and justifications" (Rawls, 2010: 97). While as Rawls does Turowitz and Maynard give special attention to the essentials of self-definition and commitment to the interaction, they do acknowledge another layer that may bear on the momentary interactions. They stress: "How members use a code—whether in a halfway house, on the streets or elsewhere—is a surface matter that enables sense-making and normative conduct, while the sense of the code's obdurate reality operates at a deeper level. The natural attitude presumes, as the deeper level, the existence of an objective world that exists apart from subjective perceptions of it" (Turowitz and Maynard, 2010: 506).

Scott and Lyman's work—again from an interactionist or pragmatic theoretical position—gives some substance to this "deeper level" with their definition and illustration of excuses and justifications ("accounts" in combination) used in interaction. "*Excuses* are socially approved vocabularies for mitigating or relieving responsibility when conduct is questioned. We may distinguish initially four modal forms by which excuses are typically formulated: *appeal to accidents, appeal to defeasibility, appeal to biological drives, and scapegoating*" (Scott and Lyman, 1968: 47). They incorporate an additional effort to neutralize the consequences of an act called "denial of responsibility" with their category of "appeal to defeasibility." "Like excuses, justifications are socially approved vocabularies that neutralize an act or its consequences when one or both are called into question. But here is the crucial difference: to justify an act is to assert its positive vale in the face of a claim to the contrary" (Scott and Lyman, 1968: 51, their emphases). Illustrations include denial of injury, denial of victim, condemnation of condemners, and appeal to loyalties.

For the sake of illustration here, a set of norms or at least conventions that both commentators and participants invoke is a type of secrecy over the process of locating, using, and concealing drug products. They use the name Omertà to refer to this code, drawn very loosely from a normative system of ostensive criminals. "It originated and remains very common in Corsica and Southern Italy where Mafia-type criminal organizations such as the 'Ndrangheta, Sacra Corona Unita, and Camorra are strong" (Omertà, Wikipedia; discussed in Chapter 5 and 6). Effectively, however, this use of the term and certainly allusions to the normative system in place within criminal organizations seems largely metaphoric and a term romantically to refer to honor which is easily compromised. Capricious firing by team management, non-fault based injuries, ready rider alternatives, and automatically potential penalties promised from agencies such as the USADA led in all cases to bitterness among riders toward superiors (and the end of such a code) and untethered confessions by riders to the legal authorities. So, the use of "interaction order" as a dominant theoretical tool, even with the prospect of normative substantives that can be identified as used strategically by the parties to interaction (Scott and Lyman and Turowitz and Maynard) can advance the theoretically informed explanation only a little further.

The second set of theoretical options displays a conflict approach, where there are those on one side of the exchange who violate formal rules (and those who prosper by the riders doing so) by employing their resources of practice and concealment. Schneier's (2012) account of the battle over concealment and detection illustrates what technical resources each side in the use and detection of forbidden products and techniques potentially can use. The institution of the World

Anti-doping Association in 1999 and the United States Anti-doping Association immediately following the Festina Affair in 1998 shows the entry and potential force of outside agencies in the control of a system of drug use and deceit. As mentioned in Chapter 4, the use of detection technology and the effectiveness of outside legal agencies, resources in the conflict of oversight groups with institutional rule violators, is mixed.

Legal authorities have figured prominently in the resolution of cases of pedophilia victims at Penn State and in the Roman Catholic and in the case of USA Swimming. One would have to judge given the time taken finally to secure at last a factual resolution of the Hillsborough case that the actors on the side of legal force moved very slowly. No penalizations there have occurred. The outcomes of utilization of record keeping in the interest of visibility of official conduct in the Church and in USA Swimming—an institutionalization of technical resources in the interest of controlling abuses of power by superiors cannot yet be determined.

The definitions of sport and religion in this project have oriented to an idealization of those institutions. But as argued if they are to be considered closer to their founding character than the character judged after the infractions then they have qualities that are unique compared to other institutions of society. Sport for millions of participants relies on the value of an internal, reciprocal method of governance and rule enforcement. Some religious denominations rely more on hierarchical control than others do. But, again, principles of religious organization give more deference to norms of trust and trustworthiness that allow stability based on reciprocity than on external sources of monitoring and penalization. Is there application to the organization of sport and religion at levels of competition where stakes of reputation and material gain grow? Can there be social contractual kinds of participation that is self-monitored and self-policed? Can the rules of conduct from Ashworth, Fisher, Ury, and John Rawls have effect?

Golf and curling, as described, are two sports now with a distribution of players and international attention to offer two models of sport where reciprocity in principle dominates over practice norms that test rules (cycling) and institutionalized security efforts to detect and punish rule violations. Golf appeared in the 1900 and 1904 Olympics and the International Olympic Committee ruled its resumption as a sport for men and women in the 2016 Olympics. Curling entered the winter Olympics in 1998 and has continued with growing popularity in participation; daily television occurred during curling competition in the 2014 Winter Olympic Games. Curling, too, historically is a self-policed sport. A memorable representation of the strength of internal rules of honor in curling is the movie "Men with Brooms" (2002), mentioned earlier. The issue in the storyline is an occurrence of a foul by a member of a team (a rink) who touched or "burned" a stone and didn't call a penalty on himself.

Despite the growing formalization of the sports, in the interests both for standardization and security, the extent of the need for standardization and security can vary. Considering the initial conditions of the sports, within the available theoretical alternatives of reciprocity, contract, cooperation, and participant control, can give illumination about existing possibilities even in these international sports. With alternatives for reciprocity and cooperation among participants in view, prospects for other sports and for other endeavors, such as within religion, can be considered.

A crucial ingredient for cooperative systems to work and sustain themselves according to Robert Axelrod in his *The Evolution of Cooperation* (1984) is the existence of an actor start-point of cooperation (rather, say, than a nuanced reciprocity that may be inimical to a common good or a stance of each or both in a party to get away with as much as possible before detection). Axelrod began with the general question about when an actor should be cooperative and when an actor should be selfish. The scale could be a literal individual, a business in dealing with another business, or a nation-state dealing with another nation-state. He simulated the general question within a Prisoner's Dilemma game. The minimal rules of the game, which examines the rewards to two players who can either cooperate or defect, allow a sequence of choices with different rewards given for both cooperating, both defecting, and one cooperating matched by the other's defection. "Together, these choices result in one of the four possible outcomes shown in [the] matrix. If both players cooperate, both do fairly well. Both get R, the *reward for mutual cooperation* [say, a value of 3 points or 3 dollars] ... If one player cooperates but the other defects, the defecting player gets the *temptation to defect*, while the cooperating player gets the *sucker's payoff* [respectively within the example, a credit of 5 versus a credit of 0] ... If both defect, both get 1 point [or such a multiple with another reward], the punishment for *mutual defection*" (Axelrod, 1984: 84 emphases his).

When participants in his study are asked to write programs with principles of interaction (cooperate or defect) the principle that turns out to be the most successful is what he terms a tit for tat strategy. He acknowledges: "To my considerable surprise, the winner [a pattern that continues through various sponsorships of the game] was the simplest of all the programs submitted, tit for tat. Tit for tat is merely the strategy with cooperation, thereafter doling what the other player did on the previous move" (Axelrod, 1984: viii). Two important conditions for the success of the sequence, and applicability generally are: that there is some predisposition at the outset that a first move will be a cooperative one; and the expectation that the actors will meet at some point in the future. Both conditions are reasonably part of the institutions of sport and religion discussed in the book.

The work of John Rawls represents a second alternative for relying on a contractual exchange among participants for creating a just social order. The contract is created with an eye to the position of each participant (sport participant or church member). He elaborates the fundamental process of identifying principles of a just (for all) social order in *A Theory of Justice* (1971), a statement issued in revised form in 1999. This requires the imagination or articulation of a system of distribution of valued resources "behind a veil of ignorance." Documented inequality, many philosophies dealing with inequality, and certainly major theoretical themes within sociology show laws, policies, judgments about distribution of resources depend strongly on the personal location of the spokesperson. Rawls' approach attempts to constrain the influence of such self-interested systems of distribution. Behind the "veil of ignorance" one must propose principles of distribution that exclude one's existing position or prospective position in the system proposed. If one considers the intense enjoyment of participating in sport at any level, and the memories of watching a sporting endeavor, a set of principles that meets these conditions of a set of rules for player conduct and patterns of reward generally will bring unqualified acceptance of the idea.

An alternative to the approach of Goffman and differing from a conflict standpoint is what Roger Fisher, William Ury, and Bruce Patton call *Getting to Yes* (2003). It is an approach to negotiation which rests on positive assumptions and practices. The majority of their examples of successful and unsuccessful negotiations and where their approach has been productive in settlements come from the worlds of politics, international relations, and business. These are fields where conflict between competing interests can be the most acute among institutions. Within sport and religion presuppositions of parties and the histories of the purposes of sport and religion lean much more obviously toward the value of reciprocity and principles and actions for the common good. They describe and illustrate four main principles: "Separate the *People* from the Problem; Focus on *Interests*, Not Positions; Invent *Options* for Mutual Gain; Insist on Using Objective Criteria" (Fisher, Ury, and Patton, 2011: 17; their emphases).

WWI began on July 28, 1914. Initial successes of Germany included overrunning Belgium in August; some short-lived success of the French against the Germans at Lorraine, Alsace, and the Ardennes; and then defeats and retreat of the French. By November the character of the conflict from mobile and reciprocal strikes to relatively stationary positioning of sides in tranches became common and, in Tony Ashworth's recounting, durable. For the four years of the war until November 11, 1918, a form of "static" war in the words of Ashworth prevailed along a trench system 475 miles long (Ashworth, 1980: 3). Writing of a pattern of warfare which has been lightly recounted compared to descriptions of major battles and victories (and defeats), Ashworth has sought to describe and provisionally explain this trench warfare which was the environment for the majority of combatants for a majority of the duration of the war. Trenches as temporary protections for infantry and as objects of gain for advancing troops has been described, he allows. What has not been given apt attention is the much more common existence of life and fighting from trenches where little movement occurred forward or in retreat: "static" again. The reasons he proposes include a major and still rather novel one, that informal group norms, illustrative of what sociology calls "primary group" developed not only among compatriots on each side between members of opposing sides: an operable pattern of reciprocity of "live and let live" developed.

Ashworth lists four reasons for the motivation and conduct for fighters in wars. One is the inducement that comes from traditions associated with military branches and units. A second comes from aggressions associated with masculinity. (The distance in time from his authorship in 1980 and the historical referents of 1914–1918 would have to lead to elaboration of psycho-social motivations that could apply to female combatants now in military service.) A third factor acknowledges wider civilian and political values of nation-state and customary ways of life. The fourth is non-obvious. In his words: "A fourth type of explanation, pursued for the most part in this study, emphasizes informal social relationships among combatants. These are often termed as primary groups, in contra-distinction to secondary groups, formed by the formal military division of labor" (Ashworth, 1980: 205). The bonds of primary association occur within aligned units; less obviously they can in his record appear between groups on either side of the lines that separate the parallel-running trenches.

Processes of primary group interaction are described within teams, friends, and management groups in cycling. The processes can occur in informal norms of discussion and concealment as in the cases of administrators at Penn State, authorities charged with serving the football venue of Hillsborough, and later preoccupied with concealing improprieties, and priests and their immediate superiors. The dynamics of same-side primary groups for periods of time and primary interactions with the enemy living in opposition tranches hold nuances in Ashworth's account. The same-side commitments were strong, as were also the bonds across the trenches. The system of same- and oppositional-association carried great import as primary group affiliations tend to do. But if there was a violation in the form of a killing or attack from the other side a norm of revenge assumed unusual strength and rapidity of implementation. The act of revenge against the enemy was not only a formal act of destruction directed toward an oppositional entity, its vehemence reflected the perceived threat to the unusual pattern of primary group relations—a pattern which was essential to presumed survival in the "Live and Let Live" normative order (Ashworth, 1980: 208).

Some Light—and Some Shadows: Continuities in the Study of Hypocrisy

Milton's anticipation (seventeenth century) still carries a foreboding weight. Contradictions and inconsistencies that may display deceit are common enough in human institutions that their prevalence may limit curiosity in sociological investigation. In the past few years, news reports of lying in two institutions whose very essence eschews such deceptions elevate the stakes for sociologists on the topic. An almost universal form of lying—hypocrisy—features in reports and criticisms of sport and religion. The general matters of lying and inconsistencies in institutions can fruitfully begin with sport and religion as limiting cases, since their defining characteristics claim consistency and fidelity as opposed to deceits. This project has approached the topic of hypocrisy along five lines of sociological inquiry. One, giving the substance, has acknowledged the value of ideal-typical cases, and here selecting two: religion and sport, with usable and illustrative instances of each. From these case selections, the additional steps from the capabilities (and obligations) of sociologists) have included attention to meanings and cultural variation; structural influences; consequences of hypocrisy; and theoretical options. Some summarization and stock-taking will hopefully invite future efforts of sociological inquiry.

Meanings and Cultural Variation

"Hypocrisy" is used loosely in many of its appearances. The term attaches to a variety of acts where some form of contradiction exists. This looseness and even commonness of usage partially come from cultural influences which elevate the salience of the implied infraction and enlarge its use as a term to stigmatize another person. When the etymological roots of the term are faithfully attended to, with recognition of its history within drama and hence fabrication, we come to two essential components of the term for analytical purposes: lying, yes; but specifically *dissimulation*, where one denies a negative act or characteristic or *simulation* where one claims, falsely and almost always to one's advantage, an act or characteristic neither accomplished nor possessed.

When all or most of the substance of dissimulation and simulation are present, an important point about meanings is that hypocrisy has broad currency across societies and the occurrences are generally condemned. The apparent universality and general condemnation receive elaboration as attention moves to different cultural contexts. The range of cultural contexts exploited in the early chapters of time and across three cultures (United States, Iceland, and France) shows variation in the frequency, or at least public preoccupation with hypocrisy. Additionally, attending to the prospect that hypocrisy may be affected by degrees of the importance of success and especially relative success, cultures yielding different salience and seriousness to hypocrisy show themselves. Judith Shklar's (1984) concept of exigency usefully illuminates how the very demands of a culture to show oneself successful—and particularly relatively so—within the values of the culture may enlarge the temptations and likelihood of excessive claims which turn out to be hypocritical.

Structural Influences

The third general sociological topic examined within the substantive domain of hypocrisy is whether and how much influences of organizational structures affect meanings, variations, and consequences when hypocrisy occurs. The primary summary point to be made here is that the negative meanings attached suggest some worry should attend to this prospect. But within the few research pieces that do address hypocrisy within the research media in the sociology of sport and sociology of religion, there is not careful attention to these structural influences. The hundreds of news items where "hypocrisy" is invoked, though, assuredly constrained by journalistic guidelines on brevity, generally do not attend to organizational influences. So the conclusions from the attention to the specific cases in the book that display strong influences from surrounding organizational components that influence the appearance and progression of hypocrisy are potentially productive. I use, to underscore the contribution of organizational surroundings, institutional or organizational *imperative*, and I think the loading of influence to be accurate. The use of "hypocrisy" when selected to criticize another person implies virtually without exception a personal failing. Omitted as the cases illustrate in the chapter coverages is the role of organizations in creating the conditions where temptations toward deceit can occur; there may be initial dismissal of the deceits, and then even concealment of the deceits can occur.

Consequences

When acts and persons identified with hypocrisy are discovered, the surrounding organizations may act forcefully to penalize or exclude the offender. This strong response, and sometimes the vehement public statements of condemnation, coincide with the negative meanings noted as the initial summary point above. The evidence of the cases described in the book, though, show a considerably more qualified picture of the role and even culpability of the surrounding organizations. Institutions may create the culture that tempts the deceit, and then as noted contribute to sustaining facades and act to conceal the lies. Given this organizational imperative it is not anticipated that the consequences for various entities are either appreciated or allowed for by organizations. Principals can experience huge monetary loses as has been the cases of Lance Armstrong and Floyd Landis. Caught in the dynamic of high expectations from culture and organizational expectations, deceitful persons may exact punishment on themselves in the form of attempted or successful suicide. Associates of the hypocrites, depending upon the degree of incorporation into the biography and the ideological trajectory of the hypocrite, may exact self-blame.

In the latest recounting by a member of the team networks surrounding Lance Armstrong, George Hincapie notes his response to a 2010 request for his legal testimony:

> I honestly felt I would never have to deal with my drug use. Four years prior, I had made a very conscious and concerted decision to stop doping. It was before the 2006 Dauphiné Libéré (now called the Critérium du Dauphiné), and after narrowly missing an out-of-competition test where I felt I would have been caught, I decided using performance enhancing drugs (PEDs) was no longer worth the price. At that time, I reached out to select team members to tell them of my decision and that I planned on becoming as an advocate for clean racing (Hincapie, 2014: 3).

Following the revocation of the Tour de France title in 2010 from Alberto Contador (then given to Andy Schleck), Cadel Evans won the 2011 event. Alexandre Kolobnev tested positive for hydrochlorothiazide; he withdrew upon the discovery, but in March 2012 received only a warning due to the judgment that there was a medical reason for the ingestion. Bradley Wiggins won the 2012 Tour, without any recorded drug disqualifications. Chris Froome won the 2013 Tour, with no drug disqualifications reported one month following the event.

Following the earlier network of drug use among Armstrong's associates, Armstrong faces continuing legal battles from sponsors who consider they were defrauded by his deceits and seek return of sponsorship money. In April 2014, Johan Bruyneel received a 10-year ban from the American Arbitration Association, retroactive to June 2012.

In ways similar to the proceedings surrounding principals within the Tour de France, the trajectories of figures within the Penn State abuse scandal continue through the courts. Graham Spanier, former President, Gary Schultz, former Vice President, and former athletic director Tim Curley await in April 2014 trials on charges against them for complicity in the Jerry Sandusky scandal for not reporting known events in 1998 and 2001. Twenty-six cases of 32 pending received portions of a 56.7 million settlement with Penn State. Three were dismissed, and two continued after the collective agreement with the 26. The predominance of legal efforts to protect principals includes the Paterno family contesting the Freeh Report which implicated the university, Mike McQueary sustaining a lawsuit against the university for wrongful termination, the former president of the university filing a lawsuit, and one Pennsylvania State Senator suing the NCAA because of its penalty. A June 5, 2014 report about Jake Corman's lawsuit estimates the trial could occur in January 2015.

BishopAaccountability.org, as mentioned above, is a vehicle in the vein of using technology for exposure and eventual control that Schneier discusses. One can observe something from the volume of reports of "Abuse Tracker," a tool within BishopAccounablity.org. An inquiry in June 2014 provides a 753 page inventory. The headline for April 30, 2014 reads: "More Documents Released Detailing Sex Abuse Allegations in Joliet [Illinois] Diocese."

The Three Theoretical Alternatives

Three representative theoretical traditions inform and are informed by the substantive themes of hypocrisy, by degree.

Within the interactionist tradition as illustrated by Erving Goffman and heirs, deceit is not a problem until it is challenged and one party veers from a consensual line of interaction. In the formulation of Anne Rawls using the concept of "interaction order," the joined action of parties even with a substance that is deceitful is a crucial analytical baseline: "There is no referee to which participants can appeal ..." (Lewis, 2010: 97). This stipulation has utility in understanding the network of exchanges among principals in Lance Armstrong's network, where they are lying to each other and knowing they are lying to each other. The utility of the stipulation is limited, however, as the durability of the exchanges in this illustrative case is so tenuous. Individuals in the network are challenged, and the very tenuous nature of the substance of their interactions generally gives way to self-protection, through the use of another layer of the social, which Lyman and Scott term excuses and justifications (1968).

Schneier's focus on information as a valuable resource appears as a representative of conflict theories, with the premium value placed on the commodity of information: liars (and their protectors) seek to manipulate and conceal valuable information; over-seers and opponents seek to authenticate and detect concealed information. The approach connects well with the cases of Penn State, appearance, concealment, and detection of pedophiles within the Roman Catholic Church, and the Hillsborough case, and very recent challenges to the fidelity of governance of international soccer, FIFA particularly. Conflict theoretical assumptions and explanations, Schneier's being one example, are indeed useful. However, the theory may underestimate the extent to which powerful organizations themselves—in their arrogance—may underestimate the potential costs of deceits.

The utility of contract theories mentioned for illuminating hypocrisy and hypocrites is less easily demonstrated than are the contributions of aspects of the interactionist tradition and embodiment of conflict theory such as those within Schneier. The title page of the June 7th–13th issue of *The Economist* (2014) reads: "Beautiful game: Ugly Business," and aptly captures what proponents of idealized sport hope for. The stories in the magazine summarize revelations of June 1, 2014 by *The Sunday Times* (Calvert and Blake, 2014) about bribery associated with the selection of World Cup sites and *The New York Times* description of "fixed football matches" though bribes given to referees, a prospect investigated by FIFA itself (Hill and Longman, 2014; Hill, 2014).

Qualifying what can be concluded to be arrangements meant to circuit transparency and compromise fidelity to rules in the examples of payment in behalf of the bid by Qatar for the 2022 World Cup and the fixed soccer matches, acts and organizational arrangements do exist to sustain sport as physical, intrinsic, rule governed, and consummative; and religion as "that which concerns us ultimately." Sports do vary in their particular preoccupations with rule adherence, and reluctance to gravitate away from self-policing to external rule enforcement. Individuals reflective of their violations within sport and religion can exact extreme self-penalties. Located within the most recent news reporting on the "Armstrong Affair" and recent biographies by key figures, along with expected self-protectiveness, are genuine resolutions to invigorate contractual norms of transparency and accommodation to the rules of cycling (Millar, 2012; Hincapie, 2014). It cannot be denied that the millions of people of all ages throughout the world who daily engage seriously in sport, with hopes of success, and finally knowing the joy of doing it believe the contract of faithfulness to the rules will prevail.

The ideal typical cases attended to in the book, as noted in the early pages, adhere to Max Weber's use of such strategic selection: they represent the theoretical questions in view, and they are strategically placed in the social systems identified (here, the United States, France, and Iceland). The meaning of a program, the enterprise sustained through the book's analyses, has received prompting from the estimation that sociology carries a level of responsibility in addressing hypocrisy, with the stakes of consequences for society and potential theoretical yield within the discipline.

The cases illustrating the program of the book have respective histories and so the case coverages have a retrospective character. This program also has a prospective feature, perhaps even a mandated one. In the first months of 2015, two highly visible additional cases of duplicity within world sport have appeared. As expressed in Chapter 1, sociology should entertain the responsibility of addressing a topic such as hypocrisy and has the requisite tools to do so.

On May 20, 2015 Loretta A. Lynch, United States Attorney for the Eastern District of New York, indicted nine officials of FIFA and five corporate officials that have done business[7] with this organization. FIFA (the Fédération Internationale de Football Association) and its six constituent continental organizations oversee the creation, marketing, management, and fidelity of world football events. The program advocated in the book is to extend the analyses now to these cases, which are closely related to those in the book, and to apply the approach of considering the cultural context of sport and the force of organizational imperatives, and to probe for social consequences and extend sociological theory.

The indictments in the document (formally unsealed on May 27, 2015) list fraud, bribery, money laundering, concealment, misappropriation of funds, and violation of fiduciary duties. The legitimacy of the US Attorney acting in this fashion comes from the record that officers were located in the United States, sales of merchandise and media rights have been made to US companies, US financial institutions were employed, and communication networks for business lie within the United States.

In the specific:

> The conspirators engaged in conduct designed to prevent detection of their illegal activities, to conceal the location of proceeds of those activities, and to promote the carrying on of those activities. That conduct included, among other things: the use of contracts to create an appearance of legitimacy for illicit payments; the use of various mechanisms, including trusted intermediaries, bankers, financial advisors and currency dealers, to make and facilitate the making of illicit payments; the creation and use of shell companies, nominees and numbered bank accounts in tax havens and other secretive banking jurisdictions; the active concealment of foreign bank accounts; the structuring of financial transactions to avoid currency reporting requirements; bulk cash smuggling; the purchase of real property and other physical assets; the use of safe deposit boxes; income tax evasion; and obstruction of justice. Within the United States, such conduct took place within the Eastern District of New York and elsewhere (United States of America against Charles Blazer, 2015: 14, 15).

---

7 Loretta Elizabeth Lynch became the United States Attorney General on April 27, 2015.

A second recent case lying within the substantive foci of the book and clearly within the purview of prospective future analysis by our discipline is the report from the Danish cycling federation about a past history of drug use within cycling by Danish athletes. Anti Doping Denmark (ADD) published *Rapport OM Doping I Dansk Cykelsport, 1998–2015* on June 23, 2015. The investigating group responsible for the report originated from ADD, the National Olympic Committee (of Denmark), and the Sports Confederation of Denmark. The investigating committee and their mandate began in 2012, following the October 2012 USADA report, "Reasoned Decision of the United States Anti-Doping Agency on Disqualification and Ineligibility," discussed in Chapter 5 above. As the date interval conveys, the report examines prospective and identified illegal drug usage by Danish Cyclists from 1998–2015, with particular focus on the performance and management work of Bjarni Riis and the cycling team CSC, a team closely associated with Danish cycling. Riis admitted in 2007 he used prohibited drugs in the 1996 event. The organizers of the Tour do not consider him to be the official winner; the Union Cycliste Internationale, though, has not revoked the championship, claiming too much time has elapsed since his victory.

The indictment document against FIFA principals cites a duration of cheating and dishonesty of 24 years. The report of the Danish group acknowledges prospects of rule violation and dishonesty from 1998–2015. The extension of the ideas of this book and specifically the elements of the program of analysis suggested, and invited, lies in the future. To this date, the record in these two main documents noted (the indictment and the Danish report), shows consistency with the reported analyses in the chapters of the book, particularly the diagrammatic summary in Figure 5.1.

1. Following the norm violation and then the dishonesty either to conceal it or to make false claims (hypocrisy), a considerable period of time transpires before official acts of surrounding institutions to redress the violation take place.

2. The individual himself/herself, his/her supporting group of peers, sponsoring groups, organizations charged with oversight, journalist reporting, and public sentiment in varying degrees and manners allow the deceit to exist unchallenged. As the discussion in Chapter 5 and Figure 5.1 display (and by analogy with Thomas Kuhn's view of normal science noted), this is the period of a set of general presuppositions that prevail around the sport or religious circumstance.

3. In the terminology of Thomas Kuhn describing the revolutions that occur in science, irregular patterns of anomalies in the sport and religion cases reported here pose challenges to the basic presuppositions of fidelity to rules and honesty in the institutions of sport and religion These anomalies may come from independent journalists (Ressiott, 2005 and Walsh, 2007 in the case of the Tour de France, the *Boston Globe*, 2002 in the case of Priest pedophilia), or they may come from claims of victims of an organization's

or organizational member's acts of hypocrisy. They also may come from athletes having general moral compunctions or from being induced to confess their own cheating with promises of reduced penalties associated with accounts of others' cheating. The sporting events covered in the book receive subsidization from major sponsors, and once suspicions emerge within the anomalous reports, they may reduce or end funding. Some sponsors resist the implications of the anomalous claims ("With Huge Sums in Play, FIFA Sponsors are Reluctant to Push Reforms, July 27, 2014). Other firms assay potential losses if the sport turns out to be dishonest, and, as with reports about Castrol, Continental, and Johnson & Johnson (Rumsby, 2015), companies withdraw support.

4. As within the cases of science disciplines, where a consistent and compelling body of new evidence tips the balance of what is considered normal in the science field, there tends to be in the cases described in the book a report or pivotal event which acts as a fulcrum to start the tipping toward an altered conception of what is considered normal or presumptively true about the sport. Within the Tour de France, a likely prospect for such a fulcrum was the October 2012 USADA report. In the case of the Hillsborough tragedy, an important political act that can serve as such a fulcrum was the admission of national culpability made by the Prime Minister in 2012. It may develop that the two documents described here, from US prosecutors and the Danish cycling group, turn out to be such a fulcrum inducing a change of presuppositions about what is normal in the sport of football, and a further embodiment of a change in presuppositions in cycling (Chapter 5).

5. Change among the range of entities that have been complicit in erecting and maintaining the prior set of presuppositions is neither immediate nor general. The relatively late internal report of the UCI recording a pattern of cheating and deceit already reported by the USADA and from two careful investigations by *The New York Times* and *The Wall Street Journal* still was resisted by some individuals and organizations (Chapter 5, note 5). Similarly, there remain nay-sayers responding to the indictments of FIFA officials. The long-time president of FIFA, Sepp Blatter, eventually was forced to resign following the report, but he remains adamant about his lack of culpability – as has Lance Armstrong, a situation described in Chapter 5. Within science fields, some still deny Darwin's theory of evolution and modifications such as those of Stephen Jay Gould. Once the fulcrum appears, though, as with the illustrative October 2012 USADA report (Chapter 5 above), related groups take steps to move their own organizations' principles and their former sets of presuppositions from the prior set of principles and "business as usual" to the new, now revised sense of normality about acceptable conduct and expectations about how other entities will proceed.

Bibliography

Books and Articles

Ahrenhall, Alan. 2001. "Hypocrisy Has Its Virtues." *The New York Times.* February 6.

Albergotti, Reed and Vanessa O'Connell. 2013. *Wheelmen: Lance Armstrong, the Tour de France and the Greatest Sports Conspiracy Ever.* New York: Gotham Books.

Anderson, Nate. 2013. *The Internet Police: How Crime Went Online—and the Cops Followed.* New York: W.W. Norton.

Andersson, Theodore M. 1964. *The Problem of Icelandic Family Origins.* New Haven, CT: Yale University Press.

Annuaire statistique de l'Eglise jusque'en 2003, puis Conférence des évéques de France.

Arendt, Hannah. 2006. *Eichmann in Jerusalem: a Report on the Banality of Evil.* New York: Penguin.

Armstrong, Lance with Sally Jenkins. 2000. *It's Not about the Bike: My Journey Back to Life.* New York: Berkley Books.

———. 2003. *Every Second Counts.* New York: Broadway Books.

Ashworth, Tony. 1980. *Trench Warfare 1914–1918: the Live and Let Live System.* New York: Holmes & Meier Publishers.

Augeron, Mickaël, Didier Poton, and Bertrand Van Ruymbeke, dir. 2009. *Les Huguenots de l'Atlantique: Pour Dieu, La Cause ou Les Affaires.* Vol. I. Paris: Presses de l'Université Paris-Sorbonne.

Axelrod, Robert. [1984] 2006. *The Evolution of Cooperation.* Revised Edition. New York: Basic Books.

Axthelm, Pete. 1970. *The City Game: Basketball from the Garden to the Playgrounds.* New York: Penguin Books.

Bacon, Francis. 2008. "Of Simulation and Dissimulation," pp. 349–51 in *Francis Bacon: the Major Works.* Ed. by Francis Vickers. Oxford: Oxford University Press.

Bainton, Roland. [1950] 1995. *Here I Stand: a Life of Martin Luther.* New York: Plume.

Bale, John and Joe Sang. 1996. *Kenyan Running: Movement Culture, Geography and Global Change.* London: Frank Cass.

Ballister, Pierre and David Walsh. 2004. *L.A. Confidentiel: Les secrets de Lance Armstrong.* Europe: Editions de La Matinière.

Balmer, Randall. 1999. *Blessed Assurance: a History of Evangelicalism in America.* Boston. Beacon Press.

———. 2002. *Encyclopedia of Evangelicalism.* Louisville: Westminster John Knox Press.

———. 2006. *The Kingdom Come: How the Religious Right Distorts the Faith and Threatens America: An Evangelical's Lament.* New York: Basic Books.

Barber, Bernard. 1983. *The Logic and Limits of Trust.* New Brunswick, NJ: Rutgers University Press.

Barry, Jason. Forward by Andrew M. Greeley. 2000. *Lead Us Not Into Temptation: Catholic Priests and the Sexual Abuse of Children.* Urbana, IL: University of Illinois Press.

Becker, Howard S. 1960. "Notes on the Concept of Commitment." *American Journal of Sociology* 66 (1): 32–40.

Bell, Quentin. 1976. *On Human Finery.* Second Edition. New York: Schocken Books.

Berger, Morroe. 1977. *Real and Imagined Worlds: The Novel and Social Science.* Cambridge, MA: Harvard University Press.

Berry, Jason and Gerald Renner. 2004. *Vows of Silence: The Abuse of Power in the Papacy of John Paul II.* New York: Free Press.

Bilefsky, Dan. 2015. "France Crosses as Threshold in Examining Strauss-Kahn's Personal Life." *The New York Times*, February 19. http://www.ny times.com/2015/02/20/world/Europe/Dominique-strauss-kahn-trial.html?hpw &rref=…

Bok, Sissela. [1978] 1999. *Lying: Moral Choice in Public in Public and Private Life.* New York: Vintage Books.

———. 1982. *Secrets: On the Ethics of Concealment and Revelation.* New York: Pantheon Books.

Bowen, William G. and Sarah A. Levin. 2003. *Reclaiming the Game: College Sports and Educational Values.* Princeton, NJ: Princeton University Press.

Brent, Joseph. 1993. *Charles Sanders Peirce: a Life.* Bloomington, IN: Indiana University Press.

Brittain, Amy and Chris Trevino. 2013. "Ex-swimming Coach Rick Curl Gets 7 Years in Child Abuse Case." *The New York Times*, May 23. http://www. washingtonpost.com/local/ex-swimming-coach-rick-curl-to-be-sentenced-in-chi…

Broad, William and Nicholas Wade. 1982. *Betrayers of the Truth.* New York: Simon and Schuster.

Brym, Robert J. and John Lie. 2007. *Sociology: Your Compass for a New World.* Belmont, CA: Thomson Higher Education.

Buford, Bill. 1982. *Among the Thugs.* New York: Norton.

Butler, Jon. 1983. *The Huguenots in America: a Refugee People in New World Society.* Cambridge, MA: Harvard University Press.

Byock Jesse L. 1998. *Medieval Iceland: Society, Saga, and Power.* Berkeley: University of California Press.

Campbell, Donald T. and Julian Stanley. 1963. *Experimental and Quasi-Experimental Designs for Research.* Boston: Cengage Learning.

Carlson, Rolf. 1988. "The Socialization of Elite Tennis Players in Sweden: an Analysis of the Players' Backgrounds and Development." *Sociology of Sport Journal* 5:241–56.

Carril, Pete with Dan White. 1997. *The Smart Take from the Weak.* New York: Simon & Schuster.

Chambliss, Daniel F. 1988. *Champions: the Making of Olympic Swimmers.* New York: William Morrow.

Chartier, Roger. 1989. *The Culture of Print: Power and the Uses of Print in Early Modern Europe.* Cambridge, UK: Polity Press in association with B. Blackwell.

———. 2003. *A History of Reading in the West.* Amherst: University of Massachusetts Press.

Christesen, Paul. 2012. *Sport and Democracy in the Ancient and Modern Worlds.* New York: Cambridge University Press.

Condon, Thomas and Stephen G. Wieting. 1982. "Morality, Justice, and Social Choice: Foundations for the Construction of Social Order." In *Structural Sociology,* edited by Ino Rossi, 183–228. New York: Columbia University Press.

Cook, Karen S., ed. 2001. *Trust in Society.* New York: Russell Sage Foundation.

Cook, Karen S., Margaret Levi, and Russell Hardin, eds. 2009. *Whom Can We Trust?* New York: Russell Sage Foundation.

Coyle, Daniel. 2010. *Lance Armstrong's War: One Man's Battle against Fate, Fame, Love, Death, Scandal, and a Few Other Rivals on the Road to the Tour de France.* Updated Edition. New York: Harper Paperbacks.

Crouse, Karen. 2013. "Abuse Victim Seeks Ouster of U.S. Swimming Officials." *The New York Times.* http://nytimes.com/2013/05/24/sports/kelley-davies-currin-seeks-ouster-of-usa-swim…

Daniels, Bruce C. 1995. *Puritans at Play: Leisure and Recreation in Colonial New England.* New York: St. Martin's.

Darnton, Robert. 1968. *Mesmerism and the End of the Enlightenment in France.* Cambridge, MA: Harvard University Press.

———. 1982. *The Literary Underground of the Old Regime.* Cambridge, MA: Harvard University Press.

———. 1995a. *The Corpus of Clandestine Literature in France, 1769–1789.* New York: W.W. Norton.

———. 1995b. *The Forbidden Best-Sellers of Pre-Revolutionary France.* New York: W.W. Norton.

Darwin, Charles. 1859. *On the Origin of Species by Means of Natural Selection, or the Preservation of Favoured Races in the Struggle for Life.* UK: John Murray.

Dauncey, Hugh and Geoff Hare. Eds. 1999. *France and the 1998 World Cup: the National Impact of a World Sporting Event.* London: Frank Cass.

Davidson, Jenny. 2004. *Hypocrisy and the Politics of Politeness: Manners and Morals from Locke to Austen.* Cambridge: Cambridge University Press.

Dowey, Edward A. [1952] 1994. *The Knowledge of God in Calvin's Theology.* Grand Rapids, MI: W.B. Eerdmans Publ. Co.

Dunbar, Graham. 2015a. "Former UCI Leader Verbruggen Defiant after Doping Report." http://news.yahoo.com/former-uci-leader-verbruggen-defiant-doping-report-155931807.html, March 9.

———. 2015b. "UCI Chief Cookson: Doping Still Endemic in Cycling." http://news.yahoo.com/cycling-leaders-slammed-letting-armstrong-win-000401640.html, March 9.

Duncan, Otis Dudley. 1984. *Notes on Social Measurement: Historical and Critical.* New York: Russell Sage Foundation.

Durkheim, Émile. [1950] 1983. *Professional Ethics and Civic Morals.* Translated by Cornelia Brookfield. Westport, CT: Greenwood Press.

———. [1955] 1983. *Pragmatism and Sociology.* Translated by J.C. Whitehouse, edited and introduced by John B. Allcock. Preface by Armand Cuvillier. Cambridge: Cambridge University Press.

———. [1893] 1984. *The Division of Labor in Society.* Basingstoke, Hampshire: Macmillan.

———. [1912] 1995. *The Elementary Forms of the Religious Life.* New York: Free Press.

———. [1897] 1997. *Suicide: a Study in Sociology.* New York: Free Press

———. [1895] 2013. *The Rules of Sociological Method.* Ed. and intro. by Steven Lukes. New York. Free Press.

Duvinage, Cedric. 2012. *Referees in Sport Contests.* First Edition. Weisbasden: Gabler Verlag.

Eder, Steve. 2013. "Governor Sues Over Penalties to Penn State." *The New York Times.* January 2.

Einarsson, Thorsteinn. [1984] 1988. *Glíma: the Icelandic Wrestling.* Reykjavík: Glímusamband Íslands.

Enoksen, Lars Magnar. 2008. *The Secret Art of Glíma.* Viking Glíma Federation.

———. 2010. *Glíma Fighting Techniques.* Viking Glíma Federation.

Erikson, Kai T. 1966. *Wayward Puritans: a Study in the Sociology of Deviance.* Boston: Allyn and Bacon.

"Fan Falls, Dies at Candlestick during 49ers-Packers Game." 2013. *USA Today.* September 9.

Farrell, Henry. 2009. "Institutions and Midlevel Explanations of Trust." In *Whom Can We Trust?* edited by Cook et al., 127–48. New York: Russell Sage Foundation.

"Fifth Down Game (1990)." Wikipedia. December 19, 2014.

Fine, Gary Alan. 2001. *Difficult Reputations: Collective Memories of the Evil, Inept, and Controversial.* Chicago: University of Chicago Press.

Finley, M.I. and H.W. Pleket. 1976. *The Olympic Games: the First Thousand Years.* New York: The Viking Press.

Fisher, Roger, William Ury, and Bruce Patton. 2011. *Getting to Yes: Negotiating Agreement without Giving In.* Third Edition. New York: Penguin Books.

Foddy, Margaret and Toshio Yamagishi. 2009. "Group-based Trust." In *Whom Can We Trust?* edited by Cook et al., 17–41. New York: Russell Sage Foundation.

Fraud Prevention Best Practices. 2012. Freddie.Mac.com/singlefamily/pdf/faud prevention_practices.pdf.

Froome, Chris. 2014. *The Climb*. New York: Viking.

Fukuyama, Francis. 1995. *Trust: the Social Virtues and the Creation of Prosperity*. New York: Free Press.

Gather News Channel. 2015. Reported by Francescas Harper on May 10, 2010.

Gay, Peter. 1984. *The Bourgeois Experience: Victoria to Freud*. Vol. I (Education of the Senses). New York: Oxford University Press.

Geertz, Clifford. 1973. "Religion as a Cultural System," pp. 87–125 in *The Interpretation of Cultures*. New York: Basic Books.

———. 1973. "Thick Description: Toward an Interpretive Theory of Culture," pp. 3–32 in *The Interpretation of Cultures*. New York: Basic Books.

Gessen, Masha. 2014. *Words Will Break Cement: the Passion of Pussy Riot*. New York: Riverhead Books.

Glanville, Jennifer L. and Pamela Paxton. 2007. "How Do We Learn to Trust? A Confirmatory Tetrad Analysis of the Sources of Generalized Trust." *Social Psychology Quarterly* 70 (3): 230–42.

Glanville, Jennifer L, Mathew W. Andersson, and Pamela Paxton. 2013. "Do Social Connections Create Trust? An Examination Using New Longitudinal Data." *Social Forces* 92 (2): 545–62.

Goffman, Erving. 1959. *Presentation of Self in Everyday Life*. New York: Random House.

———. 1967. *Interaction Ritual*. Chicago: Aldine Publishing Company.

———. 1983. "The Interaction Order: American Sociological Association. 1982 Presidential Address." *American Sociological Review* 48 (1): 1–17.

———. [1974] 1986. *Frame Analysis*. Boston: Northeastern University Press.

———. [1963] 1986. *Stigma*. New York Simon & Schuster.

Golf Digest. 2015. January 31, 2015

Greeley, Andrew M. 1977. *The American Catholic: a Social Portrait*. New York: Basic Books, Inc.

———. 1999. *The Catholic Myth: the Behavior and Beliefs of American Catholics*. New York: Charles Scribner's.

Guðjónsson, Kjartan Bergmann. 1993. *Íslensk Glíma og Glimumenn*. Reykjavík: Höf.

Gudmundsson, Halldór. 2004. *The Islander: a Biography of Halldór Laxness*. London: MacLehose Press.

Halberstam, David. 1996. *The Amateurs*. New York: Ballantine Books.

Hallberg, Peter. 1971a. *Halldór Laxness*. Trans. by Rory McTurk. New York: Twyne Publishers, Inc.

———. Ed. 1971b. *Hús Skáldsins: um Skáldverk Halldórs Laxness Frá Sölku Völku Til Gerplu*. Reykjavík: Mál og Menning.

216 *The Sociology of Hypocrisy*

Halldórsson, Viðar. 2012. *No Man Is His Own Creation: the Social Context of Excellence in Sports*. Reykjavík: The University of Iceland: Faculty of Social and Human Sciences.

Halldórsson, Viðar and Thórólfur Thórlindsson. 2013. "The Emergence of a Successful Sport Tradition: a Case Study." Ms. Reykjavík, Iceland: Faculty of Social Sciences, University of Iceland.

Halldórsson,Viðar, Thórólfur Thórlindsson, and Michael Katovich. 2014. "The Role of Informal Sport: the Local Context and the Development of Elite Athletes." *Studies in Symbolic Interaction* 42: 133-160.

Hamilton, Tyler and Daniel Coyle. 2012. *The Secret Race: Inside the Hidden World of the Tour de France: Doping, Cover-ups, and Winning at All Costs*. New York: Bantam Books.

Hardin, Russell. 2001. "Conceptions and Explanations of Trust." In *Trust in Society*, edited by Karen S. Cook, 3–39. New York: Russell Sage Foundation.

———. 2002. *Trust and Trustworthiness*. New York. Russell Sage Foundation.

Hastrup, Kirsten. 1985. *Culture and History in Medieval Iceland: an Anthropological Analysis of Structure and Change*. Oxford: Clarendon Press.

———. 1990. *Nature and Policy in Iceland, 1400–1800*. Oxford: Clarendon Press.

Hawthorne, Nathaniel. [1850] 2013. *The Scarlet Letter*. Lexington, KY: Denton & White.

Heimer, Carol A. 2001. "Solving the Problem of Trust." In *Trust in Society*, edited by Karen S. Cook, 40–88. New York: Russell Sage Foundation.

Hersh, Seymour M. 2004. "Torture at Abu Ghraib." *The New Yorker*, May 10.

Hilbert, Martin and Priscila Lopez. 2011, "The World's Technological Capacity to Store, Communicate, and Compute Information." *Science* 332: 60–65; reported in http://en.wikipedia.org/wiki/History_of_the_Internet.

Hincapie, George and Craig Hummer. 2014. *The Loyal Lieutenant*. New York: William Morrow.

Hitlin, Steven and Stephen Vaisey, eds. 2010. *Handbook of the Sociology of Morality*. New York: Springer.

Hobbes, Thomas. [1651] 1969. *Behemoth*. Edited by Ferdinand Tonnies. London: Frank Cass.

Hogshead-Makar, Nancy and Andrew Zimbalist, eds. 2007. *Equal Play: Title IX and Social Change*. Philadelphia: Temple University Press.

Houry, Cecile. 2011. *American Women and the Modern Summer Olympic Games: a Story of Obsacles and Struggles for Participation and Equality*. Open Access Dissertations. Paper 571.

Hreinsson, Viðar. *The Complete Sagas of Icelanders*. 1997. Vols. 1–5. Reykjavík: Leifur Eiriksson Publishing.

Hushovd, Thor i samarbeid med Jostein Ravnàsen. 2014. *Thor.* Oslo: Schibsted Forlag.

Hutchison, James M. 1996. *The Rise of Sinclair Lewis, 1920–1930*. University Park, PA: The Pennsylvania State University Press.

Ingle, Sean. 2014. "Kenyan Riders Maintain Tour de France Dream Despite Death of Leader." *The Guardian*, December 12. http://www.theguardian.com/sport/2014/dec/12/Kenyan-riders-cycle-team-tour-de-france.

James, William. 2000. *Pragmatism and Other Essays*. Edited with an introduction and notes by Giles Gunn. New York: Penguin Books, 2000.

Jenkins, Philip. 2001. *Pedophiles and Priests: Anatomy of a Contemporary Crisis*. Oxford: Oxford University Press.

Josefsson, Johannes. 1908. *Icelandic Wrestling*. Þórh Bjarnarson. (Original from Harvard University.)

"Kenyan Riders." 2015. www.kenyanriders.com/the-story/.

Krasnoff, Lindsay Sarah. 2013. *The Making of Les Bleus: Sport in France, 1958–2010*. Lanham, Maryland: Lexington Books.

Kuhn, Thomas S. 2012. *The Structure of Scientific Revolutions*. Fourth Edition. Chicago: University of Chicago Press.

Lakoff, George. 1987. *Women, Fire, and Dangerous Things: What Categories Reveal about the Mind*. Chicago: University of Chicago Press.

———. 1999. *Philosophy in the Flesh: the Embodied Mind and Its Challenge to Western Thought*. New York: Basic Books.

———. 2002. *Moral Politics*. Second Edition. Chicago: University of Chicago Press.

Lakoff, George and Mark Johnson. [1980] 2003. *Metaphors We Live By*. Chicago: University of Chicago Press.

Lammers, Joris, Diederik K. Stapel, and Adam D. Galinsky. 2010. "Power Increases Hypocrisy: Moralizing in Reasoning, Immorality in Behavior." *Psychological Science*. http://pss.sagepub.com/.

Landis, Floyd. 2007. *Positively False: the Real Story of How I Won the Tour de France*. New York: Simon Spotlight Entertainment.

Laxness, Halldór. [1931–32] 1963. *Salka Valka*. UK, Unwin Hyman.

———. [1948] 1983. *The Atom Station*. Brownwood, Texas: Permanent Press Publishing Company.

———. [1968, 1972] 1990. *Christianity at Glacier*. Translated by Magnus Magnusson. Reykjavík: Vaka Helgafell. (First published in 1968 with title of *Kristnihald Undir Jökli*.)

———. [1934–35] 1997. *Independent People*. New York: Vintage.

———. [1937–38] 2002.*World Light*. New York: Vintage.

———. [1943–44] 2003. *Iceland's Bell*. New York: Vintage.

Lever, Janet. 1983. *Soccer Madness: Brazil's Passion for the World's Most Popular Sport*. Illinois: Waveland.

Levine, Donald N. 2010. "Adumbrations of a Sociology of Morality in the Work of Parsons, Simmel, and Merton." In *Handbook of the Sociology of Morality*. Edited by Steven Hitlin and Stephen Vaisey, 57–72. New York: Springer.

Lewis, Sinclair. [1927] 1970. *Elmer Gantry*. New York: New American Library.

Lieberman, Jethro K. 1981. *The Litigious Society*. New York: Basic Books.

Lindenberger, Michael A. 2014. "Texas Athletic Director: With New Rules, Long-horns Would Pay Each Player $10,000." *The Dallas Morning News.* http://www. dallasnews.com/sports/college-sports/headlines/20141021-texas-athletic-direct...

Liverpool Echo. 2012. September 12.

Lukes, Steven. 1973. *Émile Durkheim: His Life and Work.* London: Alan Lane: The Penguin Press.

Luntz, Frank. 2007. *Words that Work: It's Not What You Say, It's What You Hear.* New York: Hyperion.

MacAloon, John J. 1981. *This Great Symbol.* Chicago: University of Chicago Press.

Machiavelli, Niccolo. 1997. *The Prince.* Translated and edited by Angelo M. Codevilla. New Haven: Yale University Press.

Macionis, John J. 2013. *Social Problems.* Fifth Edition. United States: Pearson.

Mackie, Gerry. 2001. "Patterns of Social Trust in Western Europe and their Genesis," pp. 245–82 in Karen S. Cook, editor. *Trust in Society.* New York: Russell Sage Foundation.

Macur, Juliet. 2014. *Cycle of Lies: The Fall of Lance Armstrong.* New York: Harper.

Magnússon, Guðmundur. 2001. "The Internationalization of Sports: the Case of Iceland." *International Review for the Sociology of Sport* 36 (1): 59–69.

Marozzi, Marco. 2014. "Measuring Trust in European Public Institutions." *Social Indicators Research.* http://link.springer.com/article/10.1007/s11205-014-0765-9/fulltext.html.

Mead, George Herbert. 1959. *The Philosophy of the Present.* Ed. by Arthur E. Murphy. Lasalle, IL: Open Court.

———. [1936] 1972. *Movements of Thought in the Nineteenth Century.* Edited by Merritt Moore. Chicago; University of Chicago Press.

———. [1938] 1972. *The Philosophy of the Act.* Edited and with an Introduction by Charles W. Morris. Chicago: University of Chicago Press.

Merton, Robert K. 1976. *Sociological Ambivalence and Other Essays.* New York: The Free Press.

Mill, John Stuart. [1872] 2012. *A System of Logic, Ratiocinative and Inductive.* Lexington, KY: Forgotten Books.

Millar, David. 2012. *Racing through the Dark: Crash, Burn, Coming Clean, Coming Back.* New York: A Touchstone Book.

Miller, David L. 1973. *George Herbert Mead: Self, Language, and the World.* Austin: University of Texas Press.

Miller, Perry. 1939. *The New England Mind: the Seventeenth Century.* Cambridge, MA: The Belknap Press of Harvard University Press.

Miller, Stephen G. 2004. *Ancient Greek Athletics.* New Haven: Yale University Press.

Miller, William Ian. [1997] 2003. *Bloodtaking and Peacemaking: Feud, Law, and Society in Saga Iceland.* Chicago: University of Chicago Press.

———. 2003. *Faking It.* New York: Cambridge University Press.

Milton, John. 1940. *Paradise Lost.* New York: the Heritage Press.

Mitchell, W.O. 1993. *The Black Bonspiel of Willie MacCrimmon*. Toronto: McClelland & Stewart. Inc.

Molière. [1959] 2000. *The Misanthrope and other Plays*. London: Penguin Books.

Montaigne, Michel de. [1910] 2003. *The Complete Works: Essays, Travel Journal, Letters*. Translated by Donald M. Fame. Introduced by Stuart Hampshire. New York: Alfred A. Knopf.

Moynihan, Iain. 2013. "Lance Armstrong, the Omerta and Truth in Cycling." *Roar* December 5.

Nichols, M. Bennett. 1999. *Glíma: Icelandic Wrestling*. New Orleans.

Olivera, Javier. 2013. "On Changes in General Trust in Europe." Ms. UCD Geary Institute. University College Dublin.

Pearson, Michael, Daniel Burke and Holly Yan. 2014. "Pope Asks Forgiveness for Church Leaders in Handling of Sex Abuse Cases." *CNN Reporting*. http://www.nbc33tv.com/news/pope-asks-forgiveness-for.

Pétursson, Pétur. 1983. *Church and Social Change: a Study of the Secularization in Iceland, 1830–1930*. Helsingborg, Sweden: Bokförlaget Plus Ultra.

Posnanski, Joe. 2012. *Paterno*. New York: Simon & Schuster.

Powell, Christopher. 2010. "Four Concepts of Morality." In *Handbook of the Sociology of Morality*, edited by Steven Hitlin and Stephen Vaisey, 35–66. New York: Springer.

Proctor, Robert N. 2011. *Golden Holocaust: Origins of the Cigarette Catastrophe and the Case for Abolition*. Berkeley: University of California Press.

Putnam, Robert. 2000. *Bowling Alone: the Collapse and Revival of American Community*. New York: Simon and Schuster.

Putnam, Robert, Robert Leonard, and Rafaella Nanetti. 1993. *Making Democracy Work: Civic Traditions in Modern Italy*. Princeton: Princeton University Press.

Putney, Clifford. 2001. *Muscular Christianity: Manhood and Sports in Protestant America, 1880–1920*. Cambridge, MA: Harvard University Press.

"'Quite a Show': Bathroom Sex Romp Caught on Video at Yankee Stadium." 2012. *CBS News*. http://newyork.cbslocal.com/2012/09/17/quite-a-show-bathroom-sex-romp-caught-on-cam...

Rawls, Anne Warfield. 1987. "The Interaction Order Sui Generis: Goffman's Contribution to Social Theory." *Sociological Theory* 5 (2): 136–49.

———. 2010. "Social Order as Moral Order." In *Handbook of the Sociology of Morality*, edited by Steven Hitlin and Stephen Vaisey, 95–121. New York: Springer, 2010.

Rawls, John. [1971] 1999. *A Theory of Justice*. Revised Edition. Cambridge, MA: The Belknap Press of Harvard University Press.

Ressiot, Damien. 2005. "Le Mensonge Armstrong." *L'Equipe*. October 23.

Revsine, Dave. 2014. *The Opening Kickoff: The Tumultuous Birth of a Football Nation*. Guilford, Connecticut: Lyons Press.

Robinson, John A.T. 1963. *Honest to God*. UK: SCM Press.

Rosentraub, Mark S. 1997. *Major League Losers: the Real Cost of Sport and Who's Paying for It*. New York: Basic Books.

"Rules of Curling for General Play." 2014. Canadian Curling Association. Orleans, ON.

Runciman, David. 2006. *The Politics of Good Intentions: History, Fear and Hypocrisy in the New World Order.* Princeton: Princeton University Press.

————. 2008. *Political Hypocrisy: the Mask of Power from Hobbes to Orwell and Beyond.* Princeton: Princeton University Press.

"Runner Recounts Leaving Race and Leaping Off Bridge." December 22, 1986. http://articles.philly.com/1986-12-22/sports/26070945_kathy-ormsby-bide-three-other-races.

Savage, Howard J. 1929. *American College Athletics.* New York: The Carnegie Foundation for the Advancement of Teaching.

Schneier, Bruce. 2012. *Liars and Outliers.* Indianapolis, IN: John Wiley & Sons.

Scolforo, Mark and Marc Levy. 2015. "Penn State Gets Football Wins Restored, Joe Paterno Again Winningest Coach." *The Associated Press.* http://www.denverpost.com/colleges/ci_27335008/penn-state-gets-football-wins-resto red-jo.

Scott, Marvin B. and Stanford M. Lyman. 1968. "Accounts." *American Sociological Review* 33 (1): 46–62.

Scott, Virginia. 2000. *Molière: a Theatrical Life.* Cambridge: Cambridge University Press, 2000.

Scraton, Phil. [1999] 2000. *Hillsborough: the Truth.* Edinburgh and London: Mainstream Publishing.

————. 2013. "The Legacy of Hillsborough: Liberating Truth, Challenging Power." *Race & Class* 55 (2): 1–27.

Scraton, Phil, Ann Jemphrey, and Sheila Coleman. 1995. *No Last Rights: the Denial of Justice and the Promotion of Myth in the Aftermath of the Hillsborough Disaster.* Liverpool: Liverpool City Council.

Sennett, Richard. 1993. *The Hidden Injuries of Class.* New York: W.W. Norton & Company.

Shakespeare, William. [1600] 1998. *The Merchant of Venice.* Ed. by Kenneth Myrick. New York: Penguin.

————. [1623] 1998. *Twelfth Night, or What You Will.* Revised Edition. Edited by Herschel Baker. New York: Penguin.

Shapin, Steven. 1995. *A Social History of Truth: Civility and Science in Seventeenth-Century England.* Chicago: University of Chicago Press.

Shklar, Judith N. 1984. *Ordinary Vices.* Cambridge, MA: Harvard University Press.

Shulman, James L. and William G. Bowen. 2001. *The Game of Life: College Sports and Educational Values.* Princeton, NJ: Princeton University Press.

Sigurjónsson, Árni. 1986. *Laxness og þjóðlífið.* Reykjavík: Vaka Helgafell.

Singer, Mark. 2012. "Is Kip Litton a Marathon Fraud?" *The New Yorker.* August 6.

Smith, Adam. [1759] 1817. *The Theory of Moral Sentiments.* Boston: Wells and Lilly.

Sokolove, Michael. 2014. "The Trials of Graham Spanier, Penn State's Ousted President." *The New York Times.* July 16.

Sperber, Murray. 1990. *College Sports, Inc.: The Athletic Department vs. the University*. New York: Henry Holt.

———. 1998. *Onward to Victory: the Crises that Shaped College Sports*. New York: Henry Holt and Company.

———. 2000. *Beer and Circus: How Big-time College Sports is Crippling Undergraduate Education*. New York: Henry Holt and Co.

Stangneth, Bettina. 2014. *Eichmann before Jerusalem: the Unexamined Life of a Mass Murderer*. Trans by Ruth Martin. New York: Alfred A. Knopf.

"Strengthening Trust in Government." 2005. OECD: Ministry of the Interior and Kingdom Relations.

Stripling, Jack. 2014. "Behind an Ex-President, a Band of Loyalists." *The Chronicle of Higher Education*. August 11. http://chronicle.com/article.

Sugden, John and Alan Tomlinson. 1998. *FIFA and the Contest for World Football: Who Rules the Peoples' Game*. Cambridge: Policy Press.

———. 2003. *Badfellas: FIFA Family at War*. Edinburgh: Mainstream Publishing.

Suggs, Welch. 2006. *A Place on the Team: the Triumph and Tragedy of Title IX*. Princeton: Princeton University Press.

Taylor, Rogan, Andrew Ward, and Tim Newburn. 1995. *The Day of the Hillsborough Disaster*. Liverpool: Liverpool University Press.

The Economist. 2014. November 15: 84.

———. 2014. December 13–19: 63, 64.

The New York Times. 2012. October 12.

"The Reykjavík Grapevine." 2013.

"The Smoking Gun." 2012.

Traynor, Ian. 2013. "Crisis for Europe as Trust Hits Record Low." *The Guardian*. April 24. http://www.theguardian.com/world/2013/apr/24/trust-eu-falls-record-low.

Treasure, Geoffrey. 2014. *The Huguenots*. New Haven: Yale University Press.

Turowitz, Jason J. and Douglas W. Maynard. 2010. "Morality in the Social Interactional and Discursive World of Everyday Life." In *Handbook of the Sociology of Morality*, edited by Steven Hitlin and Stephen Vaisey, 503–26. New York: Springer.

Updike, John. 1975. *A Month of Sundays*. New York: Alfred A. Knopf.

———. 1989. *Self-Consciousness: Memoirs*. New York: Alfred A. Knopf.

———. [1986] 1996. *Roger's Version*. New York: Random House.

———. [1988] 2013. *S*. New York: Random House.

U.S. Religious Landscape Survey: Religious Beliefs and Practices. June 2008. Washington, DC: Pew Forum on Religion & Public Life.

usaswimming.org/protect. 2015.

Van Ruymbeke, Bertrand and Randy J. Sparks. 2003. *Memory and Identity: the Huguenots in France and the Atlantic Diaspora*. Columbia, SC: University of South Carolina Press.

VeloNews. 2012.

Walsh, David. 2007. *From Lance to Landis: Inside the American Doping Controversy at the Tour de France.* New York: Ballantine Books.

———. 2012. *Seven Deadly Sins: My Pursuit of Lance Armstrong.* New York: Atria Books.

Walter, Jess. 2013. *We Live in Water.* New York: Harper Perennial.

Ward, Theresa. 2010. "Strategies for Reducing the Risk of e-Commerce Fraud," A First Data White Paper. October.

Wazeter, Mary with Gregg Lewis. 1989. *Dark Marathon: the Mary Wazeter Story.* Grand Rapids: Zondervan Books.

Weber, Max. [1905] 1958. *The Protestant Ethic and the Spirit of Capitalism.* Trans. by Talcott Parsons. New York: Charles Scribners Sons.

———. 1994. "Politics as a Vocation." *Political Writings.* Edited by Peter Lassman and Ronald Spears. Cambridge: Cambridge University Press.

———. 1994. *The Methodology of the Social Sciences.* Trans and ed. by Edward A. Shils and Henry A. Finch. New York: The Free Press.

Wieting, Stephen G. 2000. "Twilight of the Hero in the Tour de France." *International Review for the Sociology of Sport* 35 (3): 348–63.

———. Ed. 2001. *Sport and Memory in North America.* London: Frank Cass.

———. 2005. "Kenya." In *Berkshire Encyclopedia of World Sport.* Edited by David Levinson and Karen Christensen. Volume 2: 898–900. Great Barrington, MA: Berkshire Publishing Group.

———. 2012. "Hypocrisy in Religion and in Sport: Individual and Institutional Implications." Presented during meetings of Nordic Sociological Association. Reykjavík, Iceland.

"A Wedding Fit for Ducks: Oregon Fans Get Married at Rosebowl Tailgate." 2015. *US News.* January 1.

Wieting, Stephen G. and Danny Lamoureux. 2001. "Curling in Canada." In *Sport and Memory in North America,* edited by Stephen G. Wieting, 140–53. London: Frank Cass.

Wieting, Stephen G., Simona Ionescu, and Felix Sinitean-Singer "Romanian Oina and Icelandic Glíma: Preserving Traditional Sports within the 21st Century Global Marketplace." In *Sport, Nation, Nationalism,* edited by Tomaz Pavlin, 208–17. Ljubljana: Faculteta za Sport.

Wieting, Stephen G. and Thórólfur Thórlindsson "Divorce in the Old Icelandic Commonwealth: an Interactionist Approach to the Past." In *Studies in Symbolic Interactions: a Research Journal,* edited by Norman K. Denzin, 163–89. Greenwich, CT: JAI Press, Inc., 1990.

Wilcockson, John. 2004. *23 Days in July: Inside Lance Armstrong's Record-Breaking Tour de France Victory.* Cambridge, MA: DA Capo Press.

Willis, E. David. 1966. *Calvin's Catholic Christology: the Function of the So-Called Extra Calvinisticum in Calvin's Theory.* Leiden: E.J. Brill.

Windsor, Richard. 2014. "Kenyan Rider Dies after Collision with Car at Tour of Matabungkay." http://www.cyclingweekly.co.uk/news/latest-news/kenyan-rider-dies-collision-car-tour-ma…

Wollstonecraft, Mary. [1792] 2013. *A Vindication of the Rights of Women.* UK: Wollstonecraft Books.

Women in the 2000, 2004 and 2008 Olympic and Paralympic Games. 2009. East Meadow, NY: Women's Sports Foundation.

Wooden, John and Steve Jamison. 1997. *Wooden: a Lifetime of Observations and Reflections On and Off the Court.* New York; Chicago: Contemporary Books.

Wright, Bradley R.E. 2010. *Christians are Hate-Filled Hypocrites ... and other Lies You've Been Told.* Minneapolis: Bethany House.

Wuthnow, Robert. 2003. *All in Sync: How Music and Art are Revitalizing American Religion.* Berkeley: University of California Press.

———. 2007. *After the Baby Boomers: How Twenty- and Thirty-Somethings are Shaping the Future of American Religion.* Princeton: Princeton University Press.

———. 2012. *Red State Religion.* Princeton: Princeton University Press, 2012.

Zamoysky, Adam. 2015. *Phantom Terror: the Threat of Evolution and the Repression of Liberty, 1789–1848.* New York: Basic Books.

Zavoral, Nolan. 1998. *A Season on the Mat: Dan Gable and the Pursuit of Perfection.* New York: Simon & Schuster.

Zimbalist, Andrew. 1999. *Unpaid Professionals.* Princeton: Princeton University Press.

Zimbardo, Phillip. 2007. *The Lucifer Effect.* New York: Random House.

Documents

Hillsborough

1989. The Hillsborough Stadium Disaster, 15 April 1989. Interim Report. Inquiry by the Rt Hon Lord Justice Taylor.

1990. The Hillsborough Stadium Disaster, 15 April 1989. Final Report. Inquiry by the Rt Hon Lord Justice Taylor.

1998. Scrutiny of Evidence Relating to the Hillsborough Football Stadium Disaster. Presented to Parliament by the Secretary of State for the Home Department by Command of Her Majesty.

2012. The Report of the Hillsborough Independent Panel. Ordered by the House of Commons.

Tour de France Principals

2007. United States Anti-Doping Agency v. Floyd Landis.

2008. Arbitral Award Delivered by the Court of Arbitration for Sport.

2012. (June 12). Letter to Lance Armstrong and other Tour Principals.

2012. (August 24). "Lance Armstrong Receives Lifetime Ban and Disqualification ..." United States Anti-Doping Agency.

2012. (October 10) Reasoned Decision of the United States Anti-Doping Agency on Disqualification and Ineligibility. Report on Proceedings under the World Anti-Doping Code and the USADA Protocol.

2012. (October 10). "Statement from USADA CEO Travis T. Tygart Regarding the U.S. Postal Service Pro Cycling Team Doping Conspiracy." http://cyclinginvestigation.usada.org/.

2013. Full Transcript: Lance Armstrong on Oprah. http://armchairspectator. wordpress.com/2013/full-transcript-lance-armstrong.

2013. Second Amended Complaint for Violations of Federal Claims Act.

2015. *Cycling Independent Reform Commission: Report to the President of the Union Cycliste Internationale.* February.

Pennsylvania State University Issues

2012. Report of the Special Investigative Counsel Regarding the Actions of the Pennsylvania State University Related to the Child Abuse Committed by Gerald A. Sandusky. July 12, 2012. Freeh Sporkin & Sullivan, LLP.

2013. "Critique of the Freeh Report: the Rush to Injustice Regarding Joe Paterno."

2013. Brian Leigh, "USA Reveals College Football Head Coaches' Salaries for Every FBS [Football Bowl School] School." *USA Today*, November 6. Note: Updates do occur with this medium, with latest figure for Nick Saban, University of Alabama of $7,160,187. http://sports.usatoday.com/ncaa/sala ries/football/coach.

2014. *Chronicle of Higher Education*, May 16.

General Documentary Sources; Relevant Electronic Document Services

BishopAccountability.org.

The Civil Rights Act of 1964. Public Law 88–352 (78 Stat.241).

Cohen v. Brown. US Supreme Court Case, 1992.

Cycling Independent Reform Commission: Report to the President of the *Union Cycliste Internationale*. Lausanne, February 2015.

"Equal Rights Amendment." Wikipedia. http://en.wikipedia.org/wiki/Equal_Rights _Amendment.

http://factcheck.org/.

"Fellowship of Christian Athletes." 2015. http://en.wikipedia.org/wiki/Fellow ship_of_Christian_Athletes.

Graduation Success Rates (GSR) for National Collegiate Athletic Association (NCAA): Education and Research (GSR Search).

"In the United States District Court for the Northern District of California, No. C 093329, Findings of Fact and Conclusions of Law," 2014 (i. e, O'Bannon case).

Individuals Permanently Suspended or Ineligible. USA Swimming, 2014.

"Inside the 'Perversion Files: Tracking Decades of Allegations in the Boy Scouts." October 18, 2012. Los Angeles Times Staff. http://www.latimes.com/news/local/boyscouts/.

The Legacy Tobacco Documents Library. http://legacy.library.ncsf.edu.

NCAA 2014–15 NCAA Division 1 Manual. 2014. Indianapolis, IN: The National Collegiate Athletic Association.

"NCAA Proposal Number 2014–2," October 21, 2014 (unpublished document regarding new guidelines for select group of Power Conferences). http://www.politifact.com/.

http://www.politifact.com/truth-o-meter/statements/.

Rapport Om Doping I Dansk Cykelsport, 1998–2015. Anti Doping Danmark. June 2015.

http://scholarshipforathletes.com.

The Sherman Anti-Trust Act (1890). http://www.linfo.org/Sherman_txt.html.

"Summer Olympic Games." http://en.wikipedia.org/wiki/Summer_Olympic_Games.

"Thomas J.J. Altizer." 2015. http://en.wikipedia.org/wiki/Thomas_J._J._Altizer.

Title IX of the United States Amendments of 1972, Public Law No. 92-318, 86 Stat. 235 (June 23).

http://www.transparency.org/research/cpi/overview/ (Note: This site contains the "Corruption Perceptions Index").

"United States District Court, District of New Jersey, Complain and Jury Demand—Class Action Seeking Injunction and Individual Damages," 2014. (i.e., Kessler et al. case).

United States District Court Eastern District of New York: United States of America against Charles Blazer, Defendant. May 20, 2015.

"United States Government before the National Labor Relations Board, Region 13, Case 13-RC-121359" (i.e., Northwestern University labor union for football players case).

U.S. Religious Landscape Survey: Religious Beliefs and Practices. June 2008. Washington, DC: Pew Forum on Religion & Public Lie.

Icelandic Statistical Sources

Hagskinna: Icelandic Historical Statistics. 1997. Reykjavík: Hagstofa Íslands.
Statistical Yearbook of Iceland. Continuous from Hagstofa Ísland.

Web Resources

http://en.wikipedia.org/wiki/Billy_Sunday.
http://www.bishop-acountability.org/AtAGlance/timeline.htm.
http://en.wikipedia.org/wiki/Lance_Armstrong.
http://en.wikipedia.org/wiki/Floyd_Landis.
http://en.wikipedia.org/wiki/Concordat_of_1801.
http://en.wikipedia.org/wiki/Concordat_of_Worms.

http://en.wikipedia.org/wiki/Nathaniel_Hawthorne.

http://en.wikipedia.org/wiki/Omert%C3%A0.

http://en.wikipedia.org/wiki/Operaci%B3n_Puerto_doping_...

http://en.wikipedia.org/wiki/Peace_of_Augsburg.

http://en.wikipedia.ord/wiki/Peace_of_Westphalia.

http://en.wikipedia.org/wiki/Roman_Catholicism_in_France.

http://en.wikipedia.org/wiki/Rosie_Ruiz.

http://en.wikipedia.org/wiki/Hillsborough_disaster.

http://www.oikoumene.org/en/member-churches/united-protestant-church-of-france.

http://en.wikipedia.org/wiki/Travis_Tygart.

http://en.wikipedia.org/wiki/Sherman_Antitrust_Act.

http://en.wikipedia.org/wiki/Thomas_J._J._Altizer.

https://en.wikipedia.org/wiki/NBA_Collective_Bargaining_Agreement.

http://bleacherreport.com/articles/1640782-the-anatomy-of-a-53-man-roster-in-the-nfl.

https://en.wikepedia.org/wiki/Major_League_Baseball_rosters.

http://www.nhl.com/ice/page.htm?id=26377.

Video Materials

Gibney, Alex. 2014. "The Armstrong Lie." Sony Pictures.

"Hillsborough." [1996] 2009. Screenplay by Jimmy McGovern. Netwerk, A Granada Television Production.

"Men with Brooms." 2002. Directed by Paul Gross. Santa Monica, CA Artisan Entertainment Inc.

"Standard Operating Procedure." 2008. Sony Pictures.

1999. "Tour de France: An American in Paris!" (Two VHS reels). Minneapolis: World Cycling Productions.

2000. "Tour de France: Tour de Lance!" Eight Hours. Minneapolis: World Cycling Productions.

2001. "Tour de France: Mission Accomplished!" 10 hours Minneapolis: World Cycling Productions.

2002. "Tour de France: Four and Counting!" 10 hours. Minneapolis: World Cycling Productions.

2003. "Tour de France: Armstrong Joins the Greats!" 12 hours. Minneapolis: World Cycling Productions.

2004. "Tour de France: the Historic Sixth Win!" 12 hours. Minneapolis: World Cycling Productions.

2005. "Tour de France: Magnificent 7." 12 hours. Minneapolis: World Cycling Productions.

2006. "Tour de France: Floyd Landis, Hero or Villain?" 12 hours. Minneapolis: World Cycling Productions.

Index

Froome, Chris 111, 117, 119–20, 205, 215
Fukuyama, Francis 159, 161, 215

Gay, Peter 96, 215
Geertz, Clifford 8, 106, 185, 215
Glíma 39, 74, 78–80, 214–15, 219, 222
Goffman, Erving 6–8, 28, 173, 189, 205, 215
Golf 52, 80, 121, 181, 193–5, 199, 215
Graduation Success Rate 42–3, 224
Great Awakenings (religion) 59–61, 180

Halberstam, David 12, 215
Hamilton, Tyler 18, 30, 138–9, 146, 157, 188, 197, 216
Haselberger, Jennifer 11
Hawthorne, Nathaniel 33, 70, 216, 226
Hillsborough 145, 149, 151–3, 155, 166, 168–70, 175, 199, 202, 206, 209, 220–21, 223, 226
Hincapie, George 30, 120, 197, 204, 216
Huguenots 88–90, 211–12, 221
Hushovd, Thor 119–20, 216
hypocrisy
    definition 1, 9, 17, 25, 40, 54, 67, 94, 105, 124–6, 147, 157–8, 161, 165, 186
    dissimulation 17, 71, 92, 96, 161, 196, 203
    first-order 9
    meanings in context 3, 7–10, 17, 23, 25, 27, 29–31, 35–9, 47–8, 50, 58–60, 67, 69, 71, 82, 90, 95–6, 98, 100, 121, 158, 160–61, 178–9, 181–2, 189, 191, 193, 203, 213, 220
    organizational influences 6, 32, 49, 66, 97–8, 101–3, 106, 109, 111, 114, 117, 120, 125, 127–8, 130–31, 137–40, 149, 151–2, 155, 161–5, 167, 169, 171–2, 184–5, 187–8, 203–4, 208–9, 217
    second-order 10
    simulation 17, 71, 92, 96, 161, 196, 203
    sociological attention 3, 7–8, 32, 186–7, 202

Icelandic saga 72–7, 216
Icelandic team handball 39, 78, 81
Ideal type 3, 5, 31, 70

Kant, Immanuel 173, 196
Kenya 81, 117, 211, 217, 222
Kessler, Jeffrey 53–4, 56
Koran 9, 36, 149, 160, 173
Krasnoff, Lindsay Sarah 86–7, 217
Kuhn, Thomas 107–8, 208, 217

Lakoff, George 27, 94, 217
Landis, Floyd 20, 110–11, 114, 118–19, 128, 131–3, 135, 138–9, 141, 145–6, 189, 197, 204, 217, 223, 225–6
Laxness, Halldór 69, 180, 215, 217
Le Monde vii, 25, 36–7, 71, 82, 157
LeMond, Greg 129, 167
Lewis, Sinclair 70, 179–80, 216–17
lying v, 2, 6–8, 15, 17, 20, 22, 25, 27, 30–31, 40, 50, 82, 90, 105, 115, 117–18, 120–21, 127, 138, 140–42, 149, 151–2, 155, 158, 160–61, 167–8, 173–4, 188–9, 192, 200, 202–3, 205, 208, 212
Lyman, Sanford M. 49, 115, 128, 138, 143, 183, 197–8, 206, 220
Lynch, Loretta A. 207

Machiavelli, Niccolò 218
Macur, Juliet 118, 132, 136, 171, 197, 218
McCartney, Bill 1, 63
McQueary, Mike 14, 17, 24, 110, 205
Mill, John Stuart 70
Millar, David 30, 218
Miller, William Ian 95, 189, 193, 218
Milton, John 177–8, 218
Molière 30, 70, 98, 127, 160, 179–80, 219–20
Morgunblaðið vii, 36–7, 71

NCAA (National Collegiate Athletic Association)
    criticisms of 57–8, 97, 224
    early history 34, 40
    legal disputes 55–6, 110, 112, 205

For Product Safety Concerns and Information please contact our EU
representative GPSR@taylorandfrancis.com
Taylor & Francis Verlag GmbH, Kaufingerstraße 24, 80331 München, Germany

www.ingramcontent.com/pod-product-compliance
Ingram Content Group UK Ltd.
Pitfield, Milton Keynes, MK11 3LW, UK
UKHW021001180425
457613UK00019B/769